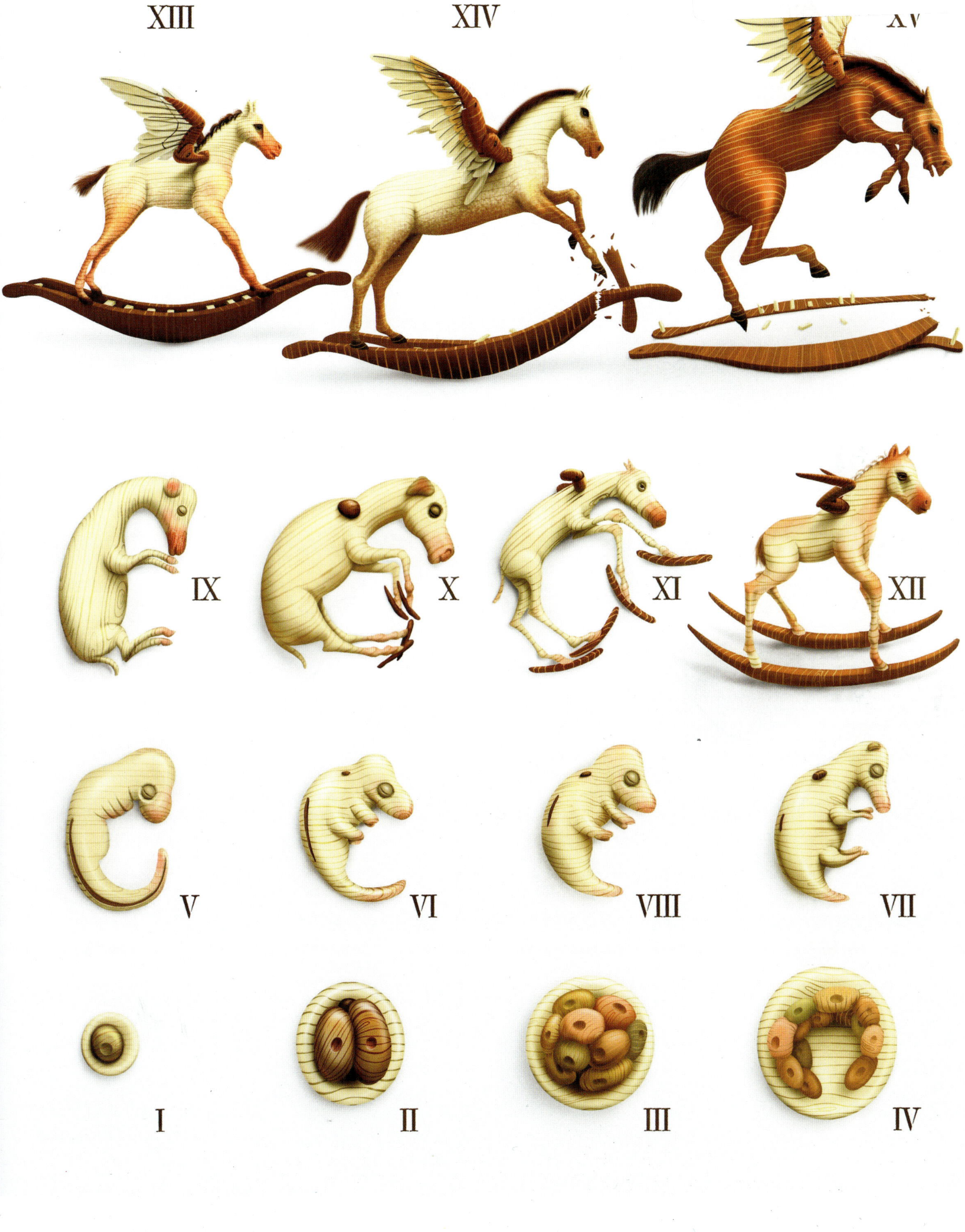
XIII
XIV
XV
IX
X
XI
XII
V
VI
VIII
VII
I
II
III
IV

To Jack

Keep Rocking!

[illegible]

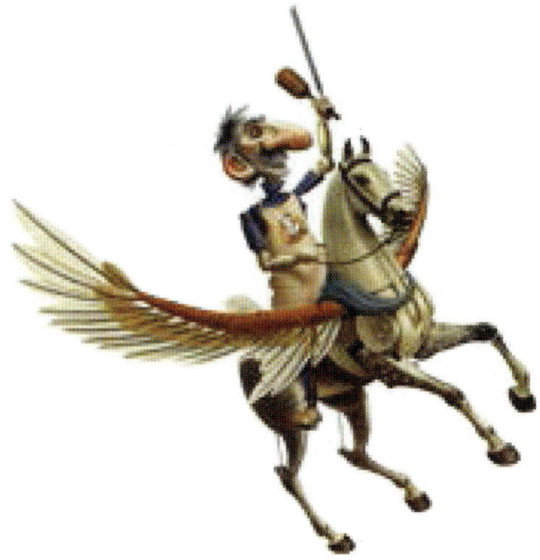

# MAKING IT with ROCKING HORSES

An intimate story of life, love,
death and rocking-horses

by

ANTHONY DEW

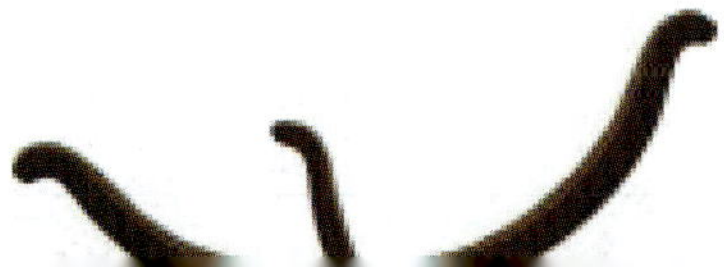

This book is dedicated to
my grandchildren:

Eva, Joseph & Margot; Abel, Aiya & Bart



ISBN 0-9545388-7-0

Published by
The Rocking Horse Shop Ltd,
Fangfoss, York, YO41 5JH, England.

Printed and bound by
York Publishing Services

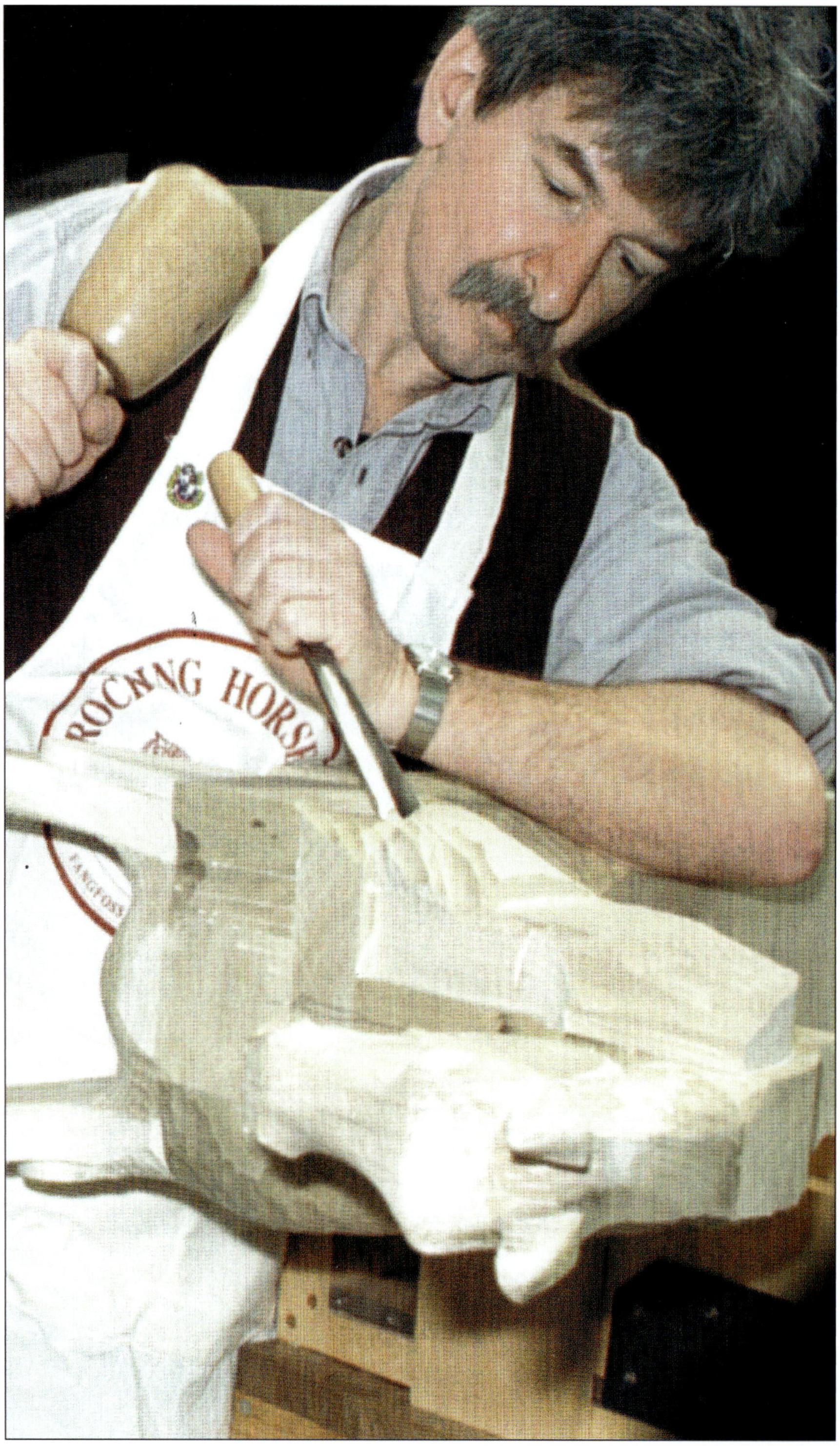

# Foreword

When I was a child the vital question wasn't, 'To be or not to be?' It was, 'What am I going to do?' I thought a lot about the possibilities: tinker, tailor, soldier, sailor… and always stopped at sailor. So, as soon as I could I left home and went to sea. By the age of twenty-two I'd been a seafarer for seven years, had plenty of adventures and stared at lots of horizons, but I still didn't know what to do with my life. Aimlessly pacing the deck of my ship, thinking about where I'd rather be, I decided to apply to college. At the interview I told them I wanted to be a maths teacher.

'I left school when I was fifteen,' I said. 'So I'm short on formal education, but I've been around the world a few times and I know a bit about maths from being a navigator. Now I've had enough of wandering the oceans and want to live ashore. I've sold my sextant.'

I was late applying but they accepted me anyway, so I quit the life I knew and drove to Yorkshire to become a student teacher, specialising in maths. Then, on my first day at college I met John Redmond Porter and changed my mind about everything. Porter was twenty, tall and charismatic, the brightest, wittiest, most insightful person I have ever known. We would remain friends for life. He had a mane of auburn hair reaching almost to his waist and wore a brown tweed jacket he'd bought for a pound at the Oxfam shop. Tweed was totally unfashionable but somehow it looked cool on him.

'Maths, Tony?' he barked. 'You're out of your mind. It'll bore you to death, now and for evermore. Get yourself transferred to art. This is where all the action is, the fun, the best women. You can't study boring maths, Tony. You're an artist.'

Nobody'd ever called me an artist before. I had no doubt Porter was an artist, the way he talked tirelessly and knowledgeably about art and music, drank prodigious quantities of liquor and smoked anything he could lay his hands on. Art was an unknown world to me that seemed impossible, ridiculous, but Porter made it sound so fascinating, so alluring, so possible. My maths tutor was dismayed but within a week of becoming a student, I was Art.

# Part One
# 1

*No bird flies too high if it flies with its own wings.*

When I became an art student I let my hair grow long, carried a sketch pad and drew all the time. I tried my hand at painting, textiles and weaving, print-making and ceramics, but it was in the 3D department I found my métier. I made sculptures in clay, cast resin, hammered copper, stone and wood. Most of my sculptures were small but what I liked most was making big wood-carvings. My art (and soul) was devoted to the naked female form and I carved some lengths of pitch pine log into chunky torsos, and a six-foot long old railway sleeper into a reclining nude (inevitably entitled 'Sleeper').

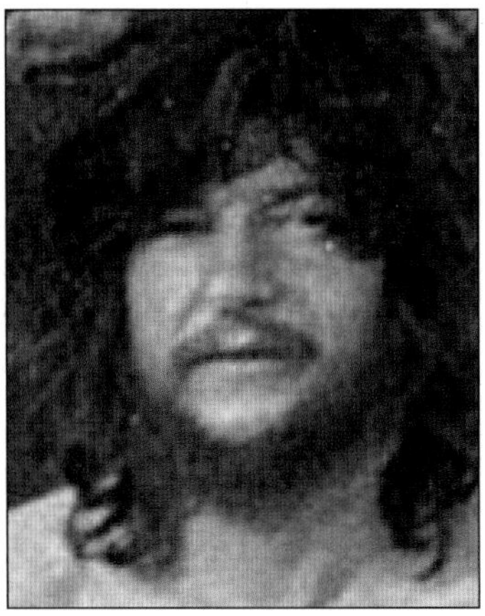

AD 1974

It was good to have a friend and to have found something I really enjoyed doing, but I also longed for someone who'd be my partner in life, to love and be loved by. One evening a couple of weeks into my first term I was in the crowded students' bar, the air thick with smoke and the juke box blaring out, when a woman sat beside me. She had a friendly smile, a lovely rounded figure and said her name was Pat. It was too noisy to make conversation in the bar so, stoned as I was, we went for a drive in my Mini. I told her I was an artist and a poet and invited myself back to her room. Although she would always maintain she was definitely not *that* kind of girl, within a couple of hours of meeting we were in bed together. I don't know if what we did constitutes love at first sight, but after that first night together we remained more or less inseparable for the next twenty-eight years.

We were 'mature' students, training to be teachers. Pat was four years younger than me but a year ahead at college, so when I started my final year she was already qualified and teaching in a Primary School, which she loved. However, I'd realised that working in a classroom full of noisy, smelly kids was not for me and was actively looking for another vocation. There was no question I'd have to do something. I couldn't be a layabout, tempting as that was, and I knew I couldn't be a boring accountant like my Dad. It seemed to me that the main thing in life, after loving and being loved, was to find something I'd love doing and get paid for it. Everything else, including happiness, would follow.

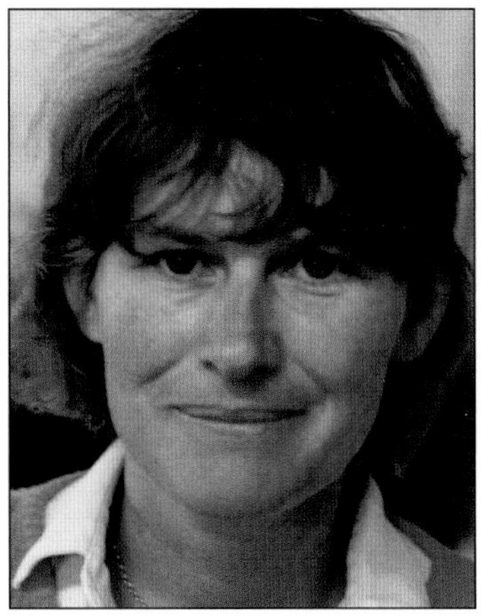

Pat Dew

Pat and I practised making children often, and talked about how many we'd have (six was mentioned at one point) and how we'd raise them. We fantasised about the idyllic house we'd own one day, in a lovely rural location where our children would grow up free, strong and happy. We'd plant an orchard and grow our own food. We'd have dogs and cats and other animals and there'd be a paddock where Pat would keep the pony she'd always dreamed of owning. I'd have a workshop where I'd create beautiful artefacts and sell them to make our living. Neither of us desired power or great riches but we did want to live a good life and these were our dreams. They seemed perfectly realistic and achievable to me.

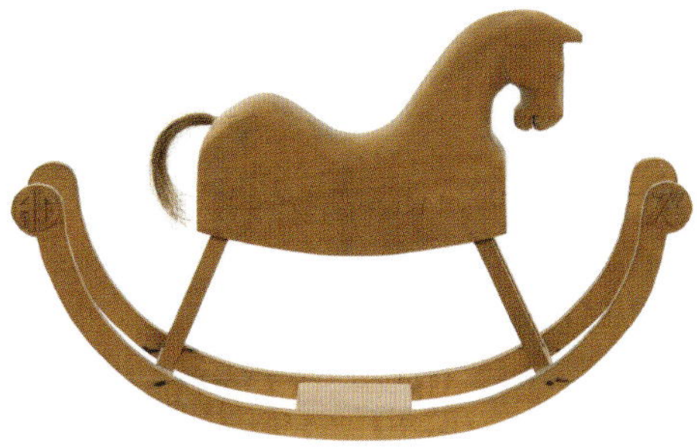

Maquette for AD's first rocking-horse - 7 inches long

With all our talk of children and Pat's love of horses - she went riding whenever she could afford it and I sometimes went with her - the idea arose that I'd make a rocking-horse for my final year art project. I drew a plan, persuaded my tutor that a rocking-horse would be art (albeit not fine art) and bought some timber from a local merchant. There were few power tools in the college workshop so I made do with what there was: a hand saw for the straight cuts, an ancient frame saw with a thin blade for the curves on the head, legs and rockers, a few chisels and carving gouges and a round wood-carver's mallet. I spent many evenings carving alone in the 3D studio, quietly absorbed in the work. George the technician kept it as tidy as he could but it was always cluttered with workshop paraphernalia and students' weird and colourful part-made projects. The room was white and stank of paint and turpentine, resin and fresh cut wood. I loved it in there.

The form and appearance of my rocking-horse had leapt into my mind right at the start. It would have a carved head with glinting glass eyes and a carved upper body with sensuous curves and contours. The lower body would be more angular, with the legs simply cut to shape, not carved at all. The hooves would be attached to long curved bow rockers which would have my initials and the year - AD 1976 - carved into roundels at the ends. My art tutor was encouraging but critical. He clearly felt my design was too idiosyncratic to succeed, and in his opinion it certainly wasn't art.

But one afternoon he invited me to his house to show me the rocking-horse he'd had since childhood. It was a very small carved dapple grey on a red stand, looking forlorn and battered from decades of use. As a child I'd never had a rocking-horse of my own, had never even ridden one: this was actually the first one I'd ever seen close up. I wasn't impressed. My rocking-horse would be a whole lot bigger and better than that sorry little thing.

As my horse took shape I experienced a very real and pleasurable sense of achievement. An idea, a sketch, a few tools, some raw timber and a powerful desire to make something, slowly transformed into a solid, rideable animal. It even took on a personality and I started to refer to this creature I was making as 'he'. Of course, just because he was hand-crafted didn't make him any good. He was a big, ugly brute, but he was my baby and I loved him. And he worked. I sat on his back and rocked with a grin on my face like a slice of water-melon. Pat sat on him and rocked and she loved him. We took him home and our friends all rode him (I insisted) and said they loved him too.

I kept wondering if making rocking-horses was the vocation I'd been looking for. Everybody seemed to know about rocking-horses and like them. I was sure that at the college's end of year art show somebody would fall in love with my rocking-horse and buy him.

Nobody did, but one visitor exclaimed, 'A rocking-horse! How lovely! Why doesn't anyone make them any more?'

That was all I needed. I became convinced that the craft was ripe for revival. So, putting aside all other considerations - such as why nobody made them anymore and whether Pat was happy to come with me on what could well be a perilous ride - I decided that's what I'd do.

However (apart from being broke, but we'll get to that) if we were going to start a rocking-horse making business we faced two big challenges: we knew nothing about business and next to nothing about rocking-horses. So we made a plan: 1. Find out about rocking-horses and how to make them; 2. Make some; 3. Sell them; and 4. Hey presto, we're in business.

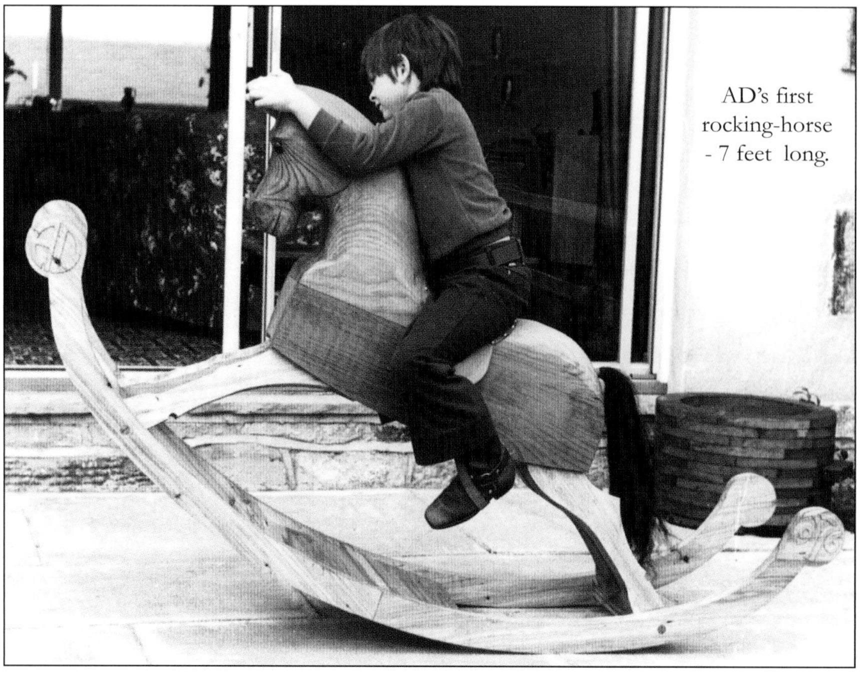

AD's first rocking-horse - 7 feet long.

# 2

*The first step is the hardest.*

The first rocking-horse was made around 1605 for Prince Charles, a sickly child who, by the age of five, hadn't learned to walk properly. The rocking-horse was intended to exercise his weak legs and teach him to ride, a necessary accomplishment for a gentleman then, especially a prince. The idea of a toy horse big enough for a child to ride caught on and that first one was followed by many more, in a huge variety of sizes and styles.

Real horses have played a major part in most human civilizations and small models of horses have been found dating back over three thousand years. Made in clay or wood, they were not intended for children but were burial artefacts, to be used by the dead to ride in the afterlife. Yet what child could resist a little model of a horse? They'd surely beg dad to make them one, not to be buried in a grave, but to play with.

Hobby horses - a wooden or stuffed material representation of a horse's head mounted on a stick - are known from medieval times right up to the present day. Some wooden ones are simple cut-out silhouettes, usually painted, and some are quite beautifully carved and detailed with a wheel at the stick's lower end. English Morris dancers had (and have) an elaborate form of hobby horse in which a near life-size horse's head and body, made from soft textile over a willow or wicker frame, is strapped round the waist of the 'rider'. The terms hobby horse and rocking-horse are often used interchangeably but I make this distinction: a hobby horse's movement depends on the legs of the 'rider' on the ground, whereas a rocking-horse is ridden, its motion simulating (albeit imperfectly) the movement of a real horse. Sometimes the simplest household object can serve as a hobby horse. I've seen children galloping round my yard astride an upended sweeping broom imagining it a horse.

The soothing value of rocking has always been known - what parent has ever *not* rocked their baby? Cradles with curved rockers were widely used by those who could afford them, but are only for tiny infants. To combine the idea of a toy horse, a hobby horse and a rocking crib, and make a moving toy horse big enough for a child of any age to actually ride, that was inspired. And, like many brilliant ideas, so obvious you have to wonder why nobody'd thought of it before.

Young Prince Charles's inability to walk properly is said to have been due to rickets, which can cause a child's bones to soften and become distorted. In 1604 when his father, King James VI of Scotland, became King James I of England and the royal family moved from Dunfermline Castle (where Charles had been born) to London, servants had to carry the little prince in a litter. Long before railways or motor cars or even metalled roads, the four hundred and thirty mile journey must have been seriously arduous for anyone, never mind a sickly child.

King James proposed bracing his younger son's weak legs with iron boots - the royal blacksmith could forge him a pair. But Lady Alletta Carey, who (with her husband) was charged with looking after the fragile prince, suggested long boots of Spanish leather, a less harsh way to provide firm support. And it was probably her idea to have the rocking-horse made. It would have arcs of solid timber for rockers (like a baby's crib), a carved horse's head on top with a seat and simple saddle, and be big enough for the boy to sit on and ride.

Charles had an older brother, Prince Henry, who was athletic and charismatic, heir to the throne and the favourite son of their parents and of the nation. While weak little Charles rode his rocking-horse or sat alone in a corner with his head in a book, King James and Prince Henry, both excellent horsemen, hunted across the royal estates with their entourage. Henry teased his brother, 'When I'm King I'll hunt and you can be my Archbishop of Canterbury'. Fine horses were much coveted, the Ferraris of the day, but poor Prince Charles could only watch and envy. He lived in his brother's shadow and little was expected of him - until Henry died.

It is said that at the start of the 17th century childhood had not yet been invented, and certainly the beneficial role of play in a child's development was not yet recognised. Children were regarded as small people whose purpose was to prepare for adulthood. Most had no toys at all and even the children of wealthy parents had only one or two - a home-made doll for a girl perhaps, a bow and arrows for a boy. Low life expectancy and a high mortality rate often led to adult roles being put upon children remarkably early. When Prince Henry died of typhoid fever in 1612, young Charles unexpectedly became heir to the throne. A year later he was running his own household, at thirteen.

Prince Charles was twenty-five when his father died and he became king, but by then his childhood problems were to a large extent overcome. The rocking-horse had served its purpose admirably: as an 'exercise machine' it strengthened his muscles and taught him balance and poise. He became known as a fine horseman and Van Dyke painted a magnificent portrait of him as King Charles I, astride a white stallion and looking every inch the imperious monarch. Both painting and rocking-horse survive to this day. There was likely also a psychological benefit: as he rocked he could imagine himself a healthier, more capable person, free of disabilities. He would always have a lisp and remain physically slight but his self-confidence was boosted, so much so that he became a supremely arrogant king and paid for it, eventually, with his head.

Lady Carey may have had the inspiration for Prince Charles's rocking-horse but the name of the man who actually made it, a carpenter on one of the royal estates probably, is lost. It could well have been the only one that man ever made, whereas the first one I made set me off on a forty-year obsession during which I'd make hundreds and deal with thousands.

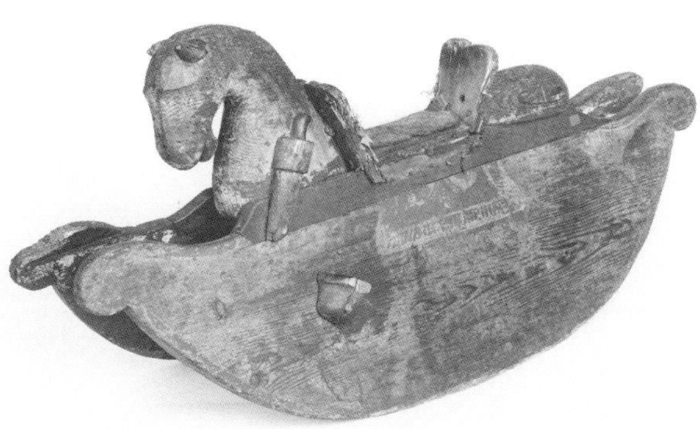

Early 17th Century rocking-horse - one of the first.

Apparently the 'Prince Charles' rocking-horse had survived nearly four hundred years and I wanted to see it, but couldn't discover where it was. However, there was a near contemporary one in the Museum of London and Pat and I drove down from Yorkshire to look at him. Surprisingly large, we judged him suitable for riders up to about eight years old, maybe ten because children were smaller then. He had footrests, a seat back and a dummy wooden pistol at one side of the neck. The curator couldn't tell us any more than was stated on his label: 'rocking-horse, early seventeenth century'. If only he could talk.

Those very early rocking-horses with arcs of solid timber for rockers, rudimentary carved heads and basic construction, soon gave way to more fully realised carved horses mounted on slender bow-shaped rockers. Pat and I went to Woburn Abbey to see Lord Grantley's rocking-horse, a marvellous example dated 1650. Two of his legs were fixed to a flat platform mounted on curved rockers, the other two raised in a high-step walk. Balanced on two legs, he had an iron support under the belly to stop him falling over and was a very fine creature indeed, with a superior attitude, head turned slightly to one side and exquisitely carved details, including flowing mane and tail. The rockers had quite a shallow arc which I guessed would not rock well, and the horse itself was more sculpture than plaything. To me this spoiled it. I was coming round to thinking that however fine and beautiful they might be, rocking-horses should be capable of being ridden and enjoyed or they had no raison d'être. I was imbuing my own still unmade rocking-horses with a purpose I didn't have for myself, yet.

I read everything I could find on the subject, which wasn't much, and wrote to every museum in the country with rocking-horses in their collections. The curator of London's Gunnersbury Park Museum very kindly showed Pat and me the museum's basement store where they had many more rocking-horses than the few on show, amid a higgledy-piggledy mass of marvellous artefacts racked to the ceiling like a vastly overstocked secret toy shop. What an extraordinary variety of sizes and styles the old-time makers had explored! They all fascinated me, but one in particular whose paintwork had completely disappeared, allowing me to examine the tool marks and joints and see exactly how he'd been made. He'd been a fine rocking-horse once, but I was surprised to see the poor quality of his underlying woodwork: ill-fitting joints crudely nailed, gaps and cracks filled with putty or other gunge, the carving remarkably coarse. The rough wooden surface, I learned, would have been hidden under a plaster-like substance called gesso, a mixture of rabbit skin glue and gilder's whiting (which is fine-ground chalk). The gesso would be painted on hot and, when set, sanded smooth and even carved before painting.

One account of the methods of 19th century rocking-horse makers described how the horses were carved in the Spring, allowed to dry out through the long Summer then gessoed, painted and tacked up in the Autumn in the run-up to Christmas. I couldn't know how factual that might be, it sounded like a wonderfully leisurely manner of working and too good to be true (which it was). Also, all the references to rocking-horse making I could find were in the past. There were mentions of several historic makers but nothing contemporary. Rather than worrying about why this should be so, I was delighted to have stumbled onto a well-loved traditional craft which, it seemed, nobody practised anymore. Great, I thought, no competition.

# 3

*Desire peace? Prepare for war.*

My days as a carefree college student ended. Pat was working while I stayed home, unemployed, pondering. If we were ever going to run a successful enterprise making rocking-horses we'd need timber, glue, paint, varnish, leather, hair and stacks of other materials, as well as tools and machin-ery to equip a workshop. And a workshop. I no longer had access to the college's facilities and every penny Pat earned went on our living expenses. We needed money.

At the end of my first year at college, when Pat and I decided to live together, we'd bought a very old stone cottage. I was relatively well off, for a student, because every college holiday I'd gone back to sea. I could always get a job as relieving Mate on a coaster and make good money, especially over Christmas and New Year when I'd be paid double for every bank holiday I worked. We found an old mid-terrace house in nearby Keighley for £450. We liked it but I didn't have that much cash so we couldn't afford it. But we learned that between us we could raise a mortgage and I had enough in the bank for the 10% deposit on a better property, which we bought.

Our old stone cottage was high on a hill overlooking Keighley and the Aire Valley beyond. We slept on a mattress on the floor and rented the upstairs bedrooms to our best friends, Porter and his girlfriend Linda, and her two dogs, Ben and Jake. We lived cheaply and all our money went on drink, music, petrol and food (in that order) but Pat and I loved each other and enjoyed each day as it came (it was only our future I worried about). Some mornings we'd wake to find fog and pollution hanging low in the valley outside so that the smokey old mill town of Keighley was obliterated, while from our bedroom window we enjoyed a glorious view across the tops of the clouds glistening in bright sunlight and stretching away into the distance. We felt like gods.

One Tuesday morning I woke up and looked at Pat, sleeping softly beside me, and decided I loved her so much I wanted to wake up beside her every morning for the rest of our lives. When she opened her beautiful blue eyes and smiled I asked her if she'd like us to marry. She answered by throwing her arms round me. We wanted a quiet wedding and weren't going to tell anybody except Porter and Linda (who were to be our witnesses). But we relented and phoned our parents, the word went round and on the Friday about fifty friends and family showed up at Keighley Registry Office. After we'd made our vows we had an impromptu party in a nearby pub and then Pat and I drove off in our little Morris 1000 van. We spent our wedding night in a hotel in Norfolk and the rest of our honeymoon touring the countryside sleeping in the back of the van. It was such a relief to me, being married. To have one sexual partner freed me to enjoy platonic friendships with other women. And Pat's father, who'd totally refused to speak to me while I was living in sin with his daughter, suddenly became all smiles and welcoming. Now I could plan our rocking-horse future with confidence knowing I had someone to share it with.

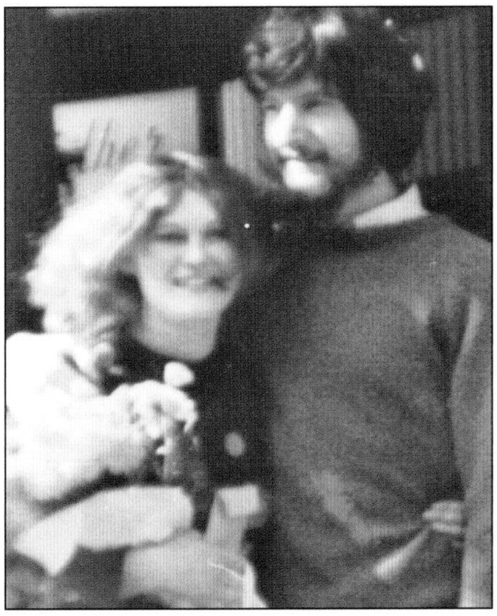
Pat & AD - wedding day..

Pat was earning and I needed to work too. I was dubious about being a teacher but was now qualified so applied for a job teaching metalwork, maths and remedial reading at a local Middle School. At least teaching promised short working hours and long holidays. I liked the kids, most of them, but the work was all-consuming and so enervating I couldn't even think about rocking-horses. My metalwork shop was a bus ride away from the school which ate into lesson time, especially when kids missed the bus and I had to go looking for them. Many of the children came from poor homes where English wasn't spoken and, despite having gone to school for up to ten years, couldn't read or even write their names. I had to deal with daily arguments and fights among the kids and at the same time a war was going on between the long-serving teachers, mostly old-school disciplinarians, and the recently appointed Headmaster. He was young, progressive and liberal, struggling vainly to introduce a more enlightened approach than the chalk, talk and whack regime of the old-timers. Tensions in the school grew worse and worse and when, after two terms, the Headmaster committed suicide, I decided I'd had enough too, and quit. I was unemployed again.

I said, 'Look Pat, making rocking-horses is the only thing I really want to do. But we need money to get started and we haven't got any. I know I promised you I wouldn't go back to sea, but it's the only work I can do where I'll earn a lot more than we spend just living. Why don't I go back to sea and we use my sea salary and yours to raise a mortgage on the biggest, the most run-down house we can afford. We'll sell this cottage, do up the new place and sell it for a huge profit so we can buy a cheaper house with a workshop but lower outgoings. That'll really get us set up. How about it?'

'You've got it all worked out haven't you?'

'Yes. No. It's a plan. I don't want to be away from you but it won't be for too long. I reckon it'll take five years at most. A five year plan (like the Russians). It'll be laying the foundations for our whole future life together.'

'By going away?'

'Well, yes.'

'For five years?'

'No, no. I'll do short trips. We'll still get to see each other.'

'But it'll be five years, at least, before we start the family we're always talking about. What am I going to be doing all that time? Waiting for you?'

She had a point. Our lives would be drifting past while we were apart. We were young and in love but until now whenever Pat had asked me when we might actually have a baby, I'd always answered, 'Not yet'.

I said, 'There probably isn't a perfect time to start a family. It might be a mistake to delay until we get everything perfect because we might wait forever. Why don't we start now?'

'You mean that?'

'Of course. We'll manage somehow.'

So we went to bed and found that sex is never so wonderful as when two people really want to make a baby.

The day I left to join my ship was the day Pat got her pregnancy test result. I was all packed, ready to go and expecting her home in time to see me off. But the doctor kept her waiting and I didn't want to miss my train, so I walked to the station. I was already on the platform, the train approaching, when at last she appeared at the top of the ramp and came running down and into my arms.

'It's true Tony! I'm going to have our baby!'

The train came to a halt and I opened the nearest door, threw my bag into the carriage and turned to hug her. She didn't feel any different but she was radiantly beautiful, her blue eyes bright, her cheeks glowing and not from running.

'Wonderful news my darling. Goodbye.'

I climbed into the train, shut the door and pulled the window right down. The train pulled away and speeded up. I leaned out to wave and look back at her. She was standing with one hand on her tummy and the other raised, quite still, until a building blocked her from view.

We found a buyer for our cottage on the hill, a plump middle-aged businessman who stank of after-shave and deodorant and wanted a 'love-nest'. His young lover stood meekly beside him smoothing her mini-skirt, saying nothing.

He said, 'I'm a cash buyer Tony, and I want to push this purchase through asap, so I won't be bothering with a survey if you can assure me, man-to-man, that the property is sound.'

Immoral arsehole, I thought, and decided not to mention the damp or the rot in the cellar.

I said, 'It's an old cottage, but cosy and comfortable. We've been very happy here.'

He stuck his hand out, 'It's a deal.'

To expedite the sale and until we could find something better, we rented a Victorian back-to-back house in Fox Street, Bingley. The front door opened straight onto the cobbled street and the neighbours' houses were joined on at either side and behind. It had four rooms: cellar, living room, bedroom, attic. No bathroom or kitchen, no yard or garden. It was damp, draughty, condemned and due for demolition, but very cheap.

I was Second Mate on mv Cervantes doing ten-day round trips carrying some twenty containers from Felixstowe to the sunny Canary Islands and back. If the ship was delayed in Felixstowe Pat drove down to see me for a night or two. The best thing about going away was always our glorious reunions, but I was enjoying my job and excellent food prepared three times a day served by uniformed stewards in a smart saloon, and a warm, comfortable bunk in my own cabin with en-suite shower and toilet. Meanwhile pregnant Pat was living in squalor. As she grew bigger she needed the toilet more frequently and had to use a bucket and carry it up the street to the communal toilet block to empty. When winter came the pavements iced over and the toilets froze. Friday evenings she'd walk to town to the slipper baths where, for half a crown, she'd be given a bar of soap, a towel and the use of a bathroom. The place stank of sweat and disinfectant but the baths were clean and deep and the plumbing huge, with unlimited municipal hot water. You could have a bath to wash the dirt off then run another one for a soak. We went together when I was on leave and it was a friendly affair, neighbours chatting over the partitions as we luxuriated, laughter echoing through the steam.

Aside from being away from Pat I liked being at sea again: the wonderful smell, ambience and constant movement of a sea-going cargo ship, my role as a watch-keeping officer, the community of crewmen. I enjoyed battling through gales with the wind in my face and I got to navigate with a sextant again and acquire a new fund of sea stories. It wasn't so bad.

Pat said, 'You're not thinking of staying at sea are you?'

'Of course not, I want to make rocking-horses and a home with you and our family. It's just, I wish I'd got to be a Master Mariner.'

'Well, you've got something better now,' she said.

I nodded, snuggling in beside her to feel the swelling life in her belly.

Pat was teaching but using every spare minute to look at possible houses for us. Several times she found a likely property but, unwilling to commit without us both seeing and agreeing, we lost it. It was very frustrating, until she found a house nobody seemed in any hurry to buy, a five bedroom semi that had been empty and for sale for four years. It stank of neglect and thick dust, cobwebs and mouse droppings littered every room, windows were filthy, paint peeled from every wall and window-frame, weeds overflowed the gutters and the garden was a rampant wilderness. Exactly what we'd been looking for.

The roof was sound, it had central heating and the location was good - near Pat's parents and a ten-minute walk from the centre of the excellent market town of Skipton, 'Gateway to the Dales'. It even had a double garage I could use as a temporary workshop. And we could afford it. But why had it been empty so long? I looked and looked but couldn't see any structural faults or major problems. I concluded that all that was really wrong with it was neglect, and we could fix that. Our offer was immediately accepted and we moved in. Pat was delighted to escape Fox Street and we had a warm, dry home into which to welcome our child.

Pat's parents helped her with the mammoth task of cleaning the house and every time I came home, after our glorious reunion, we worked to improve it. Over the next months we brightened the whole place with fresh paint, converted the small fifth bedroom into the master bedroom's en-suite shower and WC (an unusually up-market feature in those days), built fitted wardrobes, decorated a bedroom especially for the baby and installed a cot. In short, we transformed the house from a shabby dump into a desirable, well-appointed family residence.

Pat, phenomenally enormous, was growing bigger by the day. We told ourselves that the disconcerting and even alarming changes to her physique, and us being apart most of the time, were more than counterbalanced by the joy of knowing that a tiny human was growing inside her. I lay with a hand and ear against her distended belly while we studied The Everyday Miracle, photographs of a living embryo as it develops from dot to fish to fully-formed baby.

All along Pat felt it would be a boy. I was home on leave and we were building a wall in the garden when he announced his imminent arrival. Pat was mixing mortar in a wheelbarrow when she suddenly dropped the shovel, gripped her belly, let out a groan and ran inside. I carried on laying bricks until she poked her head out of a bedroom window and shouted.

'The pains are coming close together Tony. We should go to the hospital.'

'Don't want to waste this fresh mortar, my love. Half an hour?'

I laid a few more bricks but she came out carrying her overnight bag and the look on her face was so urgent I abandoned the wall and we jumped into the car. I drove fast.

'Take it easy, Tony,' she said. 'I want us to get there alive.'

'Sorry. But you know I can handle the birth in

the car if we have to. *The Ship Captain's Medical Guide* says all we need is scissors and string. Don't you worry if it pops out early.'

'Don't call our baby it,' she wheezed. 'You even call your damned rocking-horse he. Anyway, look at the state of your hands.'

They were thick with muck and grey cement dust congealing in sweat. Five minutes from the hospital Pat announced that her contractions had ceased, so we detoured into the countryside and for an hour drove round in circles, the hospital at the centre of our anxious orbit, until she gasped and grasped the edge of the seat.

'He's coming. Let's get there now. Now.'

A nurse ushered us into the delivery room and helped Pat onto the bed. We'd learned some breathing exercises together but I couldn't remember how they went. The minutes ticked along slowly. Pat's face creased up with increasing frequency and I squeezed her hand, trying to play the calm, encouraging husband.

'Ow, you're hurting me.'

When the contractions came Pat screamed and cursed, not at all like her. She grimaced, her face flushed with pain and embarrassment.

'Here comes the head,' the midwife said, concentrating at the other end. 'One more big push now, dear. There! Perfect.'

There was a flurry of anxious activity as midwife and nurse grabbed the slithery newborn. I must have forgotten to breathe and staggered, fainting. I'd never imagined it would be this emotional, not for me. A nurse helped me from the room to slump onto a chair in the corridor and breathe deeply for a minute. Back in the room, now transformed into a remarkably tranquil scene, Pat was sitting up beaming, exhausted and relieved, damp hair clinging to her rosy cheeks and a huge smile lighting her face as she hugged our son, gently stroking him. He was perfect.

Later, at home alone, exhausted, drunk and exhilarated, I held up my glass and told the wall, 'I promise I'll always try to do my best for you, my son. I won't let you down. There are bad people out there who might want to hurt you but I'll never, never let anyone or anything do you harm. Not you, not my beautiful darling boy.'

Pat had said it was the happiest day of her whole life and I was feeling the most overwhelming emotions I'd ever experienced. Stumbling upstairs to bed it hit me how badly I'd treated my own Mum and Dad. Since I'd left home fifteen years before I'd done whatever I wanted and given them hardly a thought. I took it for granted they'd always welcome me with love whenever I chose to visit them, and they always did. Would my son treat me with such disdain? I hoped not. Would I always be here for him anyway? Yes. Would I be a good father? I'd try. I managed to get at least some of my clothes off before falling onto the bed. A few days later I fetched Pat and baby Sam home, my leave ended and I went back at sea.

I was now 2nd Mate on the Baltic Jet, a small general cargo ship taking leather hides, steel and other raw materials to Gdynia in Poland, bringing back ready-made machinery and household goods including tens of thousands of pairs of shoes. It was open stow, not containers, so shoes were easy to steal, but if a customs officer caught you without a receipt for your new footwear you'd be in trouble. Like Cervantes, the Jet did a regular round trip of about ten days calling at Felixstowe and Hull. Hull was less than two hours drive from home, the dockers there went on strike at the slightest excuse and delayed the ship, which was good news for us since it meant Pat and I often had time together.

She came with me on several trips to Poland, bringing Sam along. He was a tiny baby on his first sea voyage and later took his first steps and spoke his first word, 'Hammer,' on board the Jet. He was spoiled by all the crew and we were never short of someone to babysit. Gdynia was a concrete town, drab and grey, but the people were friendly and everything was so cheap on the black market that Pat and I did some smuggling.

We'd go ashore with Sammy in his pram and when we came back he'd be six inches higher, perched on top of sheets, towels, glassware, screwdrivers and chisels. In that way we acquired a great many items for our home and hand tools for my workshop. It was illegal to change money on the black market, never mind buy all this swag, but the companionway guards would sling their machine guns behind their backs and be so busy chuckling at the cute little baby in the pram they never thought to look under his mattress.

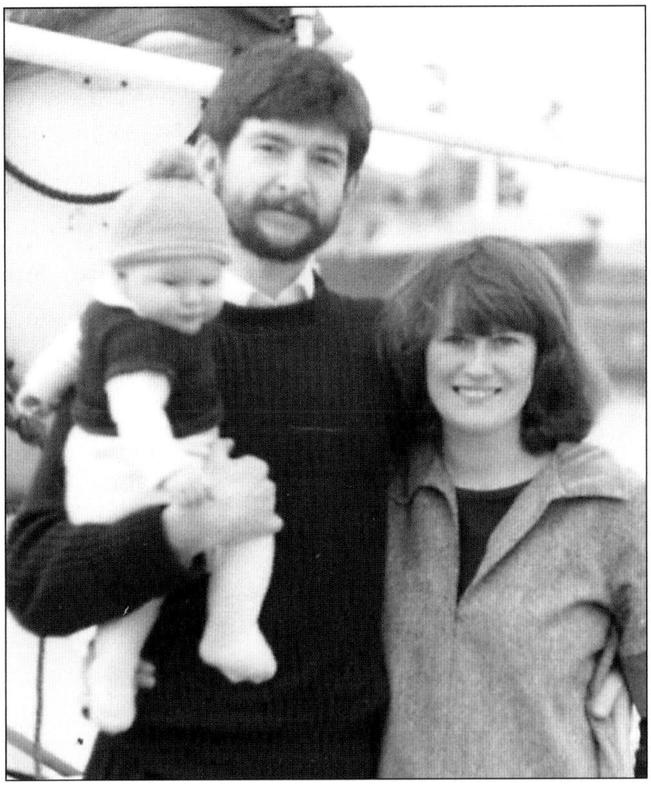

Sammy, AD & Pat on board the Baltic Jet.

# 4

*To know how to do something well is to enjoy it.*

For months I'd carried in my wallet a newspaper article entitled, 'End of an Era as England's Last Rocking-Horse Maker Retires'. I'd written to him, via the newspaper, and told him about the rocking-horse I'd made. He'd replied:

*'Dear Mr Drews, You should always enclose a stamped self addressed envelope if you write to me. Its only common politeness or should be. I get lots of letters and its my firm policy never to reply to anyone who is as inconsiderate and disrespectful as you have been in failing to send me a stamped self addressed envelope. However I've decided to make an exception in your case because you may be an impoverished student who can't afford a stamp. Also you have actually made a rocking-horse which most of the people who write to me haven't. If ever you are near Ipswich you may call and see me at my workshop, Sincerely, Jim Bosworthwick'.*

As well as docking at Felixstowe, the Jet occasionally went upriver to Ipswich and on one of these trips I got a full day off - my chance to meet a real live rocking-horse maker.

The bus driver dropped me at a stop he said was the nearest he got to Jim's village, still twelve miles away. The day was sweltering hot and not a single car passed for me to try to hitch a ride. I was loaded with unnecessary clothing and the arms of my jumper, jacket and coat were tied round my waist. Seamen don't walk much and I was really unfit, desperate for water, sweating from every pore, feet squelching with painful blisters in unsuitable shoes. But thirst and discomfort were forgotten when, well into the afternoon, I rounded a bend and saw Jim Bosworthwick's house and workshop.

White painted rocks lined the verge of a grassy track leading to a white thatched cottage. Smoke wisped from the chimney even on this hot day and I stepped under a fragrant arbour of pink and red roses to lift open the ancient wooden gate. A mass of colourful flowers surrounded the house and climbed the walls. A wooden farm cart overflowing with geraniums rotted gently in one corner. To the side a vegetable patch with neat rows of peas, carrots and onions. Runner beans swarmed up long canes tied together at the top. Chickens clucked and scraped in the yard and I could see a goat tethered in the orchard beyond. A sleeping dog raised his head to look over his shoulder at me, then slowly closed his eyes, dropped his head and went back to sleep. Even the bees buzzed softly. Everything was cared for but unkempt. Weeds were discouraged, not destroyed. I'd never seen anything remotely so idyllic for real, and I fell in love.

There seemed to be nobody about, but the door of a tin-roofed wooden shed hung open on broken hinges below a faded sign: 'James Bosworthwick. Toymaker.' As I stepped through the door I was blinded by the darkness inside.

'Hello-o.'

No reply. I sucked in the mingling smells of garden and animal, sawn timber, leather, and the stronger stink of fresh paint. As my eyes adjusted a great herd of white horses slowly emerged ghost-like from the gloom.

Dozens of them, forty at least, maybe fifty, not on rockers but standing on the dirt floor. I walked in amongst them. The heads of the biggest were as high as my chest but many were smaller and some tiny ones hardly knee-high. One or two were painted dapple-grey, some bare wood with empty eye sockets, but most plain white with glinting, staring glass eyes. They were wooden, so quite motionless of course, but they had a weird living presence, especially those with eyes, and I felt gripped by a silly fear that any sudden movement of mine would set off a stampede. I stepped carefully. They were all pointing in different directions, some looking into the darker recesses of the workshop, some towards the door as if they might make a bolt for it, some staring straight at me. I was surrounded by them in silent close-packed assembly and I felt like a god with his flock. The moment confirmed what I would do and be.

A squat, elderly figure emerged from the shadows and turned on a smile.

I said, 'Jim Bosworthwick? I'm Anthony Dew. I wrote to you a while ago and you very kindly wrote back.'

He wore a brown coat covered in paint blotches and held a dripping white brush in one hand. He thrust the other out to be shaken. It felt limp and sticky. He was clean shaven, short, plump and bald, and though I felt the awkward reverence of a young disciple before the Master, I was as disappointed as Dorothy when she met the Wizard of Oz. I don't know what I expected, some kind of larger-than-life Father Christmas look-alike perhaps, but I told myself it's not how he looks that matters, it's what he does.

At least his voice was impressively deep and encouraging. 'So young man, you want to make rocking-horses?'

'I do.'

I stammered with embarrassment and handed him a photograph of my first effort. He glanced briefly at it and handed it back, now with a big white thumb print in one corner.

'Good start,' he said.

He was lying, but I was ludicrously pleased and flattered. He put his brush down on the back of a horse and pulled a dirty rag from his pocket to wipe at his hands. I watched the paint drip from the brush and run down the horse's side. It was sacrilege, but it was his horse, he'd made it, so he could do what he liked with it.

'At least you've made one. I get a lot of people here. They stand where you're standing and tell me they want to do what I do, and you know what? They've never made a damned thing in their lives. Never even carved a roast chicken. They haven't the faintest idea. Non-starters. Time-wasters. And if they do give it a go they soon give up. It's hard work, see. They're all afraid of hard work these days. Are you afraid of hard work, young man? Then you might be the exception.

'Mark my words, young man, if you can make a good rocking-horse the world will beat a path to your door. There's enormous demand out there. Do you know I've a waiting list two years long? I can't make them quick enough. There's nobody left, nobody, only me, and I'm nearly done. After next Christmas I'm retiring. Mark this young man, the craft is ripe for revival. Who will carry the torch after me? You?'

As I sucked up his words I was looking round, desperate to take in everything and store it in my memory. There were wooden horses and parts of horses at every stage of construction heaped on every bench. Stands and rockers, body parts, heads and legs, tools, board patterns hanging from nails, long curved bow rockers in various sizes, other shapes I didn't recognise. What tools did he use? An ancient band-saw, a planer, a lathe and a big old Singer sewing machine appeared to be all the machinery he had. But hand tools littered every bench and hung all over the walls: saws, axes, adzes, gouges, mallets, rasps, drills, and tools whose names or use I couldn't even guess at. Everything covered in dust or rust but there for a purpose, to work. This was no museum, it was a living workshop. I noticed turned stand posts, metal fittings, rows of paint pots, leather hides hanging in a corner by the sewing machine, hanks of black hair.

'See these?' he said. 'Here's a tip for you.' He walked to a pile of cardboard boxes with Foreign Made stencilled on them and pulled out a couple of wooden spinning tops. 'I get so many time wasters. They're never going to buy a rocking-horse so I make them buy a top. Sometimes I make them buy two or three. You've got to get something out of them, eh? Business.' He chuckled, rubbing a thumb across his fingers.

I laughed but I wasn't interested in bought-in spinning tops. I had a million how-do-you-do-it rocking-horse questions but my mind was numb and I couldn't think of a single one to ask. Having made his little speech Jim appeared to be waiting for me to leave. The audience was over. I apologised for taking his precious time and thanked him profusely. I was kicking myself that in my hurry to leave the ship that morning I'd neglected to bring him a gift, a bottle of whisky or something.

I said stiffly, 'I hope to be able to call and see you again.'

'Anytime', he said. 'Anytime you're passing. Goodbye.'

He turned away abruptly, picked up his paint brush and I winced as he banged the bristles hard down at the congealing paint drips on the horse's back. I was dismissed. As I went outside, back into the bright sunshine, I heard him swear. Cursing me for a time-waster?

Marching away down the road my mind was a whirl of rocking horse images, plans, and workshop ideas. My fingers itched to wield mallet and gouge. Blessed are the ignorant for they know not what obstacles lie ahead. I'd learned such a lot. I knew I would carve the most beautiful rocking horses and they wouldn't be like my first one, that ugly brute. I laughed out loud and danced a jig along the road. I felt ridiculous and self conscious but there was no-one watching. The sun was still high in the afternoon sky and I was soon soaked with sweat again, my hurting feet squelching in sweat and bursting blisters and my mouth parched. I hadn't thought to ask him for a glass of water and he hadn't offered one. I longed to be back home with Pat, excitedly confiding what I'd seen and all my new rocking-horse ideas to her. She'd purse her lips and smile, 'Mmm ...'

# 5

*If the highest aim of a captain were to preserve his ship,*
*he would keep it in port forever.*

All the talk on the Jet was of redundancies. The company once had thirty ships, now it was down to five, all for sale, no longer viable. It was the same all over and I couldn't understand it. We were an island dependent on trade, weren't we? But Britain's once great merchant fleet was shrivelling. Sad Sid, the Jet's other Second Mate, lived in the cabin next to mine. He was forty-five and single, a skeleton of a man who drank two cases of beer a day and posted the empties out of his porthole in the dark believing nobody noticed. His unfastened sandals rattled a warning of his approach as he shuffled along the ship's alleyways.

'What will I do if I lose this job?' he wailed. 'What else can I do? I'm a professional seaman, this is all I know, all I've ever known.'

He hovered behind me swigging his beer, looking over my shoulder at my rough sketches of the rocking-horses I'd make one day.

'You're going to leave the sea to do that, Tony? You must be out of your tiny fucking mind.'

I shrugged, 'I know.'

I felt sorry for him. At least I had something to look forward to.

In the Summer of '79 the Baltic Jet was sold to Greek shipowners and we docked in Hull for the last time. I'd been on the Jet a year and would have happily stayed longer but went home on leave wondering what next. Sam was now walking and talking, a constant delight. I could hardly believe how much I loved that little boy, our son. After Sammy was born Pat had decided to stay at home to look after him rather than go back to teaching, and she was pregnant again. Every penny I earned went into the house and our living expenses and we had nothing left. We'd completed the main improvements to the house but there was a long list of finishing-off jobs still to do and we were constantly broke. I hoped I wouldn't have to go away to sea for the whole of the five years we'd talked about but we weren't at all ready to take the plunge, not yet. Another ship for a year, maybe two, and we'd be able to get properly set up.

I'd been at home a few weeks, working on the house, when the company's marine superintendent phoned to say he had a Second Mate's job for me.

'Great,' I said. 'Short trips?'

'Not what you've been used to,' he said. 'It'll be four months away and this ship doesn't come back to the UK at all.'

'Oh,' I said. 'That's disappointing. You know Pat's pregnant again? Our second.'

'Congratulations,' he said.

'Thanks. I really don't want to be going away for four months at a stretch, not now.'

'I understand,' he said. 'But I'm afraid I don't have anything else I can offer you.'

'In that case,' I said, and hesitated for about three seconds. 'You can keep your job. My seafaring days are over.'

That same afternoon I drove to the builder's yard in town and ordered timber for six rocking-horses. On the Jet I'd drawn plans for a more traditional-looking rocking-horse than my first unappealing effort, one I was sure people would love enough to buy, and I had a cutting list ready. I owned a mallet and a few carving tools and hand-saws bought in Poland or picked up in junk shops, and a huge old workbench with a massive cast iron vice with a lion on, mounted on a bench I'd bought for £5. It cost me £10 to have it delivered and was so heavy I'd near broken my back getting it in. We put the house up for sale and started looking for a cheaper one, with outbuildings or a big garage I could use for a workshop. Until it sold the garage at home would have to be my rocking-horse workshop so I set about equipping it with next to no budget.

My first woodworking machine was a lathe. I bought an ancient head and tail stock for a fiver at an auction, bolted them to a six-foot length of secondhand roof beam and powered it with a motor salvaged from a scrap washing-machine. Turning tools are specialised so I had to buy a couple new and Neil, a friend from my college days and a brilliant engineer, made me a long steel tool-rest. The lathe had some odd quirks but worked well enough. I taught myself to turn and the lathe served me well: I'd make all our rocking-horse posts on it for the next ten years.

I needed a bandsaw to cut out all the odd-shaped parts and bought one new, a three-wheel table-top model and the cheapest I could find. From the moment I started to use it I wished I'd gone for a better one. Every horse I made it broke at least a blade or two which was annoying, expensive and time-consuming to replace. It was a lesson to always buy the best professional equipment I could afford. But having paid good money for the thing I had to use it. My equipment was far from ideal but you can always make do - that was my second lesson.

A rocking-horse is a rectangular hollow box with a solid wooden head and neck on top and four legs jointed into the lower corners so they splay out. With cardboard from old wine boxes I made full size patterns for the parts. When the timber arrived I drew on the shapes, cut them out and glued and cramped them together. I soon ran out of the few cramps I owned so had to buy more and learned my third woodworking lesson: you can never have enough cramps. With my mallet and gouges I carved the horses and sanded them smooth by hand - a laborious and dusty job. I gave each horse three coats of white primer, two of dark grey and applied white dapples on top with a stencil brush. The inside of the mouth, ears and nostrils were painted red, as I'd seen on many old rocking-horses.

I cut steel rod to length with a junior hack-saw and bent it in a vice to make the swing irons on which the horse rocks. It was hard to get the bends right and a pile of failures accumulated in the corner. I cut steel strips to length to make brackets to secure the horse to its stand and used a device made by Neil to squeeze them into shape in my vice. I painted the metalwork black and the wooden stands bright red. I drove to a tannery in Hull to buy a couple of cowhides and with a craft knife cut strapping to make bridles and reins, stirrup leathers and simple saddles padded with foam rubber and nailed onto the horses' backs.

I enjoyed the smell of leather, paint and wood dust and the way my garage/workshop was filling with rocking-horse clutter, but there were always more things to buy. My horses couldn't be blind and bald but I was stuck for eyes and hair. I phoned Jim Bosworthwick and he sold me half a dozen pairs of glass eyes and some swatches of the hair he used. It came from the heads of Asian women who, he said, grew and harvested it like a crop. We didn't like the idea of human hair and it didn't look right, hanging limp and tangling easily. And it was all pure black rather than the grey I wanted, but I had to use it until we could find something better. Jim also sold me stirrup irons. Work-ing flat out from early morning to late evening every day, my first six rocking-horses were completed in six weeks. One a week. I was exhausted and exhilarated. At that rate we'd be in business - once we'd sold them.

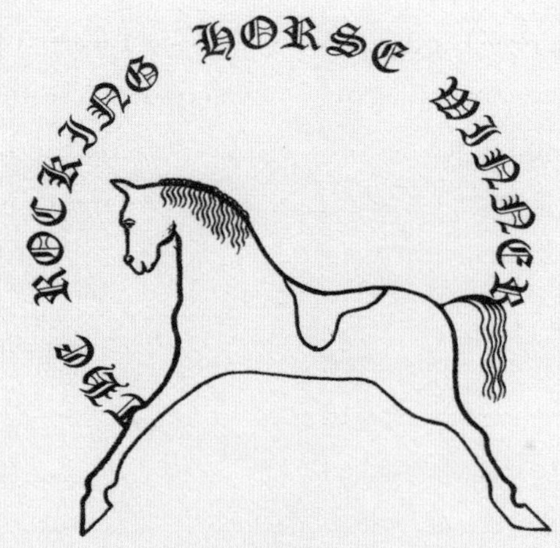


**A Real Rocking Horse — The toy that will delight your child and which will be cherished for many years. Entirely hand made in the finest tradition of English Rocking Horse making, using best quality timber throughout, with a painted dapple grey finish and real leather saddlery. The Rocking Horse stands about forty inches high and is mounted on a firm stand four feet long overall.**

They stood in line in the hallway like the start of the Grand National and we thought they looked marvellous. Eyes glinting, ears pricked, ready to rock. I fetched Sam and lifted him onto one for a test ride, pushing him gently back and forth and holding him steady. It rocked beautifully and I was disappointed that Sam looked nervous and uninterested. After only a few seconds he held up his arms to be lifted off.

'Is that all for now, little man? You can have another go later. Whenever you want.' He toddled off to play with toys nearer the ground. I was deflated.

'Never mind, he'll get used to them,' Pat said.

We called our embryo business The Rocking Horse Winner and had a brochure printed which Pat distributed to shops and notice-boards around town. She phoned our local newspaper, the Craven Herald and a reporter and cameraman came round. Next issue the paper's back page was dominated by a photograph of a very serious-looking Sam sitting on a rocking-horse, and a glowing write-up headlined, Horses in the Bedroom. Next came a reporter from the Yorkshire Post, our 'local national' newspaper, resulting in another big picture feature under the headline, 'The Rocking Horse Winner'. Then a crew came from the BBC's regional television news programme, Look North. Pat hid in the kitchen while I nervously answered the interviewer's questions and pretended to carve. Sam was carried in to sit astride a horse, unsmiling and unmoving, like he too was made of wood.

'Now then young man,' the cameraman said. 'Are you going to rock the nice horsey and give me a nice big smile?' Sammy stared at him.

'I'll take that as a no, then.'

The reporter said, 'It must be wonderful to do what you love doing and get paid for it.'

'It must be,' I said stiffly.

I watched myself later on the TV and squirmed with embarrassment, but Pat said, 'Just think how much we'd have had to pay for such great advertising exposure.'

Pat's Dad phoned, 'Saw you in the paper and on telly. Brilliant, bound to do you a lot of good.'

Porter phoned, same message.

I said, 'Thanks Porter, but we're sat here waiting for customers to call. Get off the line will you.' He hung up and the phone didn't ring again all evening.

Next morning we were having a silent breakfast when there was a knock on the front door. I jumped up and found a little old lady on the doorstep. She peered up at me and said, 'Oh there you are! Mr Dew! I recognise you from the television…'

She handed me a paper bag and I pulled out a large hank of the most beautiful wavy auburn hair, nearly as long as my arm. Her own hair was thin, wispy and white.

'... and I thought oh, he's only round the corner, I must go and see him. I do love rocking-horses. My grandchildren are too big for one now unfortunately, so I've nobody to buy one for, but I'd like you to have my hair.'

'It's, well, it's lovely.'

'My mother let me grow it. It was down past my waist. I had it cut in 1921 when I went to big school and kept it ever since. When I saw you on television I thought oh, you're just the person. You can use it on one of your beautiful rocking-horses.'

I doubted there was enough to make a mane and tail but I thanked her profusely and give her the last £10 note from my wallet. For the rest of the day we worked distractedly while we listened out for the phone, which didn't ring, not once. However, later that evening as we sat silently on the couch it did suddenly ring. We both started up and Pat answered it.

'A customer!' she screamed when the call ended. 'He's coming now.'

I dusted the horses again and we told each other to keep calm, but by the time the doorbell rang we were in a high state of excitement. Our customer was a smart young businessman in a suit and tie. We ushered him in and pointed to the six horses lined up along the hall.

'I'm up here on business,' he said in a clipped Birmingham accent. 'Happened to see you on the TV in my hotel room. We've two little ones at home. The item took my eye. Yes. Interesting ...'

Pat and I gushed, eager to show him all the finer points and offering him colour choices, discounts on the price, free delivery, anything he could possibly want, anything. He said he'd have to check with his wife before he ordered, glanced at his watch and said, 'Very nice. Thank you so much. I must be off. I'll be in touch.'

We closed the door behind him, held hands and danced in circles laughing. Our first customer! We sat discussing how long it would take him to get back to his hotel, phone his wife and then us to confirm his order. When he didn't phone we started to wonder if maybe we should have asked him for a deposit. Then we thought maybe he'd decided to leave phoning us to the morning. He didn't phone then either. Or at all. Of course he didn't. We'd frightened the life out of the poor man and would never hear from him again. We hadn't even thought to take his contact details so we could do a follow-up.

All the years I'd been at sea I'd been proud to call myself a seaman. Recently I'd been telling people I'd quit seafaring and was now a rocking-horse maker. It felt good and right. But my confidence wobbled.

# 6

*Ignorance of thine ignorance is thy fiercest foe (and a blessing).*

I'd once applied for a job as a dishwasher in a back-street greasy-spoon cafe in Dover and when they turned me down thought I couldn't get any lower, job-wise. But this was worse, far worse. Now I spent every Tuesday in the Department of Health and Social Security waiting room, waiting. I was almost horizontal on an uncomfortable plastic chair, legs stretched out, thumbs in belt, beard on chest, hair overhanging chair back, staring at my sandals. The room was near-silent though filled with people. Across from me sat a young woman who also spent Tuesdays there, waiting. She was trying to keep her writhing baby on her knee and every so often whined at her other kids, a two and a three-year-old, to shut up and keep still. They ignored her. Everyone else stared silently at their feet or the ceiling. The air was thick with tobacco smoke and stank of sweat and fart. Nobody spoke except for the occasional breathy curse. Each Tuesday I arrived at the appointed time and waited two or three hours to see an official, a different one each time. Each week I repeated my story.

'I'm applying for unemployment benefit to help me through a difficult period.'

'Are you out of work, Mr Dew?'

'I'm broke.'

'I asked, are you out of work?'

'Well, I'm working at trying to start a business.'

'So you are working in your own business.'

'I'm working at it, yes. But I'm not earning anything.'

'But you are working'

'Yes. But I have no income.'

'But you are working, Mr Dew, and as such you are not available for work, is that correct?'

'I have a wife and baby and another on the way. I'm hoping the business I'm working at will support us all, but it doesn't, not yet.'

'The work you are doing in your own business Mr Dew, renders you ineligible for unemployment benefit. You have to be available for work.'

'Well I am. I'm broke. I need money.'

'What sort of work are you available for Mr Dew?'

'I don't know. I won't go back to sea again.'

'You have refused the gainful employment for which you are qualified, is that correct?'

'Yes. No. I'm trying to find something better.'

Each week my claim was rejected. Our situation was becoming increasingly desperate.

One week the official, slightly more sympathetic than usual, said, 'You know Mr Dew, your claim would have been accepted if you hadn't told us you were working in your own business. Why did you do that?'

'Because it's public knowledge. We've been all over the papers and on TV. If I hadn't mentioned it you'd be accusing me of fraud.'

'I'm afraid you're suffering the penalty of honesty.' He smiled, sniffed, nodded, and rejected my claim again.

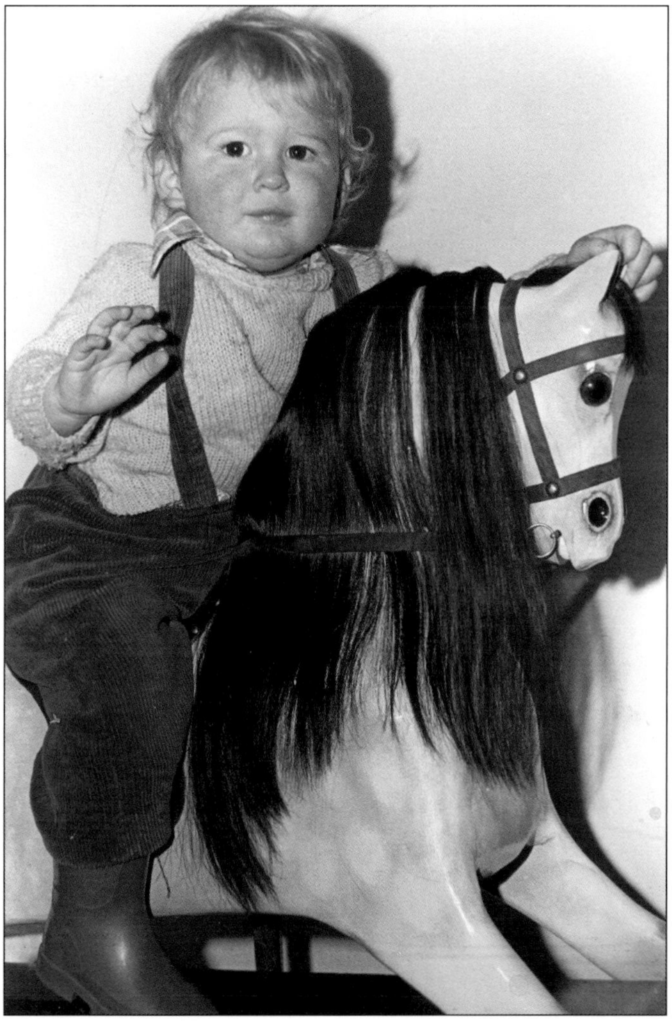

'Good luck,' I said to the young mother on my way out. She stared up at me, her eyes dead. Her claim was rejected every week too, although she was clearly in dire straits. Outside I gulped some fresh air and tried to shake off the paralysing, depressing frustration that threatened to overwhelm. We were in limbo. No customers so no incentive to do anything in my workshop. No income. No prospective buyers for our house either. I promised myself that if I ever got out of this hole I'd never enter a benefits office waiting room ever again.

I saw a job advertised in the Craven Herald for a maintenance joiner in a lift factory in Keighley and applied, telling the Personnel Manager I'd done all sorts of woodwork including making rocking-horses.

'Really?' he laughed. 'Then I'm sure you'll be able to handle this. Only thing is, this factory is a closed shop, you'll have to join the Union.'

'I've no problem with that, when can I start?'

There were two maintenance joiners - the other was an old man who'd been there thirty years. He pottered about chatting while I got on with the work - repairing broken furniture, putting up shelves and making workbenches. I also learned how lifts were made, including using an enormous automatic panel saw and router that precision-cut the huge plastic-faced plywood sheets that lined them. We were continually shifting furniture and machinery around the factory and when I got home at the end of each day I flopped into a chair exhausted. No energy to make rocking-horses, even if there was any point. The job didn't pay well and I was terrified of being stuck in it forever, but at least we were holding our own financially.

A few weeks into the joinery job a letter from the DHSS informed me that my claim for un-employment benefit had been allowed. For a week cheques arrived in every post, often two or three together. Some were for less than £10, one was over £300, and all sorts of amounts in between. There was never any indication of how the sums had been calculated and they were a bit late, now that I was in regular paid work, but very welcome. We paid off our debts, stocked the larder with quality food, bought some good music and went to the pub. After a week the cheques stopped coming and instead, a letter informing me, 'There appears to have been a system irregularity resulting in overpayment of your claim'. Then a stream of letters with increasingly strident demands for repayment, which I ignored.

When I started at the lift factory the shop steward had given me an application form for Union membership. A month later he came to see me and said, 'You haven't filled in the section about where you served your time.'

'That's right, like I told the Personnel Manager, I haven't served an apprenticeship.'

'if you haven't served an apprenticeship you can't join the Union. You can't work here.'

'But I do work here. I've been here a month, you know that. I can do the job, you know that too.'

'I can't help that. You can't work here.'

'I've a wife and baby and another on the way. I need this job.'

He shrugged and walked away. The next day the Personnel Manager called me into his of fice.

'I'm sorry, Tony. I didn't think they'd push it.'

'I'm already working here. What's the problem?'

'The problem is they're threatening an all-out strike if you stay.'

'I need this job.'

'I know. But the last thing the company needs is a strike.'

'Are you going to fire me?'

'No. I can't fault your work and I won't fire you, but I am going to ask you to consider resigning. If you leave now, before they call a strike, I will pay you a month's wages and another month on top.'

'Can I give you my answer tomorrow?'

'Of course.'

I didn't care to be bullied and was tempted to dig my heels in and tough it out. On the other hand maintenance joiner wasn't much of a job and it would be unpleasant, to say the least, to be working where I wasn't wanted. The Personnel Manager had been very fair with me. On my way home I called at a firm I'd noticed advertising for a joiner. Not a large factory this time but a small family company employing half a dozen men. I told the boss what was happening to me and he said, 'I'll give you a job. When can you start?'

'They want me to leave immediately. Monday?'

Around this time Pat's older brother John came to visit and we showed him our six unsold rocking-horses lined up along the hall. A confident businessman, John had emigrated to the USA several years previously and was now living the full American dream: he drove a monster car, played golf with his business associates, lived in a big house, had big debts, ulcers, a huge alimony bill and two bratty kids. He'd made himself rich building British-style houses in the US, lost it all and made himself rich again. He talked business all the time and he knew what he was talking about. We could learn a lot from him.

He said, 'Tony, you can make the finest rocking-horses the world has ever known, which by the way I don't think you are, but if you're not selling them and making a profit you're not in business, you've got a hobby. Business is about selling. It doesn't matter what your product is.'

I wondered if that was true. I needed to make something and supposed I could make something else, but this was what I'd chosen.

I said, 'I'm a rocking-horse maker, John. What you call the 'product' matters a lot to me.'

He snorted a laugh, 'Sure, but nobody's buying them, are they? Whatever your product is, you have to sell it and it has to be good enough to persuade your customers to get their wallets out.'

'I dare say we've got a lot to learn about selling. But why won't anybody buy my rocking-horses? What's wrong with them?'

'Honestly?'

'Yes.'

'They lack the wow factor. The colours are insipid. Their heads are too small.'

The bluntness of John's comments shocked me. After he left I sat and looked at my six unsold horses. I'd made them - six horses in six weeks! - and I'd been so proud of them. I tried to see them as he did, as others would. I realised I'd been so close to them I'd lost all objectivity. John was right. They simply weren't good enough, they looked bland and their heads were too small. I took a big hammer and smashed the heads off two of them. I mustn't be precious. I cut out new larger heads and tried to carve them with more definition, more character. I re-examined the paintwork and suddenly realised I'd got the dappling completely the wrong way round. Black dappling on a pale grey background would be far more striking. I re-made the bridles and saddles too, improving them. I looked and looked and practised and practised and became a whole lot more self-critical. I recalled one of my art tutors at college talking about 'working through the point of despair'. Now I knew exactly what he'd meant.

I was heartened and energy flooded back. However tired I was from my day job I wanted to be in my rocking-horse workshop. The problem was that all the improvements I was making took time. It wasn't viable to take so long over every horse, I'd be working for pennies. It was going to be hard enough to charge a realistic price for a new rocking-horse when good old ones could still be found in second-hand shops at £5 or £10, or even in skips for nothing. But I was a novice and needed to master the craft. I decided to concentrate on making my rocking-horses as good as I could get them. Then, after we'd won some customers, I could think about increasing my efficiency and prices. It was going to be a hard slog, but we'd get there.

As the first of my new improved rocking-horses neared completion Pat's Dad called in. He was a Cockney, slightly built but very strong. 'Feel that neck!' he'd boast, explaining how he left school at fourteen to be a porter in Billingsgate Fish market. He'd started out carrying a case of kippers on his head, eventually graduating to seven stone of turbot, and he had a neck like a tree trunk. He and Pat's Mum would call by daily to see baby Sam and pregnant Pat. They were aware of our rocking-horse struggles and had observed the progress of my first six with mild interest. Now he took a good long look at my upgraded horse.

'Oh I do like that,' he said. 'So much better. Do you know, I think I'll buy one.'

'Oh come on Dad, you really don't have to.'

'No, no, I want to. I insist. That horse is a real beauty and I want to buy it. I'll have it at my house for the grandchildren to ride whenever they come.'

He wouldn't be dissuaded. Maybe he was Pat's Dad but he was our first paying customer so we opened a bottle of wine to celebrate. Pat was getting bigger all the time and little Sam sat in his high chair watching us, gurgling happily and shouting, 'Hammer, hammer.' I fetched a box of brown price tags with strings I'd bought in anticipation of this moment, pulled one out, wrote £250 on it with a red felt-tip pen, crossed it out and scrawled SOLD in big letters.

'The first of many. Cheers.'

We clinked glasses. 'How many more price tags in that box?' Pat asked.

'Nine thousand nine hundred and ninety-nine.'

'That's a terrifying lot of rocking-horses.'

'I know, but we're out of the start gate. We're off!'

# Part Two

# 7

Herberry House sounded grand but was actually a decrepit roadside cottage with four dingy rooms and doorways we had to duck to get through. The kitchen and bathroom were in a lean-to at the rear under an asbestos roof, and far from having a pleasant eco-connection with herbs and berries, 'Herberry' was the run-together names of a previous owner's sons, Herbert and Terry. It was run down and neglected but for a tiny cottage boasted a very large garage, my future rocking-horse workshop. Unfortunately the cottage was a long way away from our friends, Pat's parents and Yorkshire's beautiful dales - not where we wanted to be at all - but we could get more for our money in the flatlands of the East Riding and I was prepared to go anywhere to further my rocking-horse ambitions. Pat said she liked the village, the cottage oozed character and had a decent back garden where the kids could play.

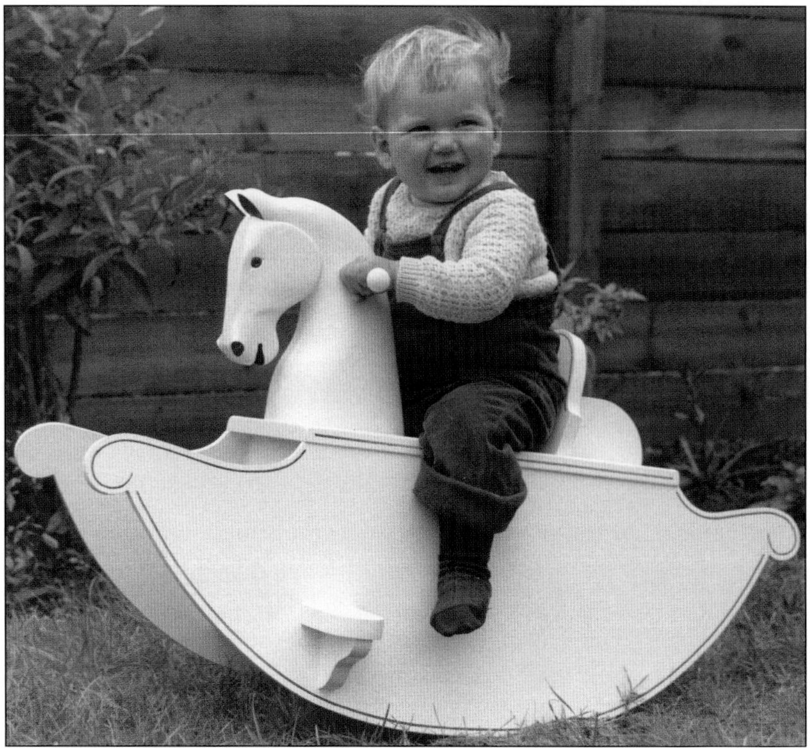

Our move coincided with the birth of Kate (short for Kathleen, after my Mum). Not great timing, but we were delighted to have a daughter who'd be a friend for Sam. Kate proved a much more demanding baby than he had been, crying a lot and staying awake all hours. Pat took her and Sam to stay at her sister's house in Leeds while, with the help of our friends, the ever-voluble Porter and the near-silent John Stentiford, I moved all our possessions in our old transit van. I slept in the van in the yard for a few weeks while I damp-proofed the cottage and tried to make it habitable. As is always the case with old houses, Herberry House was in a much worse state than had been apparent before we moved in. It was still a mess when Pat and the children joined me but we were together in our own home.

Selling our Skipton house was the single most profitable business I'd ever do in my life. We'd owned it only twenty months and near doubled our money. Of course we'd spent a lot improving the property, but we'd done all the work ourselves, so no labour costs. I thought, if we go into the house improvement business we'll be a whole lot better off financially. But no, I'd set my heart on making rocking-horses. Anyway, we'd achieved the first part of our plan: we had a home for our family and a workshop for our rocking-horses, paid for almost entirely out of the profit from the Skipton house, so our outgoings were greatly reduced.

Sam toddled about getting into everything. The day after we moved into Herberry House we found him playing with a box of mothballs he'd found, the white stuff all round his mouth. We phoned the doctor who told us to get him to Selby hospital, fast. The consultant there said he'd spoken to one of the big London hospitals specialising in poisons and learned that, if ingested, napthalene can irreparably burn the stomach lining. We must try to flush it through Sam's system by getting him to drink lots of milk. Unfortunately Sam hated milk.

Through his tears and splutterings we forced as

much milk into him as we could. Then Pat went home with baby Kate while Sam and I (still in my filth) were driven in an ambulance with blue lights flashing and sirens blaring to York Hospital to spend the night under observation. Sam slept in the bed and I crashed out next to him. He slept well, as he always did, and in the morning seemed perfectly well. We concluded he probably hadn't actually eaten any of the foul-smelling stuff after all, and Pat came to fetch us home. We'd had an awful fright and felt terribly guilty.

Before we left Skipton we'd managed to sell four of my original batch of six medium size carved rocking-horses with the bigger heads and better paintwork. To expand our range in both directions I now made a large version and a very small and simple rocking-horse for toddlers. The Toddler's design was based on the original 17th Century style of rocking-horse with slab sides. It was easy to make, mostly out of plywood, and inexpensive. I was keen to make the rocking-horse experience accessible to all, not only the rich. It upset me that Sam was still wary of my big rocking-horses but the Toddler's rocker had an exciting action and he, my chief tester, loved it. We now had three rocking-horses to offer customers: the low-priced 'starter' Toddler's rocker with either simple cut-out or carved head, a Medium fully carved horse, and a 'Large Special', our top-of-the-range model.

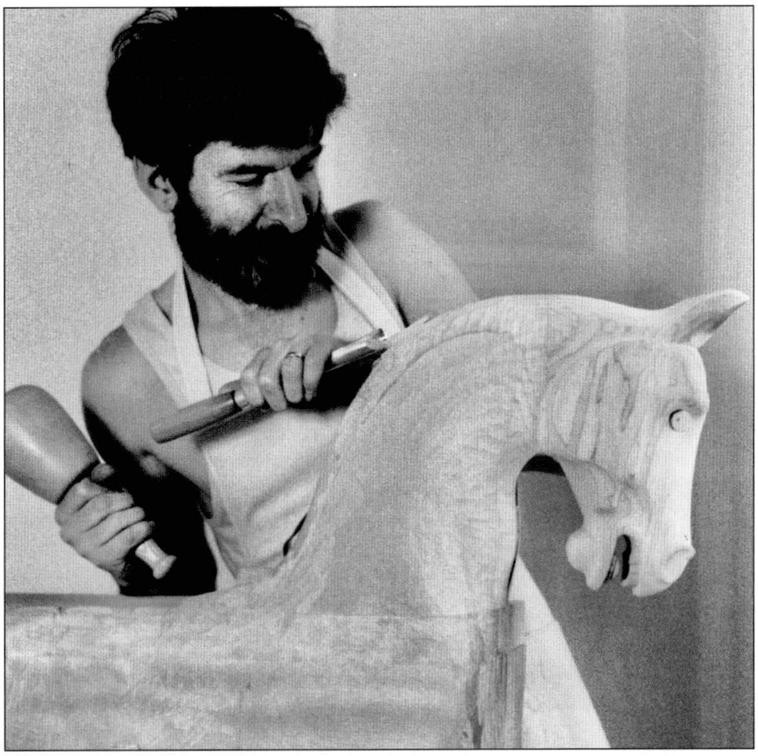

It wasn't only size that made the large horse special. A customer, seeing an unfinished horse in my workshop, said what a pity it would be to cover all that lovely wood and careful carving with paint. So instead of the usual painted dapple-grey, I said I'd make her a horse with a varnished natural wood finish. This presented extra challenges because there'd be no chance of hiding mistakes and blemishes in the woodwork under filler, gesso and paint. If all my wood joints were to be on show they'd have to be good. That first natural wood finish horse was made in pine and it turned out surprisingly well. I realised I could use other types of timber, and stains too, and so enhance the be spoke service we wanted to offer by giving our customers the choice of a variety of different finishes.

I worked every hour I could in my workshop at Herberry House and my rocking-horses were improving, each one a little better than the one before. But sales were still few and far between and we couldn't make a living out of them, not yet. John Stentiford, our soft-spoken and highly intelligent friend, was a postman. The work, he told me, mostly out in the fresh air, kept him fit and gave him plenty of time on his own to think.

'The pay's not great and I'm up ridiculously early,' he said. 'But the people are friendly and after I've finished my round I have the rest of the day to myself.'

I liked the idea so applied to Selby Post Office, passed the entrance exam and started sorting letters and delivering them. I had to be up at four, six days a week, cycling and walking many miles carrying a huge bag of mail. On a good day I'd run my post round and be home by mid-morning to devote the rest of the day and most of the evening to the rocking-horses in my workshop. We paid our way and I was never so fit, albeit perpetually tired. When customers came, as they started to do a little more frequently, Pat looked after them. Most of the house-keeping, cooking and child-care fell to her as well. She said it was all getting to be too much, she was worn out.

I said, 'I know it's hard but this is the best way to divide our labour while we build our business, and don't forget it's not just our business, it's our life. It will come good eventually, I promise, for both of us. Anyway, you know I'm always here for you and the children and I will try to make more time for you, OK?' She pursed her lips, smiled weakly and nodded.

I took time out from the workshop to build a sandpit for the children and a shed in one corner of the garden. Pat planted flowers and I cut back the overgrown holly hedge and started training part of it into the shape of a horse's head. Beyond our garden fence, in what had once been Herberry House's garden, local builder Cyril was building a pair of houses. Sam and baby Kate loved playing in the garden and whenever the weather allowed they were out there digging in the sand or standing at the fence watching Cyril and his men at work, fascinated to see the new houses taking shape.

Peggy, our immediate neighbour on one side, was a reclusive middle-aged spinster lady who'd looked after her mother until the old lady died and now lived alone. As Cyril's houses neared completion we heard that he had a problem. He'd had an understanding with Peggy's mother that when the time came he'd run the dirty water pipe from his new houses through her garden to join up with the main sewer in the road at the front. But the agreement was only verbal, Peggy knew nothing about it and she didn't like Cyril. So when Cyril asked her if she'd stand by what he'd agreed with her late mother, Peggy said, 'No, go away'.

'He's stuffed,' I told Pat. 'If Cyril can't connect to a sewer he'll never be able to sell the houses he's building. The only alternative route is through our garden. We can expect him to pay us a visit.'

Cyril duly knocked on our door and we ushered him into the kitchen. He was a hard-working East Yorkshireman who'd lived and worked in the village all his life, buying cottages with very big gardens (like ours had been) and building one or two houses at a time. From what I'd seen he was a fine builder who cared a great deal about the quality of his work as well as making money. I respected that and liked him. He took off his flat cap and Pat made him a mug of tea while he explained his sewer problem.

I said, 'Oh dear.'

He said, 'I was thinking, Tony, if you agree to let me run the pipe under your garden, well, I'd have to dig a trench for it, but I'd make it good after. I'll replant the border for you, new plants, and replace turf where we disturb the lawn. You'll not know we'd been there.'

'Mm,' I said.

He said, 'I was thinking, Tony, that drive of yours. It's a bit of a mess isn't it? How about I lay new tarmac right across. A proper job. Really tidy it up, you know.'

'That'd be good,' I said.

Cyril was quiet for a minute then he said, 'I was thinking, Mrs Dew, yon cooker of yours, it looks to me like a bit of an old model. How would you like a brand new fan oven? Top of the range. I'll have it all wired in for you.'

We shook hands all round and when he'd gone and was out of earshot, Pat and I burst out laughing. Cyril was as good as his word.

One morning Pat was sitting on the couch in the living room breast-feeding baby Kate. Sam was with her and a friendly neighbour and her two small children. The floor was totally littered with toys and nappies and furniture and a mass of other stuff. When the phone rang, the friend answered it and said, 'One moment please, I'll pass you over to Mrs Dew.'

She whispered, 'It's a Mrs Fanshawe, a rocking-horse customer,' and handed the phone to Pat.

Pat gently prised Kate from her nipple and, with one breast hanging out, passed the baby to her friend and searched for a pen and something to write on.

'Good morning Mrs Fanshawe. How may I help

you?'

'Good morning Mrs Dew,' the customer said. 'As I was just saying to your receptionist, I'm enquiring about your rocking-horses and I…'

'Our receptionist!' Pat said later. 'If that woman could have seen the chaos in our living room. Oh my god, our receptionist!' She laughed and laughed, loud and long, but her laughter had a bitter edge.

'Well,' I said. 'Maybe one day.'

To make our rocking-horses known to potential customers we took stands at agricultural, home and gift shows around Yorkshire and sometimes further afield. We usually attracted plenty of interest, especially if I was demonstrating carving, but few paying customers, sometimes none. We weren't at all comfortable with selling and the shows were always expensive and time-consuming to prepare for and attend. We often came home deflated, trying to justify ourselves: 'It gets our name out there. We've given out lots of brochures. At least three people were genuinely interested. Maybe they'll come back and order. It's good marketing.'

I thought that if we had something low priced to sell at these shows, that people would buy without too much thought, we might at least cover our costs. I remembered the wooden spinning tops Jim Bosworthwick sold to every visitor. At an auction we bought a load of bankrupt stock toys including some splendid Pelham string puppets, colourful kites and other playthings at give-away prices. I made a market stand with a canvas roof and the next show we went to, as well as our rocking-horses, we had puppets, kites, jigsaws, plastic dolls and balloons to sell, even some tops.

We sold plenty and made ready money, but soon realised the downside: people bought the cheap toys but ignored the rocking-horses. The good stuff sold well but we were left with the trashier items and re-stocking with good quality profitable toys wouldn't be easy. After a few shows we decided we'd best forget cheap toys and concentrate on our rocking-horses. I was undoubtedly making better rocking-horses, but customers for them were still too few and far between and we neede sometyhiung less expensive to sell to help our cash-flow problem.

Visitors to the shows often asked lots of questions but we soon realised these people were never going to be customers for a rocking-horse. They were home woodworkers who wanted to know about my methods of construction and the tools I used because they wanted to have a go at making one themselves. They often asked if there were any plans available.

'There are no plans,' I told them. 'If there were I'd have used them myself!'

To Pat I said, 'I could draw some patterns and write a set of instructions. If we can't sell these people a rocking-horse, we can at least sell them what they want, a plan to make one of their own.'

'But you've worked so hard to learn how to do it, how to get it right. Won't you be giving away all your secrets?'

'Yes, some, but they've still got to pick up the tools and do the hard part themselves. Telling someone how to carve a horse and them actually doing it are two different things.'

'I suppose you could run courses, teaching people how to do it.'

'I could, yes. And I'm thinking that everyone who makes a horse will also want accessories: saddlery, stirrups, manes and tales, glass eyes, all that. All specialist things we could sell to them.'

'And wood.'

'Timber, yes of course. We could sell them the wooden parts already cut to shape.'

'But wouldn't you be encouraging competition?'

'I suppose. There may be a few out there like us, crazy enough to try to go into business making rocking-horses, I don't know. Anyway, if they do they'll soon find out how hard it is.'

We bought some rolls of thick lining paper and with a ballpoint pen I drew round my patterns for the head, neck, legs and the rest of the parts, and labelled them. I wrote some step-by-step in-structions and Barbara Johnson, a lovely lady who with her coalminer husband and their children had moved into one of Cyril's new houses, typed up my longhand notes. We took the typed sheets to the public library and made a dozen copies and back home on the kitchen table collated and stapled them together, folded them so they fitted in a poly bag, put in a photograph of the finished horse and made a poster saying: 'All You Need to Know to Make your own Rocking Horse. Patterns and Instructions.' Now at shows we could say to amateur woodworkers, 'All your questions will be answered when you buy this pack, only £15'.

The take-up was surprisingly good; the first show we took them to we sold out. We made up more sets of plans and sold them too. I wrote an article about making rocking-horses for Practical Woodworking magazine and more orders came in. Soon people were sending us cheques to pay for accessories and fittings they needed for the rocking-horses they were making. We were buying all these things anyway for my own rocking-horses, but with increasing demand we were able to order more and consequently get better prices from our suppliers.

With my finished rocking-horses there was often a terribly long wait between pay-days. With plans and accessories payment came with the order. We had to carry stock so we didn't keep mail-order customers waiting, but our turnover shot up and our cash flow problems were essentially solved. It was seven years since I'd made my first rocking-horse and every year since then we'd lost money. Now, for the first time, our rocking-horse enterprise was making very slightly more than it cost us. Things were definitely looking up.

# 8

Any small profit our rocking-horses made went straight back into the business and we were always short of money. I still couldn't consider quitting my postman's job but I was tempted to try to earn money from my woodwork by making things other than rocking-horses. When neighbours mentioned they'd been unable to find a large dresser/sideboard unit for their dining-room, that they liked and which fitted, I offered to design and make one for them. It worked out well and they were pleased. But when I added up all the hours this one-off project had taken, which filled all my 'spare' time and my workshop for three weeks, we'd made very little.

I decided on a rule-of-thumb for costing cabinet-making work in future: after estimating the time and cost of a project, I'd double the time and treble the price. Surprisingly, it worked. And far from scaring customers away, my quotes gave them a sense that they'd be employing a fine craftsman who must be worth the price. Also, I could take the time to make the job as good as I could, knowing I'd receive a reasonable return for my effort.

Around this time I befriended Eric, a confident Yorkshireman who, bored to death with his office job, dreamed of being a designer and maker of modernist furniture. To this end he'd built himself a splendid workshop in his back garden, equipped with excellent woodworking machinery and hand tools. He showed me photos of the first few pieces of fine furniture he'd completed. Very impressive, and he'd sold them easily. Emboldened, Eric quit his day job, but soon found he wasn't attracting enough customers for his bespoke furniture designs to make a living. Like us, Eric couldn't afford to advertise and he ran into a problem we faced too, that once he'd made a piece and it had gone off to its new owner, he had nothing but photographs to show the next prospective customer.

What Eric did have was people bringing him damaged furniture for repair. Most of this stuff really wasn't worth the time it would take him to fix. But, desperate for work, he accepted it all. His workshop soon filled up with cheap broken furniture and started to look like a second-hand furniture store. This spoiled his image as a fine craftsman and since he didn't dare charge much for these repair jobs he wound up working all day every day for next to nothing. The struggle became too much for him and within months Eric's fledgling business died. He took a regular job as a salesman.

Eric's example taught me a lot. Diversification was tempting and we needed to get our pricing right, but there simply weren't enough hours in each week for me to be a cabinet maker *and* make rocking-horses *and* be a postman *and* spend quality time with Pat and the children. I decided to forget cabinet-making and specialise exclusively on rocking-horses.

We'd make new ones and restore old ones, sell plans and instructions for home woodworkers to make and restore them, as well as all the accessories and fittings. If they wanted to buy a fully-carved horse for £1000, great; but if all they wanted - like the customer who boasted that he'd made his rocking-horse for next to nothing using wood from old pallets and a discarded school satchel for the saddlery - was a pair of eyes for £1, we'd still be happy. We'd sell anything to anybody, so long as it was rocking-horse related. We'd deal with all enquiries in an open, friendly and informative way, and hope that the word would spread that for anything to do with rocking-horses, we were the people. Our expertise would be narrow, but comprehensive. An inch wide and a mile deep.

Pricing could be difficult, especially with restoration work. People often brought in their own well-loved childhood plaything which had been relegated to a shed where it had languished, often for decades, until a new grandchild came along and the old rocking-horse was remembered. By this time damp and woodworm had got to it, leatherwork had perished, paint fallen off, joints come apart. Once or twice people arrived with horses completely in bits so I'd be confronted with a 3D jigsaw puzzle. I said yes to every rocking-horse restoration, regardless of condition, because each of the old-time makers had their own approach to construction, quality and finish and I learned a great deal from close examination of these battered old nags. But we refused to underestimate the cost. I worried about scaring customers away, but as our expertise grew, and our confidence, we found the vast majority of customers accepted our quotations. If they wobbled we'd tell them we'd never charge them more than quoted and they could expect a first-rate job from one of the few real professional rocking-horse specialist restorers in the world.

Pat looked after our home, children and customers, ran a mother and toddler group in the village and did an evening job on the side to make extra money. She was constantly exhausted. I was up at four every morning and working late every evening, trying to make do with less and less sleep. Life seemed to have become a relentless grind and we were still a long way from the idyllic lifestyle we'd dreamed about. Then, when I'd been a postman for two years, I read an advertisement in the Selby Times: 'Part-time Woodwork Master required for Boys Independent School.'

Years earlier, when I'd quit teaching, I swore I'd never ever enter a classroom again - except maybe as part-time woodwork teacher in a private school. I'd thought I was joking, but now I said to Pat, 'Here's my job advertised.'

As soon as my post round finished the next morning I went to meet the Headmaster. Mr Green was new to Reed School and keen to make his mark. He showed me round and took me to the school's woodwork shop, an old Methodist chapel in the village a few minutes walk from school.

He said, 'It was closed around ten years ago during a cost-cutting exercise. Over the years people have borrowed tools and not returned them so we're a bit short of equipment. But I believe it's important for the boys to do a practical subject like woodwork as well as art and sport and all the academic subjects we teach.'

'Oh so do I,' I said enthusiastically. 'It's the only subject where kids get to actually make something.'

Mr Green told me he'd hired the local joiner to teach the boys woodwork. This man was a good craftsman but he couldn't hack teaching and quit after only a fortnight. I thought it was a big mistake to have hired him in the first place, since being good at something is altogether different from being able to teach it, but I didn't say anything, just made a face and nodded. Mr Green had then hired a supply teacher to look after the woodwork classes, but he could only stay until Christmas, hence the ad in the paper. All this sounded very promising to me. I'd only have to teach two days a week and the workshop was such a mess that whatever I did could only be an improvement. I told the Headmaster about my rocking-horse work, my teaching qualifications, my current job as a postman and that I was very interested. I went home feeling positive and excited, but not at all sure that my friendly chat with the Headmaster had actually amounted to a job interview.

Next day Mr Green phoned and said, 'This woodwork Master's post, if I were to offer it to you, would you accept?'

'Yes sir.'

'Good. The job's yours. I'll have to run it past the Governors but that's a formality. You can hand in your notice at the Post Office and start teaching here after Christmas.'

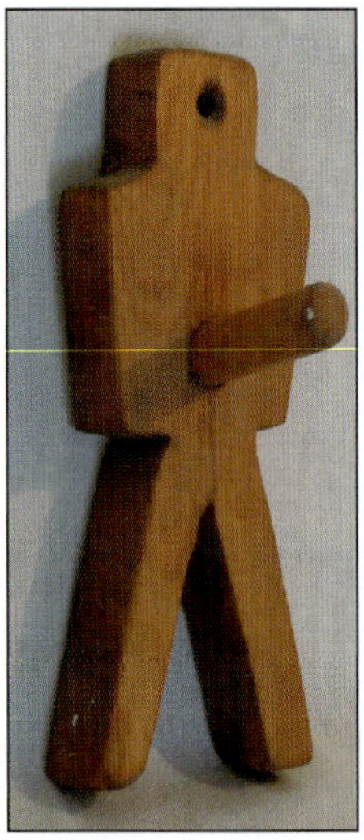

Twenty-five eleven-year-old savages in short trousers stampeded into my chapel workshop over-flowing with loud enthusiasm. Educating them whilst retaining my sanity was a formidable prospect. But I'd devised a simple project to get them started and when I held up a sample I'd made earlier they stood listening in silence.

'We are going to design, make and completely finish this project in two lessons so you can take it home to your Mums,' I told them. 'See, it has a base with a screw hole to fix it to the wall and a short length of round dowel glued into a hole angled so that whatever's hung on it won't fall off. First, you must draw a plan like this, with front and side views. The base can be a simple rectangle, a triangle, a diamond, in fact any shape you choose, so long as it's all straight lines and easy to cut out, understand?'

The project was designed to introduce them to setting out, sawing and planing, drilling, sanding and finishing. Merely a wooden coat-hook, but the boys were so excited they cheered and stamped their feet. I gave out pencils and paper and it took most of them about five seconds to draw a plan. As I approved each drawing I handed out pieces of softwood for the base. Most drew geometric shapes as I'd suggested but one lad, John, produced a very neat drawing of a man.

'Nice drawing, John,' I said. 'And all straight lines. But rather complicated for this first project. I doubt you'll be able to complete it in the time allowed.'

'Oh I know I can do it sir,' he said. 'I've done woodwork at home with my Dad.'

I said, 'OK, let's see how you get on.'

John was able and careful and made an excellent job of it. When finished he had a neat little man with a screw hole in the centre of its head, like the Cyclops, and the dowel sticking out below its waist, like a huge erection. I had a hard time not laughing out loud, but eleven year old John had no idea what he'd made. I thought, there's no way I can let him take this home and show it to his Mum.

I said, 'Well John, you've done a splendid job. Well done! In fact it's so good I'd like to keep it here as an example of how well a boy can do in this first woodworking project. What do you say?'

He agreed, smiling. I have John's coat-hook still, and its innocent vulgarity makes me smile every time I catch sight of it.

I soon settled in at Reed School and surprised myself how much I enjoyed teaching. It was full-on, but after two years as a postman the relief of getting up at a civilised time and working short hours only two days a week was immense. I loved devising projects for the boys and learned a great deal about explaining techniques and methods in straightforward language, which helped enormously when I came to write instructions for my rocking-horse designs. The best thing was that two days of teaching paid better than six days a week as a postman and gave me the rest of the week and all the long holidays to devote to my craft. The pressure eased.

One of our early customers was a Mrs Baker who taught two reception classes at an Infant School in Selby. She liked to give the children rewards every time they did anything good or promising and her principal reward was to let them ride the rocking-horse we made for her. He stood at the front of her classroom and was ridden six hours a day every day the school was open. This was far more use than in a normal domestic setting, an excellent test. We stayed on good terms with Mrs Baker and promptly fixed any problems that arose, and learned from them. I was continually making minor changes and improvements to my horses and slowly the flow of customers increased. My teaching salary comfortably paid our way and our rocking-horse enterprise was starting to turn a modest profit.

At first I'd naively thought we were lone practitioners of the craft but we kept hearing about other rocking-horse makers around the country. Jim Bosworthwick, so encouraging to me, had retired, but he turned out to have twin nephews who'd set up in business as rocking-horse makers in Kent. Starting with their uncle's designs - apparently they'd paid him £1000 to teach them everything he knew - the Stevenson Brothers were developing their own style of horse. They approached the craft with great skill in both making and marketing, and with very high ambitions. It wasn't just the two of them either: they hadn't been in the rocking-horse business as long as me but were already employing people. They were serious competition.

Pam and Stuart MacPherson traded as APES (the initials of their and their two children's names) from a remote workshop in the hills of North Wales. They made excellent traditional-style wooden rocking-horses and some more unusual designs of their own which they modelled in clay and cast in fibreglass resin. Based on breeds of British pony, these had fat bodies and skinny legs and were much more realistic than the stylised traditional rocking-horse. They were very cute, but not commercially successful, I gathered. When customers wanted a rocking-horse, they went for a proper one.

Fibreglass rocking-horses of a more traditional appearance were being made by a company called Haddon. (Jim Bosworthwick told me Haddons had approached him to make a rocking-horse in sections, for them to use to make a master mould for their fibre-glass castings, and he'd told them to piss off.) Another company, Relko, was selling a striking and unusual laminated ply-wood rocking-horse designed by Tim Orlando-Reep. And then there was Margaret Spencer.

Margaret not only made and restored rocking-horses in her workshop in Somerset, but sold plans and accessories for do-it-yourselfers. Her horses looked somewhat different from ours but her price list of accessories and fittings was shockingly similar. We met her in person at some of the shows we attended and got to know her a little. She was the daughter of Andrew Booth, who'd retired long ago but whose name I'd come across as having been an active and well-known rocking-horse maker in his time. Oddly, given that she must have grown up surrounded by rocking-horses, Margaret declined to credit her father with any influence over her choice of career and claimed to be entirely self-taught. She was a very pleasant middle-aged lady with a great passion for her craft. I wasn't concerned about the quality of the work she was producing compared with ours, but the breadth of it was worrying. She was direct competition and I always regarded her with a certain wariness.

Rocking-horse people were appearing all over the country it seemed, but we were the only ones in Yorkshire. Anyway, the world was surely big enough for all of us. Still, we couldn't be complacent. We'd have to work harder to stay ahead of the game.

'You're like Boxer, the Shire horse in Animal Farm,' Pat said. 'Always repeating the same mantra: we must work harder.'

## 9

I bought a proper drawing board and produced plans that looked more professional than the ball-point pen patterns we'd been selling. We had them printed, first on an old-style blueprint machine, then a dye-line machine and later on a large photocopier, improving the look and quality every time. We also had the instruction booklets typeset and printed by the thousand. As plan sales increased so did the demand for rocking-horse accessories and fittings. These things were often hard to find and I was constantly on the lookout for suppliers.

We needed stirrups and I found a Birmingham foundry making splendid pear-shaped brass castings, originally designed as strap-hangers for London buses, but which served beautifully. We needed bits (the metal part of a bridle that goes in the horse's mouth) so I made a device from scrap steel to form small rings in the ends of short lengths of brass rod. We'd nip these small rings tight round large brass rings to attach to the bridle at each side of the mouth. The device worked well and would remain in everyday use for forty years.

We needed brackets (to secure the swing-irons on which stand-mounted horses rock) that would be more decorative than the bent steel strip brackets we'd been using. I made patterns in clay, cast them in resin using plaster of Paris, and had a small foundry in Birmingham cast them in solid brass for us. We had some plated to give customers a choice of either polished brass or chrome. They looked splendid.

We found good suppliers of buckles, rivets, bit rings, dome and fancy nails. We haggled for the best possible price wherever we went and before closing every order we learned to ask, 'Can you do it for less?' It surprised me how often this simple request produced a further discount. To get the best price we frequently ordered more than we wanted. I was confident we'd sell it all eventually but storage became a problem. We had boxes of rocking-horse accessories everywhere, stacked in the hall in the cottage, up the stairs, even under our bed.

Some of our requirements were peculiar. The stirrup leathers of wooden rocking-horses hang from giant steel staples hammered into the horse's side under the saddle's leather skirts. I'd been making my own by sawing off the heads of 4-inch nails, grinding the cut end to a point and hammering them into shape in a vice, a time-consuming process. I asked Bill Stubbs, owner of an excellent ironmongery shop in York which still sold loose nails by the pound, to find a nail manufacturer to make me four-inch nails with points on both ends. They queried the order several times: 'You're sure you want nails with points on *both* ends?' When they arrived I made a simple steel device to do the final bending and stirrup staples now took seconds to make and the unit cost was negligible. However, there was a minimum order of 100kg, which meant that our first order for double-pointed nails kept us in stirrup staples for twenty years.

We'd never liked using human hair for manes and tails, and it only came in black. Looking for horsehair I drove to a farm on a hill above Bradford in West Yorkshire, a 'Pet Food Manufacturer'. Dozens of ponies grazed in the surrounding fields and behind the building the air was thick with flies and the stink of rotting meat and horse shit. On a bloody concrete apron lay the corpse of a very large brown horse steaming in the chill air. The slaughterman, dressed in brown overalls, green boots and a long black blood-stained leather apron, took out a small knife, sharpened it with a few strokes on a leather strop hanging on the wall and squatted over the corpse to slit the skin. When he'd loosened the hide he attached the carcass with chains to a ring in the building's wall, the hide to a hook behind a tractor. He kicked the chains and the horse's head so they aligned to his satisfaction, heaved himself up into the tractor and drove away very slowly.

He stopped several times to jump down and use his knife to ease the skinning as the hide came off the flesh of the animal with a low tearing noise, like peeling off a huge wet rubber glove. When the hide came clear the only parts of the carcass still with skin and hair on were the head and upper neck, lower legs and the tail. He killed the tractor's engine, folded the slimy hide into a neat bundle, lifted it with a loud groan and carried it to a refrigerated container. He came back carrying an axe and hacked off the dead horse's tail at the thick end where it joined the body. The hair was very long and thick, deep brown with a slight wave, but filthy. He picked it up and thrust it at me, a dismembered horse tail slimed with blood and shit. It was very heavy and I tried to hold it away from myself.

'That do you?' he said.

Every month after that I drove to Bradford to collect ten or a dozen tails from the horse slaughterer. He didn't talk about much except killing horses. He told me most of the animals that came to him had been pets, bought by indulgent dads for their daughters. After a while the daughters lost interest, the dads didn't want the cost or hassle of a pony and nobody else wanted them. The slaughter-man made his money from the meat and the hide but before I showed up he'd dumped the tails. I told him I particularly wanted large greys and whites but I'd take some browns and blacks as well. He said I could have as many as I wanted for £1 each, cash, he'd keep them in a freezer for me.

Back at Herberry House I hammered some double-ended nails into the fence posts in our garden and hung the tails up to skin them. After skinning, tanning and washing - I had dustbins full of industrial detergent and tanning solution made with borax, alum and salt - I hung them up in the shed to dry. Once they were clean and brushed out they were beautiful and I could make two or three fine long rocking-horse manes and tails from each large dock. But the process of getting them was utterly disgusting, so I was delighted when, some months later, I found Charlie Piper.

Charlie supplied horsehair for the bows of violins, cellos and double basses. He bought tails from a horse slaughterer same as I did, skinned and cleaned them and hung them up in front of a light to pluck the longest of the hairs, one by one, until he had enough for a bow. He charged an extraordinarily high price for the bow-hair he sold, but the docks he was left with were useless to him, although they still had plenty of hair on for rocking-horse manes and tails. Also, they were all white or light grey, the colours customers wanted most. I bought all Charlie's surplus docks. He was glad to sell them to me and although I paid him a lot more than £1 each I was more than pleased not to have to skin, tan and clean the horrid things myself.

We also bought horsehair from a dealer who supplied the brush trade. It came in neat, clean bundles of uniform length and I devised a method of layering it and making it into a mane, and securing it in a slot cut in the rocking-horse's neck. For tails we simply glued a bunch of hair round a wooden plug that was glued and wedged into the rocking-horse's tail hole. It was important to make both mane and tail fixing secure so that a child couldn't pull the hair out.

Eyes were an ongoing problem, a small component but vital, the window on the soul after all. Jim Bosworthwick had sold me enough to get me going but he only used a couple of sizes and his price was high. We found a cheaper glass eye supplier in Brighton with more sizes and we'd been buying from him. But Margaret Spencer was selling even more different sizes and at a lower price than we were buying them for. To compete with her we dropped our price to match, but that meant we were selling our eyes at a loss and I didn't like that at all.

Our supplier wouldn't give us a better price even when I offered to buy 100s or even 1000s from him. I contacted glass manufacturers associations, every glass maker and supplier I could find, and even wrote to foreign embassies, but nobody knew anything about glass eyes for toy animals. I couldn't use plastic, they were cheap but horrid, so I started looking at kilns in which to melt glass and make my own, but it clearly wasn't going to be easy. What I really wanted was to know where Margaret Spencer bought hers, but I couldn't ask her. The glass eye problem gnawed away at me for months.

Remarkably, nobody had ever written a book about rocking-horses. I loved the craft, had a good understanding of the basics and wasn't burdened by excessive knowledge. I reckoned I knew enough to write the first full-length book on the subject. It would be a big challenge but my teaching job should allow me the time to do it in spite of more and more orders for rocking-horses arriving daily. In Selby library I found that David & Charles in Devon published excellent non-fiction books so I posted them a proposal and by return received a positive reply. Perfectly normal politeness I thought, unaware that publishers routinely ignore all enquiries except from established writers and media personalities.

I sent D & C an outline synopsis which, after a few changes, they accepted. I then signed a contract with them to write a full-length how-to-do-it book entitled Making Rocking Horses. It would include scale plans and instructions with about 150 step-by-step photographs for making several hobby and rocking-horses, plus a chapter on restoring old ones. I started writing, determined to make my book as interesting and informative as I could.

The ink was hardly dry on my book contract

when a letter arrived from Margaret Spencer to say she was busy writing a book about making and restoring rocking-horses. She said she intended to have an appendix listing contemporary makers and restorers and asked me to send her a brief résumé of my work, together with contact details.

'Oh my God look at this,' I said to Pat. 'She's shadowing us.'

'What are you going to do?'

'I'll send her what she's asked for but I won't tell her I'm also writing a book. I'll have to speed up and make sure my book gets published before hers.'

Sam, now five, was a beautiful, loving, active little boy who had recently started big school and, with me running behind, learned to ride a bike. Kate was into everything, a typically energetic two year old, delightful but more difficult than Sam. She'd quietly listen to the stories we read them at bedtime but when Sam snuggled happily down to sleep, Kate wanted to be up and doing for another three hours. I was still teaching, and so totally immersed in my rocking-horse work that I hardly thought about anything else. Pat and I were both working desperately hard but I believed that at long last we were making real progress. Then she told me she was pregnant again.

# 10

I lay awake nights pondering. How do we fit a new baby and all the stuff that goes with one into our crowded little cottage? How do we make time for him or her? What about Sam and Kate? How can I finish all our orders for new rocking-horses in time for Christmas? Can I put off some of the horses awaiting restoration until the New Year? How can I possibly find time to teach another day a week (which the Headmaster had asked me to)? Where on earth can I buy glass eyes? Where does Margaret Spencer buy hers? How can I get my book written before hers with all this going on? How can I illustrate it when I don't even own a decent camera?

I could at least try to find an answer to that last question. On my way home from school I called at the camera shop in Selby.

'I'm writing a book about rocking-horses that has to have lots of pictures, but I know nothing about photography.'

'Hmm, there might be someone at the photography club in town willing to help you out. The chairman is Dr Allan Robson.'

'You're kidding!'

At that time some General Practitioners took a close interest in their pregnant patients, visiting them at home for regular check-ups and even attending the birth. By a fine coincidence Allan Robson was our family doctor and due to come to Herberry House to see Pat the following day, one of my non-teaching days. When he arrived I side-tracked him into my rocking-horse workshop and told him about the book I was writing. He expressed great interest and by the time he got to see Pat - waiting on the bed upstairs for the best part of an hour wondering where on Earth the doctor had got to - Allan and I were on first-name terms and he'd promised to lend me a camera and tripod and teach me how to process my pictures.

Allan taught me all I needed to know about developing and printing and how to manipulate the black and white photographs during the process to get the best results. He even gave me a key to his house so I could let myself in whenever I wanted to use his darkroom. I set the camera up permanently in my workshop and as I carved stopped at frequent intervals to take photographs so I'd have step-by-step pictures of the whole process. At the same time I was writing the words and our neighbour Barbara typed them up. An artist friend Brian Thompson helped to polish my drawings and by Easter '84 the book was finished and sent off to the publisher.

I hadn't told Margaret Spencer about my book but in January of that year I took a phone call from her. She didn't mention her book but asked me if I'd do her a big favour.

'Of course, Margaret' I said. 'What is it?'

She told me she'd been extremely busy in the weeks running up to Christmas and had employed a woman in her workshop to fix the saddlery and manes and tails onto her rocking-horses. The woman had messed up and several horses had gone out with poorly attached manes. Hair came out in handfuls and customers had complained.

'What a disaster,' I said. 'You must feel dreadful.'

'Yes,' she said shortly. 'Anyway I've fixed all the faulty manes except one, on a horse I delivered to a family in Yorkshire, not too far from you as it happens. And since it's such a long way for me to come just to fix a mane, I was wondering if you'd be prepared to do it for me. Whatever you charge, it'll be cheaper than me driving all the way from Somerset to Yorkshire and back again.'

I said, 'Of course Margaret, just tell me what you'd like me to do. I'm more than happy to help.'

Pat said, 'She must have had to really swallow her pride to pick up the phone and ask you a favour like that.'

'I know. If it had been me I wouldn't have asked her.'

The postman brought a packet containing Margaret's replacement mane and a note on how to fix it; different from my method and not as good, in my opinion, even if done correctly. I drove to her customer's house and in less than half an hour fixed the mane. While I was there I had a good look at Margaret's rocking-horse but didn't criticise it. I was very polite and even refrained from asking how come they'd bought one from her and not their local Yorkshire rocking-horse maker.

When I got home Pat said, 'You could charge whatever you like for that job. How much are you going to make her pay?'

'Nothing at all,' I said. 'I'm going to ask her where she buys her glass eyes.'

Margaret couldn't refuse and even seemed happy to tell me. Perhaps she'd been more worried about the size of my potential bill, and of course she couldn't know quite how much the glass eye problem had been bothering me. Her supplier turned out to be in East Germany, a factory which manufactured a huge range of glass eyes for use by toymakers and taxidermists. Their catalogue and price list revealed that Margaret had been making better than 700% profit on some of the glass eyes she'd been selling. I immediately ordered several thousand pairs in a dozen different sizes, styles and colours, having decided we must draw customers to us by offering a wider choice of rocking-horse accessories than anybody else, including Margaret. You want a horse with big blue eyes Madam? No problem. We even bought 1000 cat's eyes, green glass with oval black pupils, although I had no idea what we'd do with them since rocking cats were not on my agenda, or likely to be.

From being loss-making, glass eyes suddenly became the most profitable of our rocking-horse accessories. They were only a very tiny part, but they gave us a whole new insight into the relationship between pricing and profit across the board. The eyes have it! Prices didn't have to be, as we'd fondly believed, costs plus a modest margin, soon swallowed up by overheads and other expenses. Clearly it was possible to make a good profit margin, even an enormous one, at the same time as giving the customer good value for their money. If we could minimise costs wherever possible, and provide a high level of service and quality in all our products, we could nudge our prices up overall and not just survive, but make a decent living out of our craft. It wouldn't be easy: the eyes were exceptional and we were unlikely to find another product with that extraordinary level of profit. But our plans were selling well and the rest of our rocking-horse enterprise was beginning to make money too. It looked as if by the end of the financial year (April) we'd not only be making enough out of rocking-horses to live on, but a comfortable surplus on top.

Pat loved children and had loved being a teacher. She'd planned on going back to it once our kids were old enough to go to school, but with a new baby on the way, that intention was pushed back another five or six years. But, I argued, now that our rocking-horse enterprise was coming good at last, wouldn't it be better if she forgot about teaching altogether? We'd both be working from home so we'd both be around to help look after our children. If the business kept growing it would need the full-time efforts of both Pat and me, and if it kept doing well we'd be able to afford to hire someone to help with the domestic chores. The time had come for us to pursue rocking-horses all-out. Swept along by my enthusiasm and ambition, she agreed.

I told the Headmaster that I really enjoyed my work at Reed School but it was becoming impossible for me to both teach and make rocking-horses. I'd been pursuing my rocking-horse enterprise for so many years, now that it was coming good I just had to go with it and I'd be leaving at the end of the school year. Mr Green was very understanding, thanked me for giving him plenty of notice, said he'd be sorry to see me go and that he'd give me an excellent reference if ever I needed one.

'I sincerely hope I won't,' I laughed. 'This is boat-burning time again for me. With a lot of effort and a bit of luck I'll never be a wage-slave again.'

We started looking for a house big enough for our soon-to-be family of five, with outbuildings for a much bigger rocking-horse workshop and space for an office, even a showroom. It would have to be cheap enough for us to afford, meaning another run-down property we could do up. After a lot of searching we found a former butcher's shop in the village of Holme upon Spalding Moor, about ten miles away. Above the shop was a quirky but good-sized flat with three bedrooms and outside, across a garden and yard, a range of buildings, formerly the slaughterhouse, preparation rooms and foldyard. Behind them was a barn and some more garden, all wildly overgrown. The slaughterhouse had closed and the butchery had moved out several years before, leaving most of the property derelict, festooned with spiderwebs and filth, graffiti all over the walls. But the living accommodation had been rented out and was habitable. The place had great potential and I fell in love with it immediately.

We put in a very low offer and the owners, having apparently given up hope of ever selling, accepted right away (prompting me to think I should have offered even less). We put Herberry House up for sale and applied to Humberside Council for Change of Use of the HoSM property from butcher's shop and slaughterhouse to toyshop and light industrial workshop. We quickly found a buyer for the cottage, subject to contract, but when our application for Change of Use was supposed to be decided by the Planning Committee, it was deferred. We waited anxiously for the next meeting a month later, when they deferred again. We didn't dare move if permission to run our business in the HoSM shop was going to be denied, but by now our buyer was threatening to pull out.

In a state of extreme anxiety we asked the planners to give reasons for the delays. They wouldn't say. We asked Mrs Engalls the local Tory Councillor what the problem was. She didn't know. But she did say she wholeheartedly supported our application and would 'have a word' with the planners. A month later, at the next Planning Committee meeting, the day before we were due to legally complete or else lose the whole thing, our application was finally approved. We were elated, for about ten seconds. The approval was hedged round with so many conditions it was worthless. I rushed over to talk to Mrs Engalls.

'They've given with one hand and taken away with the other,' I told her. 'They're saying I can make wooden toys, but only from 9 to 5 weekdays, and only with hand tools, no fixed machinery. Nobody has run any kind of woodworking business for two hundred years without machinery. I can't do it. What's going on?'

'You really shouldn't worry,' she said blandly. 'I understand your frustration but the planners don't know you and are wary of anything unfamiliar. They're afraid you'll run machinery 24/7 and cause a nuisance to the neighbours, which leads to complaints. They don't want that.'

'They're afraid I might be successful?' I said. 'Look, we're a small family business struggling to grow. We're going to live on the premises, above the shop, so we certainly don't want to upset the neighbours. In any case we've spoken to them and they've all told us they'd much prefer a toymaker's workshop in the back yard than dead pigs and cows and tubs of stinking offal. I can live without running machines outside normal working hours but I have to have woodworking machinery or I can't make a living. If that condition stands I'll have to abandon the whole thing.'

'No need for that, Mr Dew,' she said. 'The important thing is you've got your approval. The conditions sound bad, but I'm sure that once you're in and working and people get used to you, there won't be any problems.'

'You think so?'

'Yes.'

Mrs Engalls seemed completely untroubled by what I saw as a terrible set-back. But it wasn't her risking everything.

I said, 'I must have machinery. If I can't… I don't know.'

She said, 'I tell you what I'll do, Mr Dew. You write a list of all the machinery you think you're ever likely to need and send it to me. I'll 'have a word' with the Head of Planning. He'll approve it, because I'll tell him the Council has to be seen to be encouraging enterprise like yours in the area and this is an excellent use of a redundant slaughterhouse. I'm sure everything will be fine.'

It was decision time.

I said, 'OK then.'

We shook hands.

I went home and told Pat that if Councillor Engalls was as good as her word (which she was) we'd soon be moving again. We opened a bottle of Prosecco to celebrate and even though she wasn't drinking on account of the coming baby, Pat had a small glass. I quaffed the rest.

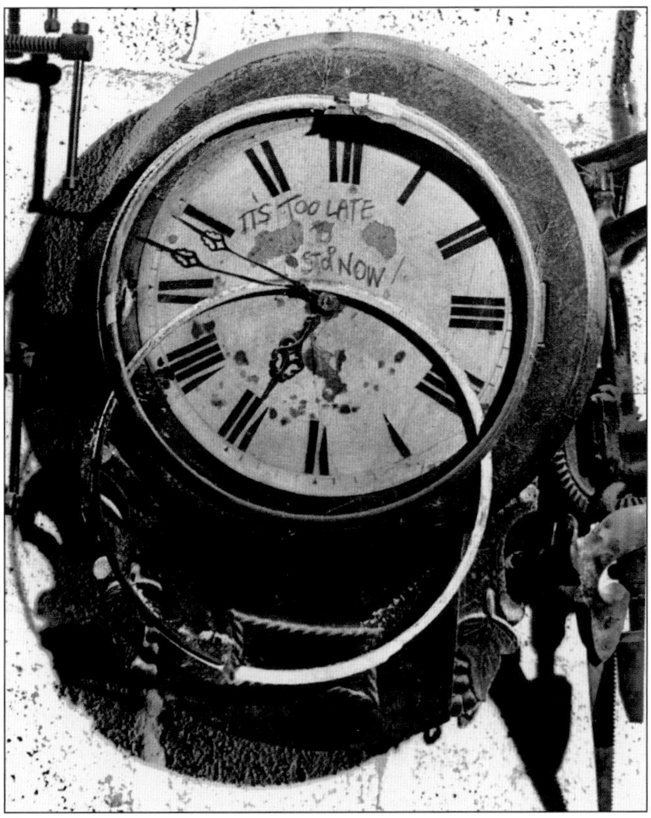


AD's workshop clock.

# Part Three

## 11

Sam was excited to have a bedroom of his own overlooking the back garden and our new workshop. Kate too, and she didn't mind that soon she'd be sharing with a new brother or sister. We were all excited about that. Pat was six months pregnant and huge again, but she set about scrubbing the graffiti off the walls and cleaning our new home top to bottom.

From the beginning we'd called our business 'The Rocking Horse Winner' (after D. H. Lawrence's short story). Now we decided to lose the dark connotations of that tale and change our trading name to something better suited to our enterprise and the new shop. 'Anthony and Pat Dew's Remarkable Rocking Horse Emporium' was too much of a mouthful; 'Ned's' or 'Rocking Ned's' too corny; 'The Dapple Shop' too twee; 'Bucephalos's Atelier' too pretentious. We wanted a simple, descriptive name and settled on 'The Rocking Horse Shop'. Not a trading name we could register and protect since there were many other Rocking Horse Shops, but did any of them actually sell rocking-horses and the array of exclusively rocking-horse related products we did? We were unique, or thought we were. 'The Rocking Horse Shop' was neat and unfussy and described exactly what we did.

Summer term ended and so did my part-time career as a teacher. One of my last tasks at school was to pick a prize-winner. The best woodworker I'd taught that year was a skinny lad, nearly fifteen, named Tim Chatham. He'd always listened to what I said and was one of the few able to grasp immediately what he should do and quietly get on with it. I'd never had to reprimand him and he'd completed some excellent woodworking projects. He was clearly pleased when I told him he was to take that year's school prize for woodwork.

'So Tim, are you staying on to do your A levels?

'No sir, I'm not much cop at academic work. I'm leaving.'

'To do what?'

'I don't know. My Dad's a coal merchant so I'll probably take over from him eventually.'

'You're going to be a coal man?'

'Yeah. But not yet, not while he can still lift the bags.'

'Really? It's a hands-on job? Sounds hard. Listen Tim, you've heard I'm leaving Reed School too? I'm going to concentrate on my rocking-horse business and I could do with a really good woodworker. How would you like to come and work for me?'

'I'd like that sir. Yeah.'

'Excellent, shake on it. And you can stop calling me sir.'

So Tim became our first employee. There was far more to do in the new workshop than I could handle on my own, even without the teaching, but employing a whole other person full-time was a big leap. Tim was a hard worker and proved every bit as useful and conscientious as I'd hoped. If I went out for a while I knew he'd get on with whatever he could - cutting out rocking-horse parts, stripping the paint off an old horse, sweeping the floor, whatever. That was the best thing about having an employee: the workshop didn't come to a standstill in my absence as it had previously.

Along with the filth and abandoned clutter we cleared out of the old slaughterhouse to make way for my rocking-horse stuff was a cow crush, used to hold the animal still while it was killed. It was a large steel contraption and while it stood in the yard outside awaiting removal as scrap the children used it as a climbing frame. I could hear their playful chatter as I was working outside one fine afternoon, making a new pair of doors for the workshop, when I became aware of their shouts increasing in volume and alarm. Then four-year-old Kate came into view, walking slowly, her face completely covered in blood. It was running down her cheeks, dripping off her chin, splattering her blouse.

'Oh my Christ what's happened to you?'

I dropped my tools, swept her up in my arms and carried her into the house, calling for Pat to fetch the first-aid kit and a bowl of clean water. We were appalled, and had Kate been able to see herself she'd have been horrified too, but she was happily chatting away, telling us how she'd slipped and banged her head on a rusty old bolt sticking out. She wasn't in pain but there was so much blood I feared a terrible injury. As I carefully wiped the blood away we realised it all came from a single tiny wound high on her forehead. The bleeding had almost stopped already so I stuck on a butterfly closure and applied a little antiseptic cream. Pat fetched a clean blouse to replace the bloody one and Kate ran back out to play as if nothing had happened. We looked at each other, mightily relieved. To this day Kate has a tiny scar near the hairline on her forehead.

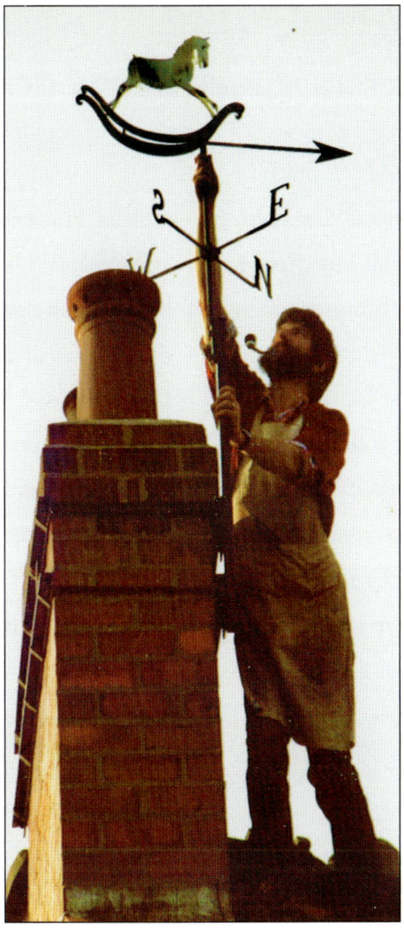

Our new baby arrived on the seventh day of the seventh month, an exceptionally hot day that had everybody sweating, Pat most of all. The birth went as well as these things can and daughter Lynn was just lovely. I was overwhelmed with love. Our family was complete.

People asked how I bent the wood to make bow-shaped rockers. Are they steamed?

'Not steamed,' I said. 'Sawn out.'

Jim Bosworthwick had generously given me a pattern for the Small rocking-horse bow rocker plans we were selling. Since they could be sawn from a single piece of timber they were easy to make, but they were shallow and really didn't rock very well. Plans for them would be in my book, due for publication in September, and I couldn't change that, but decided to design new, improved rockers anyway, with deeper bows. The new bow rockers had to be sawn in two halves and jointed in the middle, so there was more to making them, but they gave a much more satisfactory and exciting rocking action. They looked more attractive too, and were safe, with 'stops' at the extreme ends so the rocking-horse couldn't overturn - as Sam and Kate were happy to prove when they tested the prototype.

I worked my drawing of the new horse on bow rockers and the words 'The Rocking Horse Shop' into a circular design. This logo would appear on our letterhead,

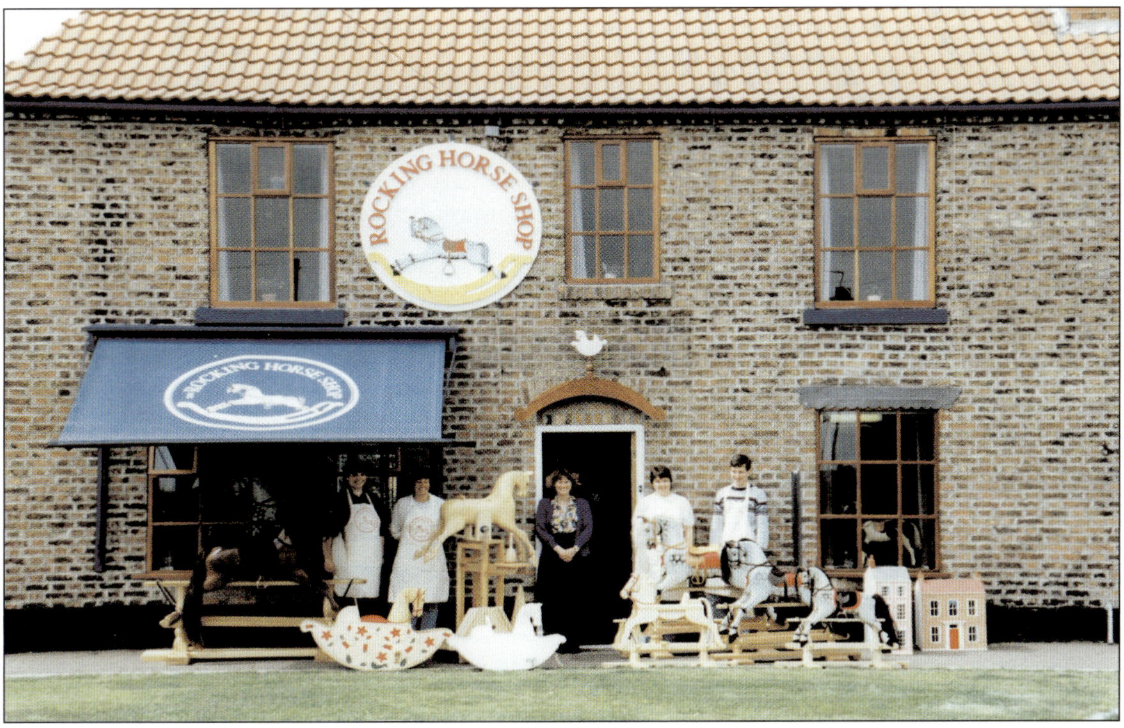

our publicity and advertising and everything we made. I made a five-foot diameter version on a plywood disc, with a relief-carved horse, rockers and letters all cut out of wood and painted. We took down the old butcher's sign from above the front door of the shop and replaced it with our new circular one. We also had our logo printed in white on the ancient blue sun blind that folded out on iron supports over the main shop window. We were in business.

Holme upon Spalding Moor was a large, long village with a primary school (where our children would go), several shops (including two butchers shops still trading) and six pubs. Our shop was a few yards from Ye Olde Red Lion where I went of an evening for a pint or three after a long day's work. I got talking to Dave Smart, local scrap dealer, and told him I was on the lookout for a large bandsaw.

'I've got one of them,' he said. 'Took it out of the British Aerospace factory when it closed. They'd not long had it overhauled so it's in good working fettle. Come and have a look. If it suits you I'll let you have it for a good price.'

'Tomorrow OK? First thing?'

Compared with my little table-top bandsaw it was a monster. Painted green, it stood half as tall again as me and had a massive iron housing holding two cast iron wheels each over a metre in diameter, spinning a blade six metres long. The cast iron doors had been broken before and re-paired and the base had holes for floor bolts because these machines are top heavy, which makes them awkward to move. This one weighed well over a ton.

'How much do you want for it, Dave?'

'£250.'

'Hmm.'

It was a lot of money for scrap, but this was a serious machine and the new bandsaws I'd been eyeing up were much smaller and up to ten times the price. I was thinking that with a saw like this I could cut *anything*.

I said, 'I take it that includes delivery?'

He laughed, 'Go on then. Seeing as it's you. I'll fetch it over tomorrow.'

He pretend-spat in his palm and we shook hands. The next morning Dave parked on the road outside with the bandsaw standing on the back of his pickup lashed with ropes. Dave's labourer John, a muscular giant, came trundling along in a fork-lift truck a few minutes later. Access to my new workshop was along a rough track between two houses at the end of the terrace, too nar-row for anything bigger than a small van. (When timber, leather or steel was delivered we had to unload it in the street and hand-haul it to the workshop.) Big John untied the bandsaw and with the fork truck lifted it off the pick-up, lowered it carefully almost to the ground and we lashed it so it couldn't fall off. He then drove down the track, very gingerly, the bandsaw wobbling alarmingly, un-til he could put it down on the level concrete apron outside my workshop. The bandsaw was half a metre taller than the door opening.

My heart sank but Dave said, 'Well now, we'd best get it inside, eh John?'

'Aye, I reckon,' Big John said, looking doubtful.

Dave moved the forks up as high as they'd go and lashed them to the top of the bandsaw. Then he took some of the weight while, by tipping it one way then the other, Big John and I walked the base across the threshold. The bandsaw tilted over more and more until the top of it was low enough to clear the door frame. We eased it in as far as we could but it was tilting at a dangerous angle and still tied to the top of the fork truck outside. Up near the roof inside and running the length of the building was a massive wooden beam set with huge iron hooks where carcasses had once been hung. I fetched more rope, threw an end over the beam and secured it to the top of the band-saw with bowlines and reef knots.

'You know how to tie a knot,' Big John said.

'I used to be a seaman,' I said.

'Did you now? Then you've gone from rolling to rocking!'

We all laughed and stared at the massive bandsaw looming above us. The fork truck was tight against the wall outside and couldn't get closer. Big John and I heaved on the rope over the beam inside and the bandsaw came up a little but was still balanced on one edge of its base. Dave clambered up the fork truck outside to untie the top of the bandsaw. Suddenly, as the machine came free, it lurched upright and started to fall the other way, towards John and me inside. If it fell onto the concrete floor the brittle iron castings would shatter and it would be ruined. There was no way I could let that happen so I threw myself against the side of the machine to stop it and so did Big John. With our combined determination and Big John's immense physical strength, we managed to push the machine almost upright and Big John held it there while I got another rope over the beam and secured it. It was then a simple if strenuous job to take some of the weight on the ropes and shuffle the bandsaw into position. By the time we'd finished we were all sweating and panting hard.

I grinned at Big John, 'That was a seriously stupid thing to do.'

He nodded, 'Aye, it would've crushed us.'

Pat came out with mugs of tea and asked how we were getting on.

'Finished, no problem,' I said. 'It just needs wiring in and bolting to the floor so it can't fall over.' We were all smiles.

The bandsaw was my first properly professional machine and would remain in daily use for over thirty-five years. It was quickly followed by a 20inch Wilson planer/thicknesser, 14inch Wadkin table and cross-cut saws and a Union Graduate wood-turning lathe to replace my primitive home-made affair. Later I'd buy a mortiser and a spindle moulder. All standard joinery machines and all second-hand, supplied by a cheerful young man named John Jenkinson who sold me the good machines I needed at prices I could afford. John was then just making his name as a dealer and we talked a lot about how to build a successful business starting from nothing. As well as dedication to the task and luck, he said, a vital ingredient was to have a partner you could totally trust who was 100% with you all the way. I agreed. He had his wife Bridget and I had Pat.

I loved the heavy old cast iron machines John sold me, British engineering at it best and built to last. We needed them for the preparation of all our timber components but the assembly, carving and finishing of our rocking-horses was (and still is) done entirely by hand. Behind the machine room we had a large workshop for hand carving and separate places for painting, making metal fittings, leather-working, tacking up, and an office where I had my drawing board. In the shop we stripped the butcher's clinical white tiles off the walls and transformed it into a toyshop. We wanted the front door to open onto a vision of childhood delight and it soon filled up with a fine array of rocking-horses old and new to show our customers.

After re-designing the bow rockers I made a stand-mounted version of the Small Horse, and modified the construction and improved the shape of the head and body of all three fully carved rocking-horses - Small, Medium and Large. They all looked good but, with a little guidance from Pat as she grew more adept at selling, customers recognised that children would soon grow too big to ride the Small, the Large was too expensive and anyway too big for many modern houses, so they veered towards the Medium, and that became our best seller.

I was constantly looking for ways to make my rocking-horses better but the improvements and extra carving took time and inevitably drove the end-price up. Keen to enlarge our range to include lower-priced rocking-horses I revisited the ideas behind my very first rocking-horse in which I'd attempted to marry a carved head and upper body to a simpler, uncarved lower body and legs. From this emerged the Little Red Rocker, which is mounted on a swing iron stand. It works well and is my personal favourite. After that I designed an even simpler rocking-horse with no carved parts at all (except an optional carved head if customers wanted) which we named the Swinger. Each new design was developed as a rocking-horse which we could make and sell complete and ready-to-ride, but also publish with actual size plans, and instructions, to join our growing series of Designs for Woodworkers aimed at amateur woodworkers.

Every design was accompanied by a Timber Pack with all the wooden parts prepared and cut to shape, as well as a range of high-quality accessories and fittings, all of which (within reason) we made in our own workshops. The search for good suppliers continued and we drove all over the country to meet them. At home, everywhere I turned there was mountains of rocking-horse work requiring my attention and I attacked every challenge with furious energy. Once upon a time I'd been a laid-back long-haired part-time hippy, lazy as a house cat. Now Pat said she'd never known anyone so driven.

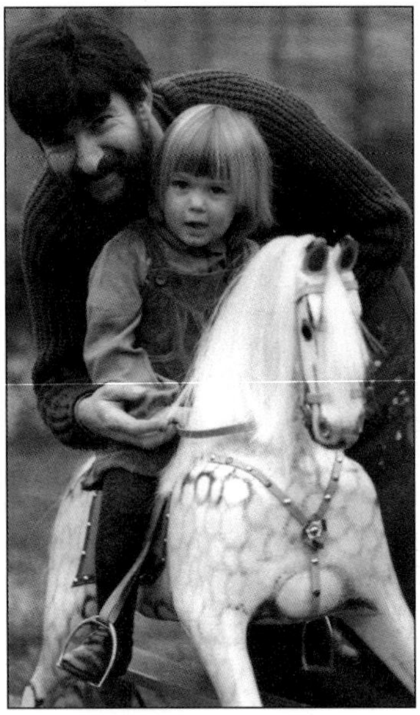

*Kate - test-rider.*

# 12

Rosie Bowser was our second employee. Intelligent, outgoing and good with people, she could easily have had a much better paid job in a bigger company. But she hated the thought of being stuck in an office; she wanted to be involved with a creative endeavour and make things. She appreciated our tiny yet expanding family business and the unusual challenges involved in making high quality leather tack for rocking-horses. Like Tim, Rosie was quick to grasp technical and aesthetic problems, and solve them. Everything was hand-crafted and that always involves risk (that's what makes it interesting) but there were many ways to become more efficient as well as enhance the quality of our products. When customers bought one of our rocking-horses, or opened one of our parcels of accessories, I wanted them to be truly delighted.

With more enquiries, orders and visitors coming every week, our growth was rapid. Tim and Rosie were soon followed by Barbara Brown, Jo, Sue and Pauline to help Rosie in the leather shop and Pat with customers. Every employee had their particular role but whenever the shop bell or phone rang, somebody had to drop whatever they were doing and deal with it. An article I'd written about making rocking-horses for Traditional Woodworking magazine made the front cover and brought in a flood of new orders for plans and accessories. In the woodwork shop I'd speeded up - I was carving as fast as I could and Tim needed assistance preparing Timber Packs. I didn't want to employ anyone over him and we couldn't afford a qualified joiner yet anyway, so I wrote to the Head of Craft, Design and Technology at the local Comprehensive School to ask if they had any rising fifteen-year-olds interested in woodwork. I'd give them a Saturday job and if they proved their worth it would lead to a full time job when they left school.

A lad named Michael Gorcik came to see me. He'd never passed an exam in his life and would leave school with zero qualifications, but he was very keen so I took him on. I had to explain carefully everything I wanted Michael to do, but once he'd got the hang of it, he really got it. And I liked it that always, if I went to pick up one end of a piece of timber, he'd leap to lift the other end. Michael had been with me a couple of weeks when another lad came looking for a Saturday job, accompanied by his mother.

'Paul would love to work for you,' she said. 'He's very arty.'

Paul said nothing and although I wanted a bright hard-worker rather than someone 'arty', he seemed personable enough so I gave him a job, thinking I had plenty of work to occupy him as well as Michael and they'd be company for each other. Paul might have had a sharp mind but he was physically reticent and would stop in the middle of whatever he was doing and stand staring idly into space. Michael had been working away cheerfully but after Paul started he went into a deep funk.

'What's eating you, Michael?' I said.

He looked at the floor and said, 'Now you've got him you won't want me.'

'Not true Michael,' I said. 'Don't you fret about Paul. You keep working like you have been and the permanent job's yours.'

Michael's energy and enthusiasm beat Paul's dreaminess every time. Paul left and Michael started with us full time as soon as he turned fifteen. I never regretted employing him.

Old friends of ours, Roger and Hilda Connell, reappeared. They were a handsome couple we'd known from Keighley who'd been away on a road trip across the USA with their two small children in a van Roger had converted for living and shipped over. The British-made van attracted interest wherever they went and before returning to the UK they'd sold it for more than it cost, a sign of their budding entrepreneurial ability. They were now living not far from us and running a small company making leather tool-holders, very successfully. Roger said he'd seen tool-holders in the US where every tradesman had one hanging from his belt, but they were hardly known in the UK. Roger and Hilda's company worked in a large unit he'd built on land they'd bought on an industrial estate, with a workforce of about six.

Roger showed me a huge old beam press he owned, which had come out of a factory making car carpets and which he used to cut out the shapes of all the leather components of his range of products. I already had a small clicking press but this machine had much bigger capacity, so I had steel cutting knives made for the parts of all our bridles and saddlery. Every few weeks I'd go over to Roger's with my car full of leather hides and my cutters, and in less than an hour on the beam press I could cut out enough components to keep my leatherworkers busy for a month. That amount of preparation would have taken three of my people working hard all day, marking the leather from wooden patterns, cutting out by hand with craft knives and hole punches, and never be as neat.

I liked Roger and learned a lot from him about leatherwork as well as running a small manufacturing workshop. He was remarkably flexible in his approach to business, always trying to keep ahead of the game. His leather tool-holders were high quality and he did very well with them while they had novelty value. But the big UK tool distributors soon caught on and the market was flooded with cheap foreign-made versions. Roger's prices were drastically undercut so he quit making tool-holders and switched to beautifully hand-crafted versions of the sort of leather game and cartridge bags hunters used, which he sold as fashion accessories through high-end retailers. Then, when he realised that competition in the rapidly growing market for designer-label fashion leather goods would likely crush a small company like his, he decided to quit leatherwork altogether and do something completely different.

He started developing a technique for freeze-drying dead animals, a sort of late 20th Century high-tech alternative to taxidermy. He made his leather workers redundant, rented his building to someone else and sold all his leather-working machinery. I knew I wouldn't find another machine like his big beam press within a hundred miles so I went to Roger's closing down auction and bought it. It was huge, weighing in at well over two tons, so it was a struggle to get it into our workshop, but it served us well. It's still in use today, all these years later.

Another valuable advance occurred after a customer named Robert Henworth visited the shop. Robert came in carrying a baby girl, Laura, only a few weeks old, and said he wanted to buy some plans to make her a rocking-horse. He needed to change and feed the baby so Pat took them through to our kitchen at the back. While he attended to the nappy and Pat warmed some milk Robert told us that his wife, Laura's mother, had died in childbirth, but he was determined to do everything he could for his daughter and bring her up on his own. He'd set his heart on making a rocking-horse for her and we said we'd be happy to supply him with everything he needed, starting with plans and a Timber Pack. Robert was a customer but he was extremely likeable; a bond of friendship formed.

In the course of the conversation Robert mentioned that he owned and ran a metal pressings company in Birmingham. I said I had all our swing iron brackets cast in brass but they were expensive and I wondered if there was a better way.

'Pressed metal,' Robert said. 'That's exactly what we do. If you send me a drawing I'll give you a quote for the tooling and what it will cost to have us stamp them out. The tooling isn't cheap I'm afraid, but once we've got it we can make any number of pressings and the unit cost will be tiny.'

Robert was right, the tooling was very expensive, but after a lot of thought I agreed to go ahead. He made us two sizes of bracket: in pressed polished brass which looked superb, and in steel which could be painted and came in cheaper. If we'd only needed brackets for our own rocking-horses the investment in tooling would never have been worthwhile, but since the accessories side of the business was growing fast I hoped we'd sell a lot that way, eventually. The unit cost would be low, as Robert had said, but we could hardly afford the cost of the tooling and I worried about paying such a high price for so small a rocking-horse component, albeit a vital one.

At a show we'd met the owner of Merrythought, a long-established soft toy manufacturing company who also made rocking-horses, cute little fur-fabric covered things on an MDF stand. I'd noticed they had rather poor quality brackets so I sent him samples of our smart new ones and said I'd do a special price for him, if he ordered lots. A few days later Robert phoned to say someone was hawking one of our new brackets round Birmingham's pressings factories looking to have it copied.

'Don't worry,' Robert said. 'Nobody will give him a better price for the tooling than I've given you.'

Shortly after that an order arrived from Merrythought for four hundred pairs of our new brass brackets. Even though I'd given a good trade discount that first order alone went a long way to covering the cost of our tooling and I knew we'd made the right decision. Next I drew the designs, and Robert made the tooling, for several other small accessories including two sizes of fancy Victo-rian-style brass rosettes for decorating the saddlery. High quality fittings like these really enhanced our rocking-horses, and our range of accessories.

A wooden horse is an awkward shape to hold while you're carving it so I designed a wooden carver's vice, properly called a chop, and we sold a plan, timber pack and the metal screw and fittings for home woodworkers to make one. (In *The Book of Lists*, novelist and woodworker Phillip Pullman listed the chop as one of his favourite tools. 'I made mine out of beech, following a plan by the excellent and learned Anthony Dew,' he wrote. Phillip made a rocking-horse from one of my plans whilst writing *His Dark Materials*.)

I designed and we made two sizes of round wooden carver's mallet with hard maple heads and ash handles shaped to fit comfortably in my hand. We made up packs of rabbit skin glue, gilder's whiting and scrim, together with instructions for making and applying gesso to the rough surface of a carved horse before painting. I carved Victorian-style pommels and Rosie covered them in leather. I visited Ashley Iles foundry in Lincolnshire, met the man himself, and we started selling their high quality carving tools, as well as sanding attachments, rasps and toy-safe paints. All these things, some highly specialised, were added to our growing mail order catalogue. Orders for our plans, timber packs and accessories rolled in. In addition, we always had at least a dozen new horses under construction in our workshop, and as many old ones being restored.

I loved it when customers made unusual demands. Canon and Mrs Norman came into the shop to ask if I could make a rocking-horse for their twenty-eight year old son, Jonathon. Despite his chronological age Jonathon was small, the size of a ten-year-old, near deaf and blind and it was uncertain who or what he was aware of in the world around him. Like many parents of disabled children, Canon and Mrs Norman worried about how they'd cope with him, physically as well as emotionally, as they got older. So they'd made arrangements for Jonathon to be taken care of in a special home for such people, then being established by a wealthy local philanthropist.

The one thing, perhaps the only thing, that

Jonathon could do, was rock. He would rock endlessly back and forth and, his parents told me, when they took him to a day-care centre, he sat upon a rocking-horse there and rocked, and seemed to relate to it. The idea was to have a special rocking-horse for him at their home, and when he eventually moved permanently into this new home, it would go with him.

The rocking-horse was a very large dapple grey and I fitted it with big handles either side of the neck for Jonathon to hold onto, and adjustable solid wooden rests for his feet instead of stirrups. The day I delivered it I was very worried. Would Jonathon even recognise what it was and know what to do? Mrs Norman kept Jonathon in the kitchen of their bungalow while I brought it in and readied it for him in the living room. Then, holding his hand, she brought him in. She led him to the rocking-horse and gently ran his hands over the horse's face, neck and saddle. Jonathon's expression didn't change but without the slightest hesitation he lifted one foot onto the footrest and eased himself up, his Mum helped push him into the saddle, his hands grabbed the handles and he was rocking. I was so relieved. It was just marvellous and remains one of the most moving moments I've experienced.

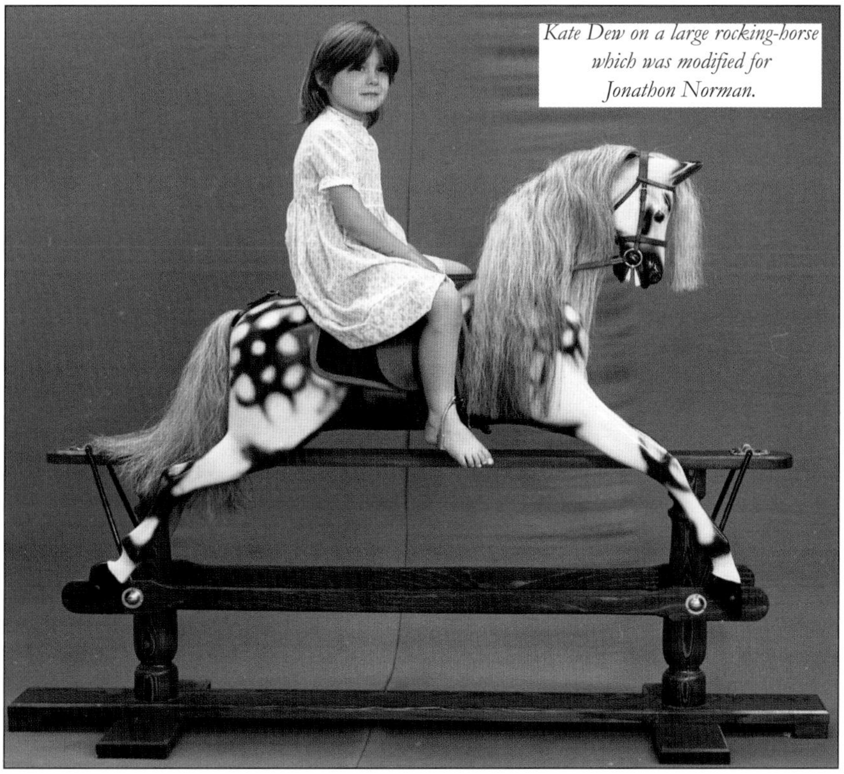
*Kate Dew on a large rocking-horse which was modified for Jonathon Norman.*

We cast our rocking-horse net as wide as we could, reaching out to sell to retail shops, professional makers and the trade as well as to home woodworkers wherever they were in the world. I boasted that there wasn't a rocking-horse made anywhere, amateur or professional, that didn't have something on it that we'd made or supplied. Pat looked after all our plans and accessories orders as well as trying to entice big store buyers to stock our finished rocking-horses. One morning the postman brought an order from the department store chain House of Fraser for nine fully-carved dapple greys. Nine! It was the single biggest order for finished rocking-horses we ever received. By this time we had our own van and drove all over the country delivering new rocking-horses and collecting old ones for restoration. Once, we collected four extremely battered nags from Paddington Green Children's hospital in London, which we restored and made safely useable again.

Home computers and the internet were the coming things so we bought an Amstrad and started to 'surf the net'. We bought the domain name rockinghorse.co.uk for £35 and Pat's nephew James, a delightful young computer geek who talked techno-babble all the time (and was clearly destined to become rich) came over to set up a website for us.

One of our first online customers was a lady in California, USA who emailed to say she liked the look of our horses and, 'Can you supply one in time for Christmas for my niece, the two-year old grand-daughter of Charlie Watts, the Rolling Stones drummer, who lives in Dorset?' Christmas was only a fortnight away and we were incredibly busy, but of course I said yes. She chose the colours she wanted, paid for the horse and the whole transaction was sorted and paid for in a matter of hours. Previously an order like that from the other side of the world would have taken weeks to arrange. We delivered the rocking-horse satisfactorily and on time.

Another customer from California came to visit our shop, arriving in a chauffeur-driven limousine with his gorgeous wife, a teenage son, a girl of about three and a nanny. He was a living caricature of an American tourist with his checked shirt, big belly and mouth to match, but I liked him immediately, he was so warm and enthusiastic. I showed him round the workshop and he kept throwing his arms in the air and shouting, 'Boy, this is so amazing. Hey, you know this is just how I imagined. Jeez, I've wanted to make this trip for so long. Wow, I'm so glad we came, aren't you kids?'

His entourage silently tagged along looking bored. He didn't seem to mind and pulled out his wallet to show me photographs of his workshop in the basement of his house back home. It looked much bigger than my workshop and far better equipped, with an extraordinary array of work benches and professional-quality woodworking machinery, all brand new. On the walls were racks of hand tools looking pristine and there were no wood-shavings on the floor nor any sign of anything he might have actually made in this marvellous workshop. I admired it anyway.

'Yeah it's great,' he said. 'Trouble is, I'm so busy with work I don't have time to get to use it. I just love woodwork though. I mean, I work with my hands all day in my regular job as a brain surgeon, but with woodwork there's no blood.' Adding ominously, 'Usually.'

Back in the showroom, the workshop tour completed, he said, 'Now Tony, I'm never gonna have the time to make them so I want to order three of your beautiful new horses. One for my boy here, that'll have to be the Large size, a Medium for the girl and a Small on Bows, a Christening present for two of my friends who've just had a baby in Iowa. You OK with that? You can arrange delivery?'

'Sure,' I said. 'No problem.'

He said, 'And how about I pay you right now? You OK with American dollars?'

'Absolutely fine,' I said. 'We can easily get a US dollar cheque changed at the bank.'

'No, no, Tony. I don't mean a bank check. I'm talking cash.'

With that he started pulling wads of US$100 bills from various pockets and soon there were piles of notes all over the desk, with Pat and I busy counting them.

After they'd gone I said to Pat, 'I know we didn't go into this rocking-horse business for the money but it looks like Christmas arrived early this year.' I couldn't stop giggling. Pat smiled at me and raised her eyebrows.

# 13

Our enterprise wasn't only about money but I'd never forgotten Pat's brother John saying that if we weren't making money we weren't in business, we had a hobby. He'd also said, 'A lot of money flies over the table but not a lot sticks'. That was our situation now, turnover increasing rapidly but the money going out as fast as it came in. We worried constantly about our bills and some weeks Pat had to use our child allowance to pay the wages. Then she went on a business development course and came back full of ideas about how to increase our profitability. The main one was we should put up all our prices.

We'd not so long since been introduced to the stupidly convoluted world of Value Added Tax, when our turnover unexpectedly exceeded the VAT threshold. This meant increasing all our prices to pay for the privilege of collecting tax for the state. Our first visit from an unbelievably officious VAT inspector had nearly crippled us. We'd survived, just, and were thriving, but I certainly didn't relish the idea of increasing our prices again.

'It'll frighten away all our customers, Pat.'

'Only what they call the bottom-feeders, the ones who always argue with us for the lowest price and often don't pay anyway. Yes, we'll lose them, but not most

of our customers who want top quality and are happy to pay for it.'

'You think so?'

'I know so. At least, that's what they told us on the course. A small price increase across the board will boost our profits dramatically.'

We took a deep breath, did it, and it worked.

By 1987 we were earning enough to take out a mortgage on a house and move out of the flat above the shop. Our new home was a modern detached property with a bedroom for each of the children, an en-suite bathroom for Pat and me and the smartest kitchen we'd ever seen. At the end of each long day we could now switch on the answer-phone, close the door on The Rocking Horse Shop and go home to a comfortable house. It was a move which only three years previously would have been unthinkable.

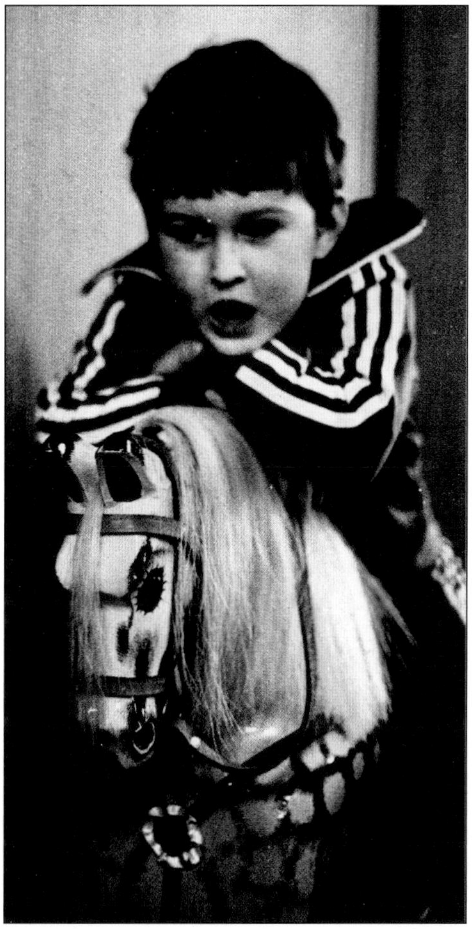

*Sam Dew.*

Our new home was a short walk from the shop, an easy commute, but I still worked every day of the week. I was at my workbench by seven in the morning and rarely finishing before nine at night. Pat complained, 'You never do anything but work.'

I said, 'We're on a roll, Pat. We've got to go with it. We can't slow down now. It's what we've been working for all these years.'

She said, 'It's not what I've been working for.'

'Well OK, our life is a bit full-on rocking-horses right now, and I know it sometimes gets to be too much. But once we've got past this phase everything will get easier, you'll see. I'm always back in time to read the kids a bedtime story, aren't I?'

'No, you're not. Anyway, I'm worried about Sam.'

Sam, now 7, had developed a stammer. That afternoon Pat had gone to meet him and Kate from school and he wasn't at the gate so she went in to find him. Hearing a commotion in the cloak-room she looked in and found a group of children surrounding Sam, taunting him for his stammer. Sam was backed into a corner, standing up straight and staring at them defiantly, unable to get away.

'It was horrible,' she said, almost crying.

I'd hardly thought about it but now Pat mentioned it I realised Sam's stammer had been getting worse. Sometimes he'd struggle so hard to get his words out that his face would go bright red and he'd be stamping his foot in frustration. We went to see his teacher. She was adamant, there wasn't a problem.

'So does Sam say much in class?'

'He doesn't actually, no.'

'And when you ask the class a question, does Sam answer? Does he put his hand up?'

'Well, no.'

'And why do you think that is?'

'He's a quiet, unassuming boy. Some are.'

'In your opinion, is he thick?'

'Oh no, not at all. His written work is excellent. He's a very bright boy.'

'We think he's very intelligent too, and we're not saying that just because we're his Mum and Dad. But we're surprised that you say he's quiet in class because at home he isn't quiet at all.'

'He's certainly one of the quiet ones in my class.'

Pat said, 'Has it occurred to you that the reason he doesn't speak up in class is because he's afraid? Afraid he won't be able to get the words out. Afraid the other kids will mock him. Afraid that you will?'

'Oh I'd never…'

'No? Well we know there's a problem here and..'

'OK. I understand. I'll make the necessary arrangements for Sam to see a speech therapist.'

'Tomorrow?'

'I'll make the calls tomorrow. It might be a week or so before we can get him an appointment.'

'OK,' Pat said. 'But please, make it urgent.'

Karen the speech therapist turned out be something of a miracle worker. She liked Sam and he took an immediate shine to her. She gave him a watch so he could time a series of speaking exercises which he practised assiduously. Within a matter of weeks the stammer was fading. The experience left Sam with an abiding memory of how awful his stammer had been at its worst, and an empathy with other sufferers that, I felt, helped to make him a better human being.

It also forced me to recognise my part in exacerbating Sam's difficulties. Karen mentioned that stammering could be brought on by stress. Obviously our move from Herberry House to HoSM had involved great upheaval for all of us, and Sam had had to try to make new friends in a new village and school. There was more. Sam had always been happy to go to bed and was always awake early in the morning. Pat and I were invariably late to bed, often after a few beers or a bottle of wine, so although I was generally up and about early in the morning, I'd often open my eyes to find Sam standing quietly beside the bed looking at me, waiting for me to wake up. I'd jokingly called him my little alarm clock.

Karen said Sam had told her that since he was often the first person in the house to wake up each morning, his job was to be the family's alarm clock. He had to make sure everyone else woke up, starting with me, because if he didn't wake me, I wouldn't wake up, then nobody would, and the day wouldn't start, it would be lost, perhaps forever, and it would be his fault.

The realisation that I'd been so bound up with rocking-horse work that I'd failed to be aware of what was happening with my son, and unknowingly put this burden on him, shocked me profoundly. I cuddled him and tried to reassure him that I would always, always wake up and be there for him, it really wasn't his responsibility. I had to hope he believed me. Anyway, with Karen's help his stammer gradually left him and he became happier, even if he always felt a little apart from his peers. I knew how that felt. I told myself I must try to spend more time with Pat and the children, and listen to them. Then I went back to work.

I tried to make the instructions I wrote for do-it-yourselfers as easy to follow as possible, but making a rocking-horse demanded a level of woodworking competence that many potential customers felt was beyond them.

They said, 'I could never make a rocking-horse. I'd love to but I'm not artistic and I haven't the tools.'

So I started thinking about how we could offer a project that would require next to no skill or equipment. Flat-pack furniture from Ikea and its ilk were becoming popular, why not a flat-pack rocking-horse? I modified the design of our little plywood Toddler's horse to sell as a self-assembly kit, complete with screws, a little tube of PVA glue and instructions. All the customer needed was a screwdriver.

Instead of cutting out the parts for each horse free-hand, I made master patterns so we could produce them in batches with consistent accuracy and all the screw-holes in exactly the right places. Jokes about ill-fitting flat-pack parts or screws missing were rife, so we took inordinate trouble to get everything right. We named our flat-pack the Little Cavalier and had cardboard boxes made-to-measure with a printed description and colour picture of the finished project on the outside. When all the flat-pack kit's contents were prepared we cleared the benches in the workshop and set up an impromptu production line with our workers packing the parts and carefully checking them.

I gave one of the first Little Cavalier kits to our doctor friend Allan Robson to test for his new grandchild. He put it together in completely the wrong order, with scant regard for my carefully prepared step-by-step pictorial instructions. But his horse came together with pleasing ease and he was delighted with it: it worked. We were ready for the orders to roll in, which they did. Not as fast as I'd hoped, but still.

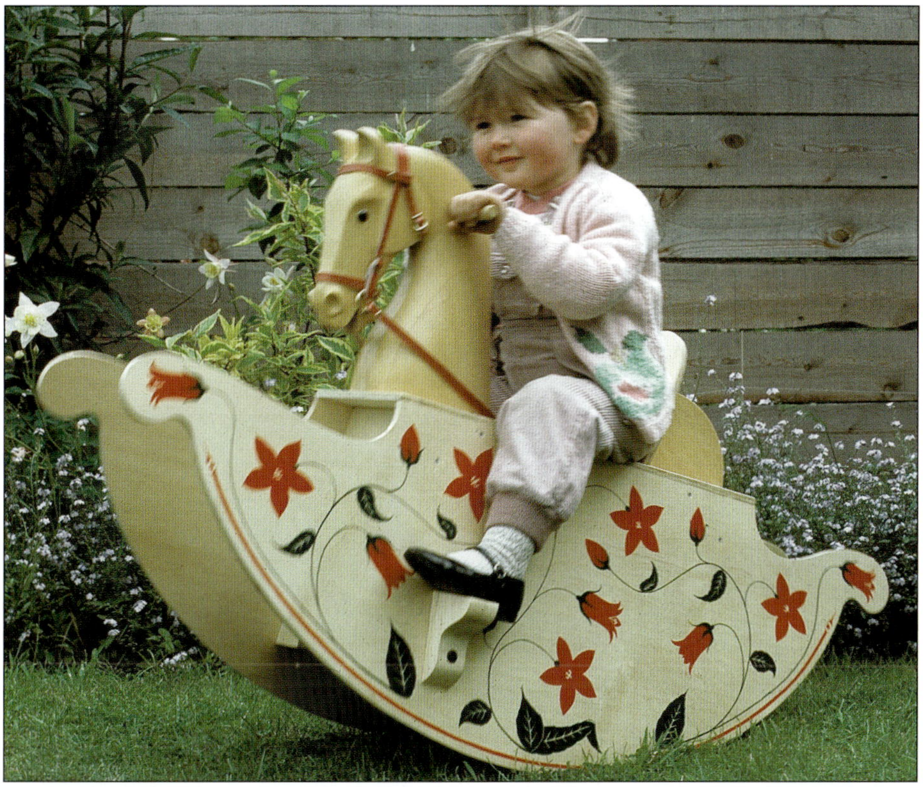

*Lynn Dew on a Royal Cavalier.*

With batch production of the flat-pack came the possibility of selling dozens, hundreds, thousands even. I made two prototypes for a larger version of the Little Cavalier rocking-horse for rising five-year-olds, we geared up to make it in batches of twenty-five or fifty and Pat set about trying to sell it to companies that dealt with schools. Rather than a flat-pack, we decided to supply the larger model in two parts already assembled, with the head and seat tucked under the rockers to make it convenient for shipping. All the customer need to do was screw the seat to the rockers.

There was a miniature horse of similar slab-sided style in Queen Anne's doll's house at Windsor Castle. That one had flowers painted on its sides so I drew a pattern of five-pointed red flowers with green stems and leaves, a pattern that worked for both sides of our rocking-horse. We had silk-screens made and printed them ourselves in the workshop, the silk-screens held in their frames with G-cramps and counterbalanced by heavy bits of machinery and tins of paint - all a bit make-shift, but it worked. I wrote to Queen Elizabeth and received an encouraging reply on quality paper with the Buckingham Palace letterhead, and we named our latest rocking-horse the Royal Cavalier.

One of the two Royal Cavalier prototypes had a carved head, the other a simple cut-out. I expected buyers to go for the simple head because it was so much cheaper, but everyone Pat showed them to liked the carved head better. There was no way I wanted to be at my bench carving the same head over and over, hundreds of times, it'd drive me completely crazy, so I started thinking about how to produce carved heads in quantity.

I'd assumed rocking-horses had always been hand-carved, as we did, but I came across a photograph of a 1920s toy factory showing six rocking-horse bodies being carved simultaneously on a large machine. With the help of the Rural Development Commission and a Technical College in South Yorkshire we designed and built our own copy-carving machine. It was intended to accurately reproduce a master head I'd carved, over and over, without complaining. All we'd have to do was fit a prepared blank into the machine and hit the 'on' button. During the several months it took to make and commission our carving machine, Pat continued negotiating with an educational supplier in Leeds and won an order from them. The Royal Cavalier would have half a page in their catalogue which went out to every school across the UK. They told us we'd likely sell a hundred or so in the first year, rising to maybe two hundred the second year and after that, who knows? We might wind up making thousands. We felt like we were moving into the big-time and could smell success.

The copy-carving machine was designed primarily to carve heads but I made it big enough to handle the largest rocking-horse components, including bodies and legs. It was a monster that dominated our machine shop, and a serious disappointment. I'd hoped to produce heads needing minimal finishing, but the heads that came off the machine were so rough that finishing them often took longer than I'd have taken to hand-carve them from scratch. Tim was spending nearly all his time preparing heads, tending the carving machine and hand-finishing, so I wasn't sorry that in its first year we achieved only around fifty Royal Cavalier sales.

Then our educational supply company was bought by a wealthy wheeler-dealer named Robert Maxwell who asset-stripped it and it went out of business. We had a re-think. If we continued with the Royal Cavalier, Pat would have to start all over again trying to sell it to a new customer, and I'd have to either redesign the carving machine so it would do a decent job (which might be possible) or junk it and invest in a better machine altogether (a huge investment).

I said, 'The carving machine is only worth having if we really are going to make multiple copies of the same thing to sell. I never really wanted to run a factory and although the prospect of all this expansion has been exciting, we don't need it. To me the best part of this work is developing a new design and overcoming all the problems that arise, so that we arrive at a beautiful rocking-horse which looks exactly right and which a customer will pay good money for.

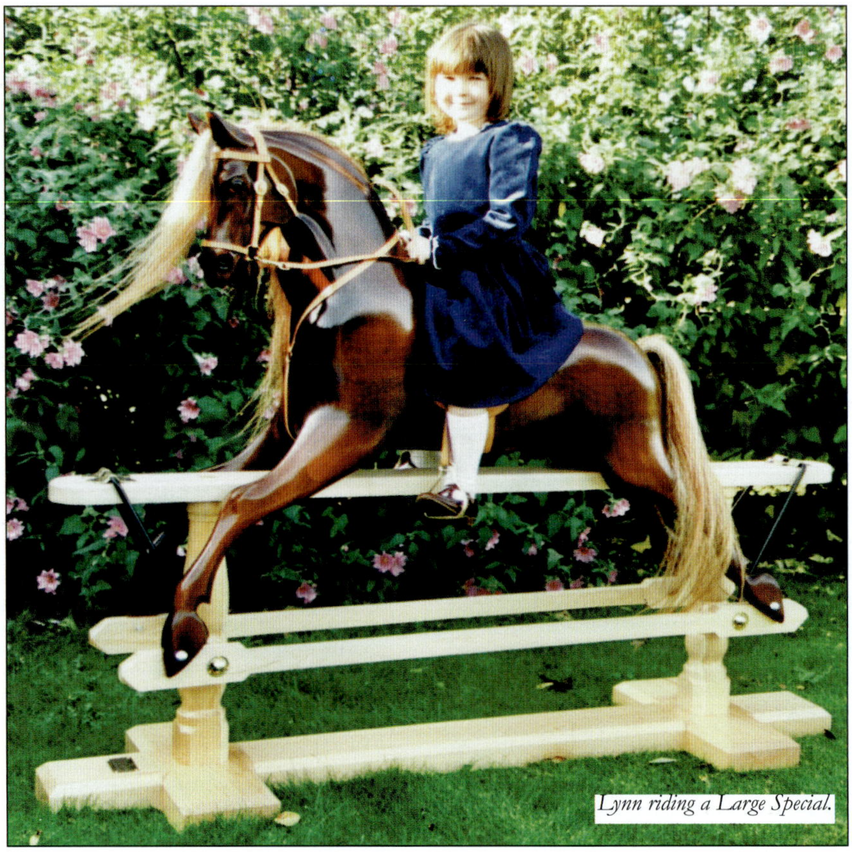
*Lynn riding a Large Special.*

I can hand-carve faster than the machine and while I'm doing that I can add something different to each new horse. That keeps life interesting and gives us a unique selling point. With all this chasing after multiple sales we've been doing we've forgotten what really matters about this enterprise of ours.'

'So you want to get rid of the carving machine and make only one-offs?'

'Yes. And while we're at it, let's dump House of Fraser and all the other shops you've been trying to sell to. Getting and fulfilling those orders gives both you and me major headaches, and all the wholesalers ever do is argue our price down. We might sell more rocking-horses to them, but what's the point when our profit's so drastically squeezed?

If we stop wholesaling and sell only to the end user, we'll be making for an individual customer we've met and know, which is always much more satisfactory than dealing with a faceless organisation. We can charge them less than the shops do, so the customer gains, but a lot more than our current trade price, so we make a better profit.'

'Sounds like a win win situation.'

'It is. Let's do it.'

It was a relief to get rid of the stress of continually chasing big orders but we could still do batch production runs of our smaller horses and needed to market them. The Design Council in London could help us with that and I sent them details of our Cavalier rocking-horses. We received a terse and dismissive response saying, 'Your rocking-horse appears to be derivative, lacking the originality we are looking for.' At the same time the Design Centre was holding an exhibition of contemporary cutlery. The shapes varied a bit but I noticed that all the knives had handles and blades, and all the forks had handles and tines. Wasn't that derivative? What's original anyway? Doesn't everything in some measure build on what's gone before?

Despite that setback the Timber Pack and Accessory side of the business was growing. Every day we shipped parcels to customers around the world. Selling the carving machine gave us back useful space in the workshop we really needed - our former living accommodation above the shop had been entirely given over to the storage of rocking-horse accessories. The profit from plans and accessories was good and they were far easier to handle and ship than finished horses, but making bespoke horses for individuals remained the cherry on our cake. The significance of this adjustment was neatly illustrated when a customer bounded into the shop and announced, 'I can make you rich!'

Jim Benson from New York City had a crew-cut, wore a smart jacket and slacks and told us he was in marketing. He waxed enormously enthusiastic about our rocking-horses, said he'd never seen anything like them at home and was confident he'd be able to sell any number to the big stores in New York and every other city across the USA. We listened politely.

'You know, you guys have got something really special here. Interested?'

'Sure, we're interested. Who wouldn't be, but...

'Great! Well how about we get down to some hard figures. Say this one here Tony, what's your best price?'

He pointed at my latest Large Special, a superior hand-carved horse in polished mahogany on a maple stand. Rosie had made him a hand-stitched removable saddle, bridle and martingale like miniature real ones and he was the best rocking-horse we'd made up to that time, our top-of-the-range model with a price tag attached to its reins showing £1995.

'See that, Jim. That's the price right there.'

'Oh I see it, sure. That's your price in-store. But I'm talking fifty units here, Tony. Go on, give me your best price.'

'That is our best price for that one, Jim. But fifty? Well now, that changes things. Let me see. If you order ten the price would be £2250. For twenty it would be around £2750. And for fifty, I think we'd have to say £3500.'

He'd been grinning broadly and waving both his hands as if drawing us toward him, but his smile faded and his hands dropped.

'Hey wait a minute. Are you guys telling me the more I order, the higher the price you're gonna charge?

'That's exactly what I'm saying.'

'But nobody does business like that.'

'We do. We're hand-craft people Jim, and we love it. There has to be compensation for the increased hassle and reduced satisfaction an order like yours would bring with it.'

He left us laughing as he closed the shop door behind him with a parting, 'You guys are plumb crazy.'

# 14

Now that The Rocking Horse Shop was feeling like a well-established business, far less fragile than in the early days, our life should have become easier. I still worked seven days a week and every morning woke up with my head buzzing with rocking-horse ideas. Although I enjoyed the family holidays Pat insisted we take, I never wanted to go away for more than a week at a time. I'd generally spend the first few days winding down and the last few days gearing up to return, so I never really got away from work, which meant Pat didn't either.

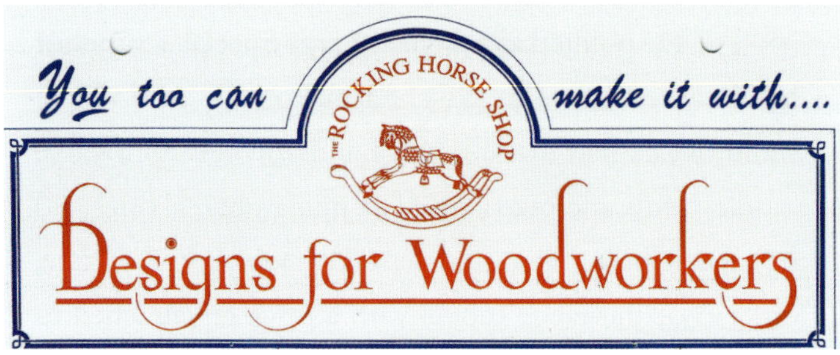


We'd updated our Designs for Woodworkers and now published eight different rocking-horse plans, and *Making Rocking Horses* was selling well . We carried a huge stock of accessories to accompany the designs as well as continuing to make new horses and restore old ones. Orders for all things rocking-horse continued to roll in and our seven employees literally never had an idle moment. We discussed running courses to teach people hands-on how to make a rocking-horse. I was reluctant to teach again but live contact with students would inform our work so we set aside some dates for courses. This led us to wonder how we might reach potential customers around the world who couldn't come on a course. The answer was to film a how-to-do-it video and mail it to them.

A media school named ARTTS had set up in a converted pig farm in a village not far away and we approached them. The owner, John Sichel, had long experience working in TV, at one time directing a popular hospital soap drama called Emergency Ward 10 which had been acted and broadcast live. He was on the lookout for video projects for his students (which would also bring in money for the school) and said he'd be happy to produce a visual version of my book. Once the contract was signed we hardly saw Mr Sichel; the work of making the video was done entirely by his students as part of their media course. Excellent film-making experience for them, an affordable production for us.

A storyboard was prepared and the filming scheduled for three days in my workshop, another day in the studio and a half day on location. The six-person crew comprised John Nolan as Director, an Assistant Director, cameraman, lighting and sound technicians and a presenter. The video would show the process of making a rocking-horse from beginning to end, with the presenter asking questions at every stage and me explaining and demonstrating. I prepared half a dozen horses in various stages of completion and we made room in the workshop for the film crew and all their equipment. They were highly enthusiastic, keen to make an excellent film and a delight to work with.

We soon learned how laborious and time-consuming film-making is; a few seconds of usable material can take hours to shoot. There were dozens of retakes when the camera or lighting didn't work, a plane flew over and spoiled the sound, the Director wasn't satisfied or I fluffed my lines. I was far from a natural performer, but John assured me that my genuine enthusiasm for the subject would more than compensate for any shortcomings in my performance. I had to hope he was right.

The final scene of the film was shot outside, in front of The Rocking Horse Shop. Half a dozen laughing children - Sam and Kate and some of their friends from school - run towards the shop window and peer in, whooping with pleasure and pointing. One of them peels away from the group and goes in through the front door while the camera pans in past the remaining children and through the window to focus on a large rocking-horse. The child inside leaps onto the rocking-horse and, with a happy smile, starts rocking. Credits roll. The scene would only last a few seconds but was by far the most difficult to set up and get right. After countless retakes John the Director announced, 'OK folks, it's a wrap'. The crew packed up their gear and disappeared back to the media school to edit the huge amount of footage they'd

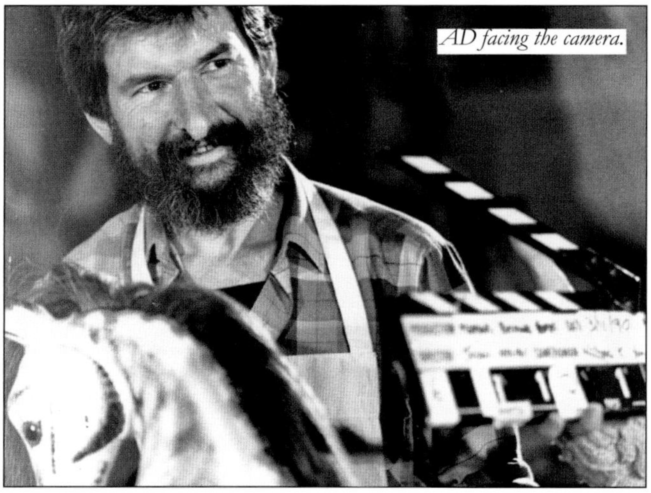
*AD facing the camera.*

shot, while we, with considerable relief, tidied up the workshop and returned to normal.

'Thank God that's over,' Pat said.

It wasn't over. A week later we went to the media school and sat in a darkened studio to view the much-anticipated film. It was excellent, but only in parts. In many scenes the camera lingered on the presenter's face or mine and not the work, missing vital parts of the construction. The film ran for an hour and a half when our agreement with Mr Sichel was for thirty minutes. As a video version of my how-to-do-it book it would not do. The students, anxious for the project to succeed, got to work on re-editing and cutting every unnecessary second. At the next showing a week later they'd got it down to just under an hour, although in the process many of their filmic highlights had been cut, including unfortunately the excellent closing scene with the children. However, I was confident that with a few more tweaks, which the students were happy to make, we'd be able to sell it to our customers. At this point Mr Sichel sent his Financial Director to see us. With slicked back hair, a designer suit and the manners of a smiling alligator, he demanded twice the fee we'd agreed for the film plus royalty payments on every copy we'd sell in the future.

I said, 'We all underestimated how long this film would have to be and we're happy to pay more, pro rata. But we won't pay you royalties. This is the first time royalties have been mentioned and even if we wanted to, calculating them would be an accounting nightmare for us, so no to that.' The alligator slammed his briefcase shut and stormed out. A stand-off ensued with us refusing Mr Sichel's demands and him refusing to release the film. Our contact from the Rural Development Commission, acting as go-between, pointed out that everyone would lose if we failed to secure agreement, especially the students who'd worked so hard and really deserved to have a successful movie project on their CVs. Eventually, a settlement was reached, to which Mr Sichel agreed so long as he didn't have to meet us again. A cheque was delivered to the media school and late one evening we met John the Director who handed over the Master copy of the finished film. It served us well for many years.

One morning a letter arrived from a high school teacher in Chicago, USA, named Brice Gonzales. He wrote that he taught 'shop' (which is to say woodwork), had read my book and wanted to visit us during the summer holiday.

'I've never carved anything but I'll do whatever you want. Sweep floors, carry out trash, if you will teach me a little about wood-carving.'

I replied that we'd be happy for him to visit and he should phone us before he got on the train from London and I'd meet him at York station. On the day he was due Pat came over to the workshop and said, 'Your American's phoned, he's already at York station. I told him you'd be quite a while and he said not to worry. He'll be waiting in the foyer at the station entrance.'

'OK, so how am I going to recognise him?'

'I asked him that and he said not to worry, you won't miss him.'

'Really? There'll be a lot of people there.'

I drove the ten miles to York wondering what to expect. I knew very little about Brice and had no idea what he looked like. But when I walked into York station I knew he'd been right, there was no way I could possibly miss him. A short, casually dressed American, sitting on a bench in the middle of the entrance foyer surrounded by a dozen suitcases, holding a long fishing pole with a flag with my name on fluttering from the top. A group of people surrounded him and as I approached I heard him say, 'That's right folks, I'm gonna see the Rocking Horse Man you know? Ant'ny Doo out at Holme on Spalding Moor. You never heard of him? Well boy, you should have, he's real famous. I come all the way from Chicago to meet him. Hey, this must be him now. Boy, am I glad to see you…'

hospital and the military, he was asked what he'd like to do. He told them that although he'd never paid much attention at school and had no qualifications, he'd always

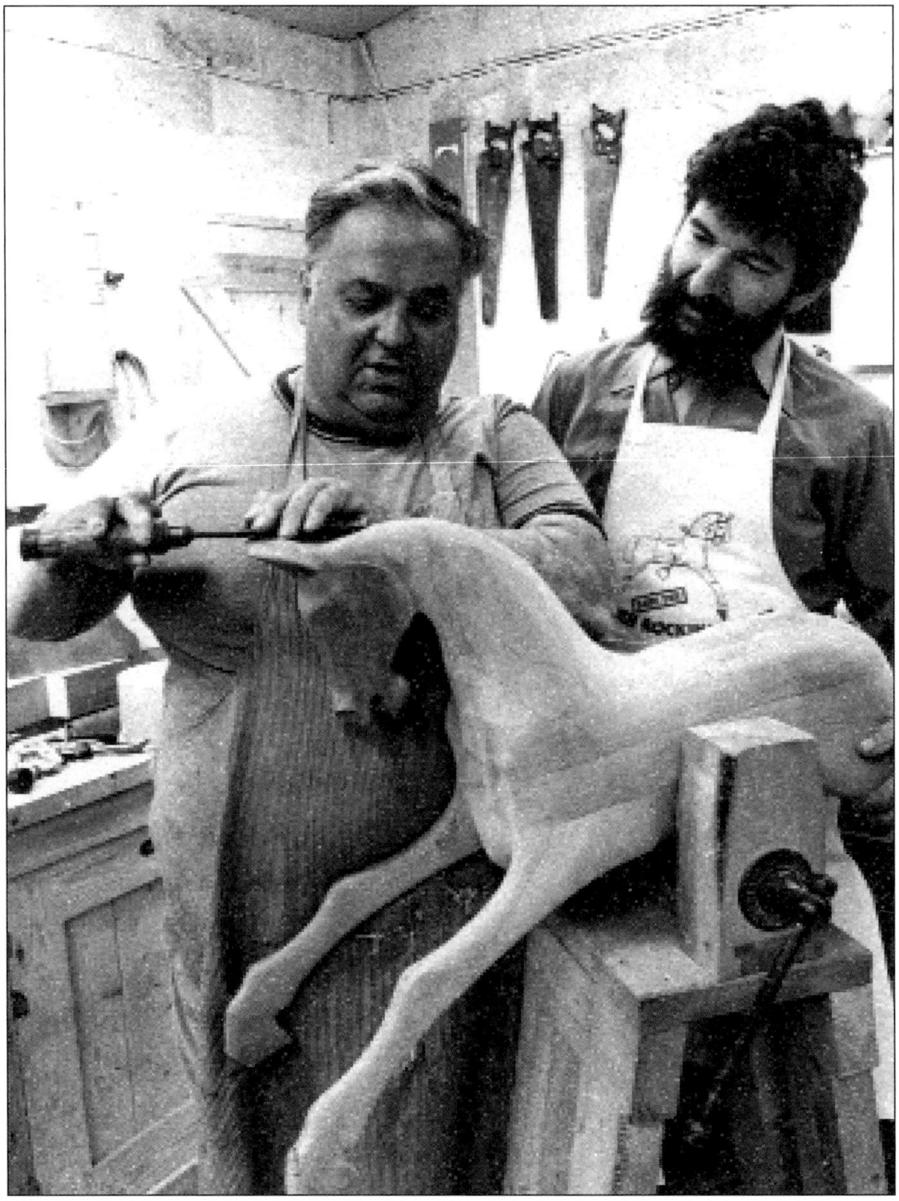

*Brice & AD.*

dreamed of being a high school teacher. The US veterans programme (a wonderfully positive initiative, unlike ours) helped him realise that ambition.

Brice was the son of a Spanish peasant farmer who had emigrated to the USA in the 1920s and wound up in Chicago, where Brice was born. During the 2nd World war Brice had joined the US Marines and was sent to the Pacific to fight the Japanese. At Guadalcanal he'd been very badly burned when an American plane crashed near him. He'd spent two years in hospital having skin grafts and recuperating, and still carried extensive scarring across the top of his head, back and arms. His face was somewhat distorted and several fingers were missing from his right hand. When the time came for him to leave

When I'd booked a room for Brice at Ye Olde Red Lion nearby, the publican asked, 'So how long will this American of yours be staying?'.

I'd said, 'I don't know. His school holiday lasts the whole summer but if we don't get on he might only be here a few days.'

Brice stayed six weeks. We took to him immediately and he soon became a firm friend to me and Pat and a favourite uncle to the children. In the workshop Brice did what he'd said he would and I helped him carve a horse's head. He was immensely enthusiastic and in contrast to our quiet British reserve, delightfully loud. He came with us when we took a stand at The Great Yorkshire Show, the biggest agricultural show in the region, very expensive and a risky venture for us, and if there was a lull in the flow of potential customers he'd march out into the crowds, take people by the arm and literally drag them in.

'Hey you folks, you gotta come see these wonderful rocking-horses. They're the best in the whole world you know? Why, I came all the way from Chicago just to see 'em.'

Brice revisited us every Christmas for several years. He was long divorced but kept in touch with his family by phone. One time I overheard him talking to his grandson Dylan, who was apparently nagging Brice about why he was spending Christmas in England with strangers and not at home with them.

'These people aren't strangers Dylan,' Brice explained. 'These people are very good friends of mine, and you're just a little pain in the ass.'

We continually strove to improve the quality of all our products, the way we presented them and the service we offered. The business was growing and towards the end of the 1980s I started looking for somewhere to expand into. A suitable building was available for rent on HoSM's industrial es-tate, but when I received a copy of the lease it was immensely complicated and the conditions onerous. Nervous about signing I grumbled about it over a beer in the Lion to Henry Nicholson, a friendly local plumber who'd done some work for us.

'I've got a unit on that industrial estate,' Henry announced. 'It's not as big as the one you're looking at but I don't use it much any more. If it suits you I'll clear my stuff out and you can have it. I won't need a complicated lease.'

'Sounds good, Henry. How much do you want for it?'

'£25 a week, hundred a month, how's that?'

'Done.'

We shook hands and the following week we moved some of our big woodworking machines to the unit. Timber was delivered there and for the next two years we handled the initial machining in the unit, then brought it in our van to the workshop for finishing. I gave Henry his rent every month and our only agreement was the handshake. The Rocking Horse Shop prospered. Every day the post van collected a stack of parcels of timber packs, plans and accessories to go out to aspiring makers all over the UK, as well as in the USA, Australia, New Zealand, Canada, South Africa and elsewhere.

Our order book for new rocking-horses was full and stretched months ahead. Restorations were also coming in at a great rate and we struggled to find space to accommodate them all, never mind the time to actually work on them. In the run-up to Christmas, the biggest deadline of the year, overseas orders had to be shipped early but we did all the UK mainland deliveries ourselves. The week before Christmas we drove all over the country and sometimes I'd be putting finishing touches to a rocking-horse's paintwork as it was loaded into our van for delivery, hoping the paint would be dry by the time we got there.

'If Santa's coming he cannot be late,' I said. 'Anyway, we're toymakers, if we weren't rushed off our feet at this time of year we'd be in trouble.'

We worked long hours right up to Christmas Eve then closed the shop until the New Year. Pat and I went home and opened a bottle of champagne.

'Cheers. Happy Christmas. Against all odds we've made this rocking-horse thing work.'

'Yes,' Pat said. 'Through your sheer pig-headed determination.'

'I know. I'm exhausted and so are you. Shall we quit while we're winning?'

'I'll drink to that,' she said.

Early in the new year we contacted a management consultant named Mike Jones and asked him to advise us on how to sell The Rocking Horse Shop.

'We've done everything there is to do with rocking-horses,' I told him. 'Now we want out.'

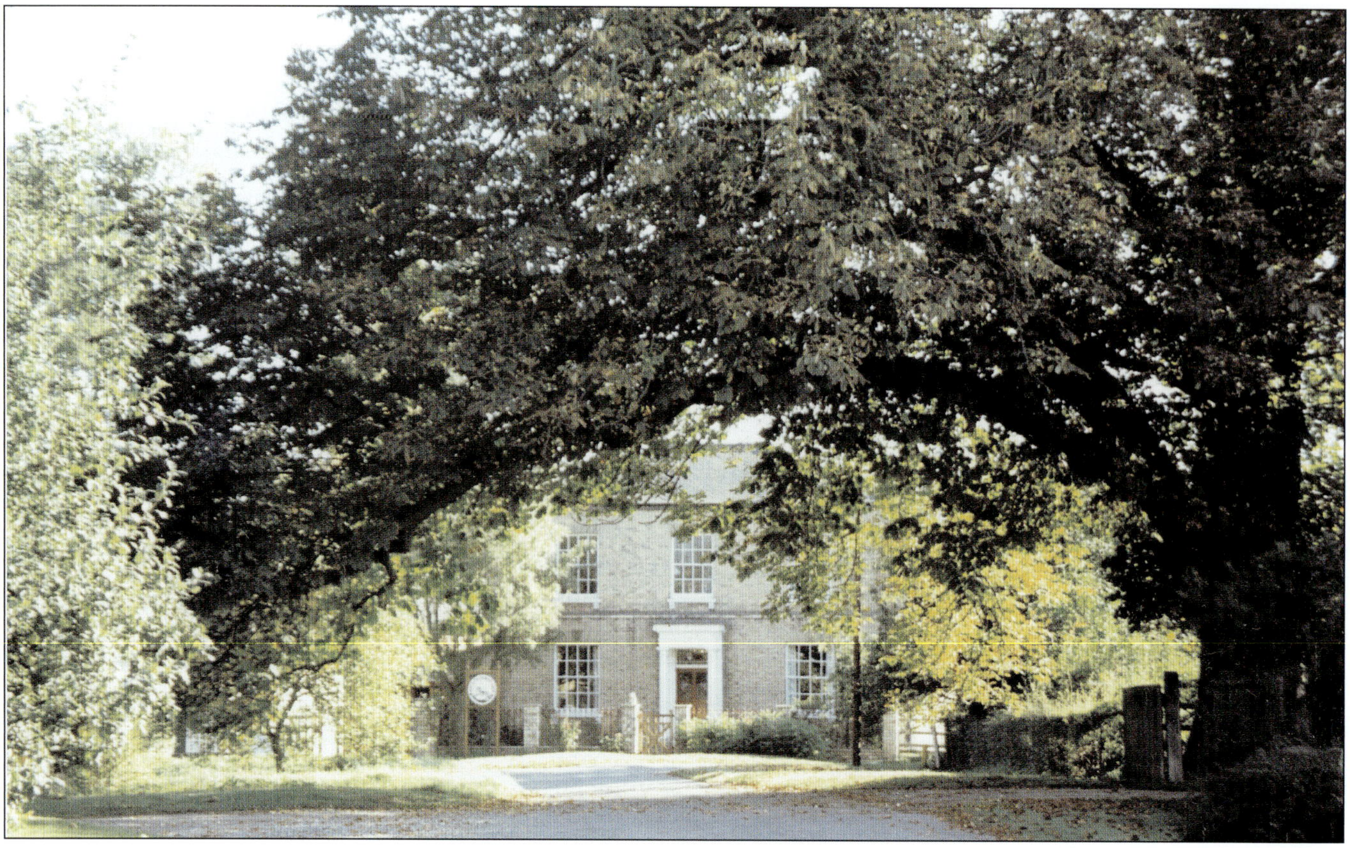

# Part Four

## 15

I saw Manor House Farm for the first time one freezing November day in 1990. It looked like a child's drawing - front door bang in the middle, a window either side and three more above, all neatly symmetrical. Facing along Fangfoss village's Main Street, the house was built in a pale yellow local brick under a black Welsh slate roof and was framed beautifully by the massive branch of an ancient horse chestnut tree overhanging the road. A low brick wall with a gate in the middle and a stone footpath led straight to the front door, which had a portico with a pair of white pillars - impressive but not ostentatious

On the left side of the front garden was a big old laburnum tree and to the left of that the drive-in entrance to the farmyard. To the left of that again was another old tree, a flowering cherry, and beside that a hedge fronting the graveyard and St Martin's church, an appropriately modest stone building for this small village. Behind the church a stand of ash, lime and beech trees, all very old and tall.

I parked by the village green and walked the fifty yards to the house, past an agent's 'For Sale' sign and into the yard. On the left squatted a large derelict brick dairy. A high fence made from railway sleepers blocked the view of the graves, placed there by one who didn't care to look on death, perhaps. Behind the dairy was a huge foldyard, its low asbestos roof supported on old telegraph poles. In the gloom a herd of cows lowed, farted and paddled in accumulated muck. Beyond the foldyard stood a very tall Dutch barn, empty but for some ancient rusting farm machines whose purpose I could only guess at. Beyond that a Nissan hut with a rusted semi-circular corrugated tin roof, crammed full of junk and empty beer bottles, and beyond that a wilderness of weeds.

On the right-hand side of the yard, attached to the back of the house and built of the same attractive yellow brick, a row of stables and a three-arched cart shed, very appealing to the eye but with a great gaping hole in the roof and a jagged crack running down the brickwork where the end wall was falling away. Next to that a long concrete animal shed with asbestos roof and several more ramshackle sheds with rotten doors tied in place with baling twine. I saw exactly what it meant: years of back-, bank- and spirit-breaking work. I also saw, beyond the neglect and dereliction, tremendous beauty and potential. I loved and wanted it.

I walked down the yard trying to avoid the worst of the mud and iced-over puddles, to find the owner. Farmer B was a thin, old-looking man, though probably not much older than me, in a mucky tweed jacket and trousers, flat cap and wellies. He was squatting beside a long hosepipe running his bare hands along it to break out the ice. He grunted a greeting and held up a muddy hand with skinny fingers. I felt I was shaking hands with a damp skeleton.

He said, 'I'll show you round as soon as I've given yon little beasts a drink.'

Aside from the fold-yard where full-grown cows stamped and moaned, every shed and building was divided into small pens made from wooden pallets lashed together with baling twine, in which over two hundred tiny calves were crying for food and water. Taken from their mothers a few hours after birth - the normal practice of dairy farmers - Farmer B fed the fragile animals for three or four months, keeping them alive and fattening them up, then he sold them on. The calves needed to drink every day but the only water supply in the farmyard was a single tap on the house wall by the door to the kitchen, and the long hose which today was frozen.

I said, 'Has the farm been for sale long?'

'About nine month.'

'I take it you're in no hurry to sell.'

'Oh I am. I'll sell it today if I get a right offer.'

I soon learned that Farmer B had been obliged to sell more than half the farm, and most of his dairy herd, as divorce settlement after his wife ran off with the inseminator (a hard thing to live down in the village, I imagined). He'd married again, now had an eight year old son and had recently bought a hundred and fifty acres of grazing land intending to start over with a new dairy herd. To do this he needed to sell what was left of Manor House Farm.

When I got home I was full of it. I said to Pat, 'The place is in a terrible state, dreadful. But that's good, because if it were halfway decent we'd never be able to afford it. The thing is though, it's potentially absolutely idyllic. Everything we've ever dreamed of. The house is beautiful, or could be again, there are enough buildings and space in the yard to make into a marvellous rocking-horse workshop, showroom and museum, and there's land, lots of it, forty-seven acres.'

'We don't know anything about farming.'

'I know, but we can learn. We can grow our own food and you can have your own horse.'

This last would be the clincher, I hoped.

She laughed, 'It seems you've got your heart set on this dream house. Can we afford it?'

'I think we can, just about, if we sell this house.'

That was a problem. The property market was in a slump; nothing was selling. Our house had been for sale while we'd been looking for somewhere else and we hadn't had a single viewing. It could take months or years to sell. Farmer B wouldn't want to wait that long.

'But I've been thinking, Pat. The land Farmer B has bought isn't far from here but he doesn't have a house to live in, not yet. He's banking on getting Ministry of Agriculture approval to build one once he's established his new dairy herd and can prove the need to live on site. That could easily take two or three years, maybe more. I can't see his wife being happy about living in a caravan in a muddy field all that time, the two of them and an eight year old boy. If they'll take this house of ours in part exchange, we should be able to raise a mortgage for the balance we'd need to buy the farm. We'd get the farm and they'd have somewhere comfortable to live while waiting for Min of Ag approval. Everybody wins.'

'You mean swap houses?'

'Exchange, yes, and pay them the difference.'

'You think they'll go for it?'

'Let's invite them here. We'll warm the house and put the coffee on. He might not like the idea but when Mrs B sees she's got a choice between this comfortable, spacious house with its gas central heating and modern kitchen, or a draughty caravan in a sea of mud for years on end, I think she'll persuade him.'

Pat laughed, 'OK, let's give it a go. I would love to have a horse of my own in our own paddock.'

The Bs came and we gave them coffee and showed them round. They looked and nodded but said almost nothing, then left. A couple of days later - I couldn't wait any longer - I called in at Manor House Farm. In his slow and deliberate way Farmer B said, 'Well now, the wife likes the idea of swapping houses and I've been thinking it over. Maybe we could do a deal at that.'

So we went into the house and sat at the table in his cluttered farmhouse kitchen. Mrs B made us mugs of tea.

I said, 'If you take our house at valuation - it's a fair valuation, check it out - and we pay you the difference in cash, which is as much as we can afford, you get your asking price. Ours is a good modern house but the market's dead at the moment and nothing's selling. But this way we'll both get what we want, and when you come to sell the HoSM house in a year or two, after you've got your Min of Ag approval, you'll probably make a good profit. What do you think?'

He sat and stared at his tea mug for a long time, then looked across at me, nodded and said, 'Aye.'

'Excellent,' I said and we shook hands.

I said, 'I'm going home now to tell Pat and sack our estate agent. We hired him to sell our house but if you and I have done an exchange deal without him, I don't need him. What are you going to do about yours?'

'I've known our agent a lot of years. I don't want to be cutting him out. I reckon he'll still be acting for me.'

'OK, if that's what you want. I'll write to him and tell him what we've agreed. If you tell him too we can get this moving along. I'd like to get it sorted and move as soon as possible, wouldn't you?'

'Aye. No need to be messing about now we've made ourselves a deal.'

'Good. We're all set then.'

I went home and told Pat. We were so excited. I wrote to our solicitor instructing him to do the necessary searches and draw up a contract. I wrote to Farmer B's estate agent setting out the deal and we waited for his acknowledgement. None came. We waited ten days but heard nothing. By now it was into December so I went to see Farmer B.

He said, 'I've told him. I don't know why he's not been in touch with you. I'll tell him again.'

We waited another week and heard nothing so I wrote to Farmer B's estate agent again: 'I'm disappointed not to have heard from you. Your client and I have shaken hands on a deal which we both want completed without delay. However, if I don't hear from you by Christmas I'll assume that in spite of what Farmer B has told me, the deal's off and we'll look for something else.'

In the run-up to Christmas we worked frantically hard to get all our orders done and delivered, all the time preoccupied with our longed-for move. I worked Christmas Eve with the staff, tidying the shop and workshop and enjoying a Christmas drink or several with them before they left for the holiday (we'd be closed until the new year) and locked the shop. The day had dragged and, sunk in depression, I walked slowly home. Pat looked up expectantly when I opened the kitchen door but I shook my head.

'Nothing,' I said. 'Not a letter. Not even a phone call. I guess that's it. I don't know what they were playing at, stringing us along like that.'

'Wanting us to up our offer?'

'Maybe. I don't know. That place in Fangfoss would have been absolutely ideal, but it's finished. Dream over.'

We sat down for our evening meal and the children cheered us up. They were jumping with excitement at the prospect of presents appearing overnight. Around nine, as we readied them for bed, the phone rang.

'Mr Dew? This is George, Farmer B's estate agent. I wanted to let you know that our client is very keen to conclude the arrangement he's made with you. He wants to move to a completion of the exchange as soon as possible in the new year. You *are* still wanting to progress this?'

'Yes, definitely. We'd about given up on you but thanks for letting me know. That's excellent news.'

'Good. I'll just call Farmer B and tell him we'll get this business wrapped up soon as the holiday's over. A Happy Christmas to you and your family.'

'Happy Christmas to you too.'

On moving day, early February, Farmer B and ourselves hired the same removal company. First thing in the morning they were to send one van to our HoSM house and one to Manor House Farm, load the two vans, drive to the other location to off-load, fill up and return. The move should be completed by midday. It didn't work out like that. Pat and I were well practised at moving house and all our smaller possessions were packed in cardboard boxes ready to go. But when the removal men arrived at the farm they found the Bs totally unprepared. Drawers full of cutlery and crockery, wardrobes and cupboards full, Farmer B's trousers still hanging over a chair in the bedroom. They set to packing and the first van didn't leave the farm until after midday. The move ran frustratingly late.

I'd been forewarned that although he was moving to a house with no open fires or need for oil, Farmer B would likely not leave us enough coal to light a fire or oil to keep the Aga in the kitchen going. So I had half a ton of coal and a thousand litres of heating oil delivered on moving day. It was bitterly cold and when one of the removal men asked if he might light the fire in the living room so we could all warm up a bit, I readily agreed.

Unfortunately Farmer B hadn't mentioned that the oil tank leaked and our newly delivered oil had been squirting out all over the coal. Consequently when the removal man, having got the fire going nicely with newspaper and kindling, threw a shovel-full of coal on, fire belched out into the room and near set the house ablaze. We killed the fire and for the rest of the afternoon thirteen year old Sam shovelled coal out into the yard for the rain to wash the oil away. I phoned the oil company to come back and pump out the tank, install a new one and refill it. Meanwhile the Aga went out and the house got very cold indeed.

It was early evening and the light was fading by the time the last removal van left the farm. The little calves had gone and the house was empty, but Farmer B hadn't taken all his possessions. He hadn't had time to fence his new holding, he said, and asked if he could leave his twenty cows behind in the fold-yard until he could sort somewhere for them. Also, he had nowhere for the billy-goat, which had been bleating at us non-stop all day over a stable door, or the dozens of chickens scratting about in the yard.

I said, 'I don't mind you leaving the chickens but I don't know anything about cows and we really don't want a billy-goat.'

'I'll look after the beasts,' he said. 'Don't you worry. I'll be back tomorrow to take care of them. But I can't take them today. Or the billy-goat.'

'Well OK then. As for the chickens, if you don't want them we'll take care of them. It'll be nice to have our own fresh eggs won't it Pat?'

Pat nodded. Farmer B said, 'Aye. Well I'll be off then.'

'One last thing before you go. Here's all the spare keys to your new house. Can you give me the keys to the farm now?'

'Keys?' he said. 'No. No keys. I've lived here thirty years and never locked a door.'

We stood in the freezing mud of the yard and watched the tail-lights of his car disappear. I told Pat we'd shove a chair under the door-knob for now and I'd fit a new lock as soon as I could. She shivered and headed for the house to make supper for us all. I filled a couple of buckets with firewood, left them on the doorstep and walked back down the yard. The cold gloom of night was settling over the yard and it stank of kerosene and animal shit. The cows and the goat had quietened down and the yard was near silent, only the soft soughing of tree branches in the breeze. The chickens had disappeared into one of the sheds and were already bedded down on rows of straw-lined shelves. They were making soft clucking and murmuring noises as they settled themselves for the night; it was the most tranquil sound I'd ever heard. I tied the door shut and went into the house. Pat was in the kitchen standing over a camping stove on top of the cold Aga, heating up a saucepan of thick soup.

'Look in there,' she said, nodding at a kitchen unit. I pulled open a drawer and peered in. It was thick with dirt and mouse droppings. I pushed the drawer shut. All our kitchen things were stacked in cardboard boxes along one wall and at least the table was clean. I found a bread knife and sliced a loaf and we loaded a couple of trays and carried our supper through into the living-room. Sam had found some uncontaminated coal and built up the fire. We huddled round, the five of us, breathing the smokey, dusty smell of this strange new house and eating our supper, not saying much but enjoying the blazing warmth and flickering light of the fire. Our fronts were hot, our backs cold. This first night we'd all be sleeping on mattresses on the bedroom floors upstairs, Sam in his own room at the back, the girls sharing. We were all exhausted and Pat said we'd go up to bed as soon as supper was over. She'd already made the beds and found some hot water bottles to warm them. I was tired out but at the same time exhilarated. I said I didn't think Pat and I would need a hot water bottle and grinned at her but she only looked at me with tired eyes. For the first time since I'd left my Mum and Dad, getting on for thirty years before, I felt I'd found a real home for myself and my family and we'd never leave.

Once the children were settled Pat and I sat in front of the living-room fire nursing glasses of whisky and staring into the flames.

Pat said, 'What are we doing here?'

'Putting down roots.'

'I know. But a year ago you were all for us quitting rocking-horses altogether and doing something else, maybe emigrating, I don't know. Now suddenly rocking-horses is all you want to do again, and all you want me to do, and you've moved us to this place which, don't get me wrong, I can see it was a lovely house once and could be again, but it will take years and years and the children will be growing up all the time and all we'll be doing is working. And it's such a dump. Life shouldn't be all about work. I feel like it's passing me by.'

'I don't feel life's passing us by. This is our life, Pat. We're making something of it, something wonderful. We're in this together. Aren't we?'

She stared into the fire.

I said, 'You remember when we had our first management consultation with Mike Jones and he told us how surprised he was that we'd built this amazing rocking-horse enterprise together all these years, you and me, and we were still happily married?'

She laughed, 'I remember. Well, we *are* still married.'

'Yes, and all I wanted to do then was quit. Not the marriage, not that, the rocking-horses. But Mike made me realise that what matters is how we manage it. It's a great enterprise, he said, and it can give us everything we want, if only we can do it without driving ourselves nuts in the process. It's about management as much as anything. How we mange the enterprise and our time. Rocking-horses aren't the problem, they're the solution.'

'You think so?'

'Yes. It's tempting to think we could quit the hassle of running The Rocking Horse Shop and do something else, something uncomplicated and easy to run that would make us enough money to live on. But I've no idea what that might be and whatever we do we have to do something. And the thing is Pat, we have this great opportunity. Our rocking-horse business is creative, challenging, absorbing, life-enhancing. Like Mike said, we've built it from nothing and established ourselves in a profitable niche market. We've got it made, potentially. And Phil's been good, hasn't he?'

'Yes, Phil's been a great help.'

A key part of Mike's advice had been that we should hire a manager to share the load with Pat and me. Mike had written a job description and sat in on the interviews, as a result of which we'd employed Phil as Workshop Manager. Phil had previously run his own small building company so he was a hands-on manager and knew how to look after a small workforce. As well as being a hard worker and a practical man he had a friendly manner and we both liked him. He'd kept the business going in HoSM while we'd been dashing about sorting the move to Fangfoss.

I said, 'Phil's doing a good job but it's just a job to him. It's not to me, it's life, our life. I know I was all for quitting a year since but the fact is I simply cannot think of anything I'd rather do than what we do already. Sure it has its downsides; I'd like our life to be less pressured and the move here will certainly make things tougher, for a while anyway. But now we've got our own little piece of paradise. I believe this is as good as it gets and I love it. Don't you?'

'I don't know Tony. Rocking-horses aren't my whole life like they are for you. I never expected our life would become such an unremitting slog. And now you've committed us to years and years more of the same.'

'Yes, there is that.'

She smirked and we stared at the fire. I said, 'Would you like me to warm your back?'

She closed her eyes, then opened them and smiled at me, 'Go on then.'

She held out both her hands and I grasped them and we heaved our tired bodies from the chairs and, with arms around each other, made our way slowly up the stairs to bed.

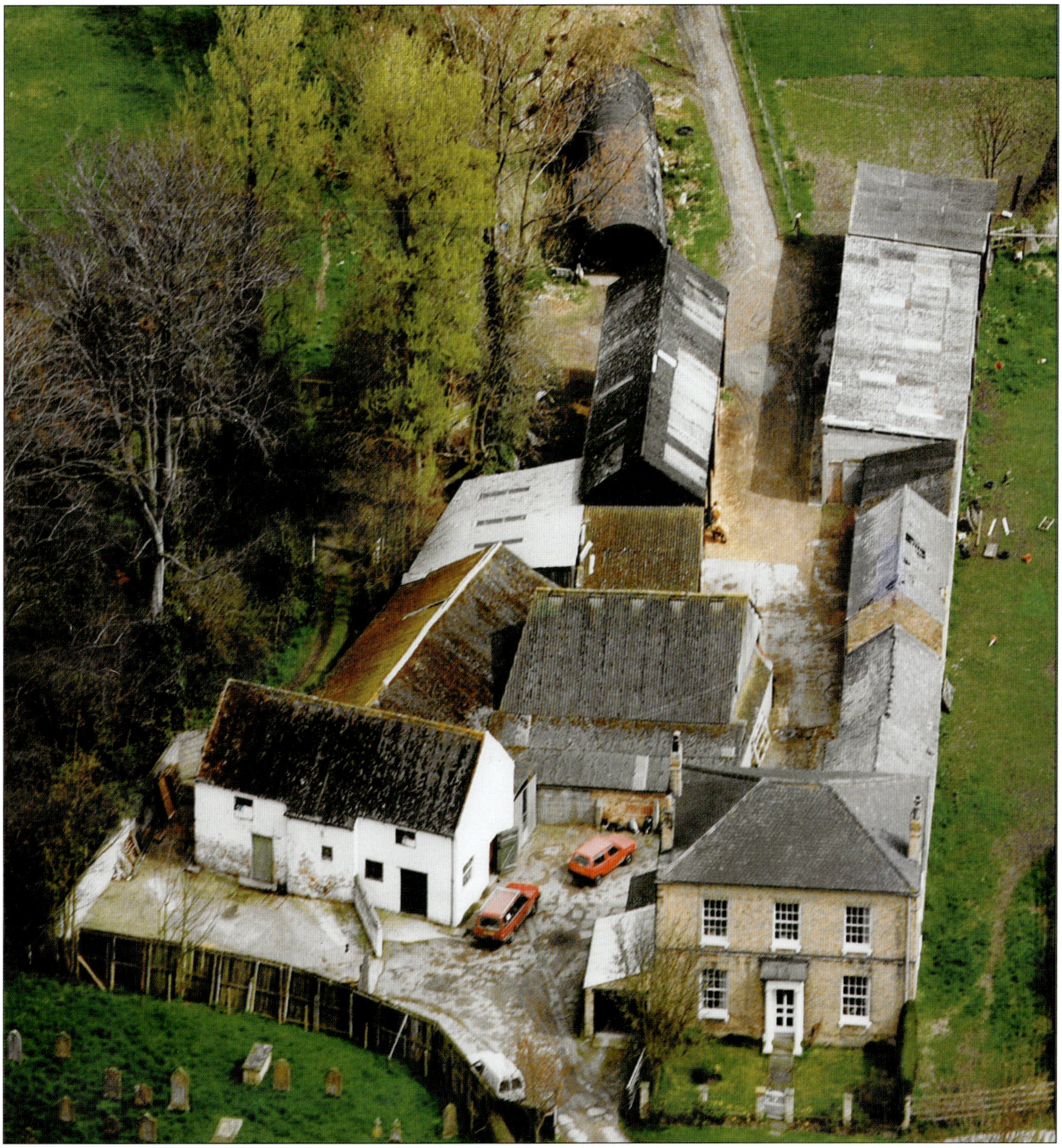

*Manor House Farm, 1991.*

# 16

Creating a rural idyll out of a badly neglected semi-derelict farm was a mammoth undertaking which we achieved, as I am fond of saying, entirely on the back of a rocking-horse. It's a fact that very few people make a decent living out of hand-craft. The vast majority of professional crafts-people have a partner with a regular paid job, or are retired and draw a pension, or have some other paid work (like teaching) or independent means. The Rocking Horse Shop provided our only income: it fed, clothed and housed us, paid the mortgage and the wages of our staff, and would have to make all the money we'd need. Alongside whatever else we did, we had to keep the business going and growing, profitably and sustainably. Manager Phil was immensely helpful in keeping the old shop and workshop functioning while we developed the new one. Our staff carried on working steadily through all the changes and upheavals. Without them we wouldn't have made it but even so it was desperately hard.

From our first night I felt at home but Manor House Farm wasn't properly ours until a couple of weeks after we'd moved in. Farmer B came every day to attend to his cows as he'd said he would, but also to take away various things from the yard he said he'd forgotten. One afternoon I found some antique hay racks loaded on his trailer in the farm yard. He'd unbolted them from the stable walls and evidently intended them for his new place. He wasn't around just then so I took them off his trailer and hid them.

When he appeared I said, 'I haven't minded you carting away the old farm machines since maybe you can use them and they're no use to us, but this farm doesn't belong to you anymore and you can't come round unscrewing fixtures and fittings and removing them. I don't want you taking anything else, except for your twenty cows and the goat. Please remove them as soon as you can. You can leave the hens.'

He bridled, then shrugged, and the following day a cattle truck came and took the cows away, and the billy-goat, and Farmer B didn't come again. The goat had been a real nuisance, several times leaping right over the stable door and escaping, and Pat had gone chasing after it down Main Street with a bucket of feed to coax it back. It also had a disconcerting habit of suddenly rearing up on its hind legs, putting its front hoofs on our shoulders and pushing its smelly nose onto our faces. It was a relief to see the back of it, and the cattle. After they'd gone I asked Trevor Craven, one of our farmer neighbours, if he'd like the muck the cows had been standing on in the fold yard. He sent his man round with a digger and a tractor and trailer. The midden was over a metre thick and it took three full days to cart it all away.

Apart from rubbish - literally tons of that - now that all the buildings in the yard were empty I could see that they were in such a poor state of repair I was uncertain how we'd be able to use them, if at all. The house wasn't great either: it had electricity but the wires were ancient and nailed onto the surface of the walls. It needed re-wiring and re-plumbing, including installing an effective heating system, and decorating. It was also filthy and needed a thorough clean but at least it had a good roof. Outside, the garden was a mess and the pillared portico over the front door was falling away from the house. In the paddocks the grass was knee high, the hedges completely overgrown and none of our fields had gates since Farmer B had taken them.

Our twenty-five acre field had a crop of winter wheat growing on it. The plants were small and would obviously need looking after but we had no idea how. And, most important, there was the family. The kids were starting new schools nearer Fangfoss but were getting to an age when Pat and I would likely spend a fair amount of time taxiing them around. As always most of the burden of our domestic arrangements fell on Pat. She and I were excited, but also alarmed and intimidated by the monstrous task that faced us, that I'd pushed us into.

We had no reserves of cash hidden away, no rich relatives to help us out and no safety net. But we did have a lot going for us. I was confident that our rocking-horses were as good as any in the world and we were on top of our game. The business was growing fast and if we could maintain its momentum we should stay solvent, if we were careful. At forty-two I was as strong and capable as

I was ever likely to be and wasn't afraid of hard work. In spite of Pat's doubts (and mine) I was sure we could succeed. Our time was now. And I knew how to approach a seriously daunting task from reading Robin Knox-Johnston.

Johnston was an ex-Merchant Navy officer like me and I respected him immensely. When he'd set off on the first Golden Globe yacht race and was faced with the mind-boggling enormity of sailing single-handed round the world, he divided the journey into manageable chunks. Whilst never forgetting his overall objective he concentrated on making as much progress as he could in the twenty-four hours immediately in front of him. Then the next day and the next and so on. I'd do the same: start with one project, one building, sort that and then go on from there. Don't forget the long-term vision - to build an idyll of creative happiness and comfort - but go for it one step at a time.

The obvious starting place was to convert the old concrete cowshed into a workshop. It should be fairly quick and easy to sling on a new roof, lay a new floor, run an electric supply to it and get it into use. It shouldn't cost too much and an excellent government scheme would help. Aimed at small businesses and administered through the Rural Development Commission, the scheme would pay a grant of 25% of the capital cost of converting redundant farm buildings to commercial use. The best bit was we could claim our own labour and in that way keep costs down. The grant would make the difference between sink or swim so we applied for it and when we got the go-ahead I was keen to get going right away.

Unfortunately, the terms of the grant insisted that before we could start we had to have professionally drawn plans and development costings, not just for the shed, but the whole site. The architect we hired came highly recommended and was highly qualified, but he took an awful long time and cost a fortune. Eventually he produced some extremely impressive, indeed beautiful drawings and I sent copies out to several builders. I told them I needed costings for everything but actually wanted to start by converting the old cowshed into a workshop. None of the builders even bothered to reply, except one named Dennis Gardham.

Dennis ran a successful local building business specialising in agricultural sheds. He had an air of competence about him and when he called round one evening and we spread the architect's drawing out on the kitchen table, he came straight to the point.

'Why do you want to renovate this old cowshed?'

'It's the quickest, easiest and cheapest thing to do. Isn't it?'

'No. For a start there are problems around putting any sort of new roof on this building. It's not square and the walls aren't straight or even parallel. That means that every roof truss will have to be manufactured individually - enormously expensive - and fitting the roof panels will be a night-mare. The building has no damp-proof course but worse than that, no foundations. That means we'll have to underpin it all the way round, a difficult and expensive job and for what? To save concrete block walls so badly built they'll probably fall over as soon as we start messing with them. Another thing, your architect has drawn an asymmetric roof and non-standard doors and windows, all of which will have to be specially manufactured, again enormously expensive. Maybe he thinks they look better that way, I don't know, but everything he's drawn is far more expensive than it need be, by a long way.'

I like straight-talking people but I was shocked and couldn't speak for a minute.

I said, 'Are you telling me it's impossible and you can't do it?'

'Oh it can be done, if it's what you want…'

'But?'

'But it will be astronomically expensive and the building will always have problems. The thing is Tony, I can put up a far better new building for you, with proper foundations, damp-proofing, insulated walls and roof, at about a quarter the cost of renovating that old shed.'

'Really?'

'Really.'

'But the architect knew it had to be affordable, I told him. Why on earth did he draw this?'

'I expect you told him you wanted to renovate the old cowshed. He's done what you asked him to do. RIBA architects don't worry about price the way you do, and since his fee will be a percentage of the overall cost of the build, he's got no incentive to keep it down.'

'I see. But what about the 25% grant, Dennis? It's approved, but it's for renovating an existing building, not putting up a new one.'

'Well, we can probably keep enough of the old shed so we can say we're renovating it. Anyway, the concrete blocks we'll use to build a new workshop will be the exactly the same as those in the old cowshed. A concrete-block shed is a concrete-block shed. Nobody will be able to tell which bits are old and which new.'

'Let's do it Dennis! You think it'll look all right?'

'It'll be a concrete-block shed. But what I can do to make your new workshop look more attractive is face the gable-end wall in brick. That's what everyone sees when they look down the yard. If we use a brick similar to your house and outbuildings it will all be in keeping. It won't add much to the cost and look better than all right.'

And so it came to pass. Dennis was right on all counts. As the new workshop neared completion we had a party to celebrate. We invited the local mayor and councillors, officials from the Rural Development Commission, Dennis and his team of builders, friends and neighbours. The building had been painted white inside and out but was still empty, a great echoey cavernous space that was actually a lot bigger than the one it replaced. Since Dennis's costings were so reasonable I'd asked him to make the new workshop longer. The extra cost was manageable and we were still eligible for the 25% grant, so instead of a converted sixty foot cowshed we wound up with a brand new workshop one hundred and twenty feet long. The visitors wandered round sipping their champagne and admiring the huge space we'd created that held so much promise, and nobody noticed that it was essentially new.

The mayor even commented, 'This building is so smart and fresh, you wouldn't think it used to be a dirty old cow shed.'

'No.' I said. 'You wouldn't.'

As well as building the new workshop, Dennis's men stabilised the falling-down part of the cart shed and fixed the brickwork, stripped off the slates to renew all the rotten roof timbers, fitted skylights and insulated the roof, then put the slates back. I was keen for us to do as much as we could ourselves so we made and fitted all the internal joinery, door frames and doors. The large space above the cart shed, formerly a granary, had been inaccessible, probably for decades, because a lean-to shed had been built right across its first floor entrance door. When we finally got in we didn't find any hidden treasure, but discovered a lovely bright room destined to be our office, accessed by a new external wooden staircase we designed and built in our rocking-horse workshop.

I'd anticipated occupying the new premises at the farm bit by bit, the woodworking machinery first, the rest of our equipment as and when we could manage it. But as the building work progressed, with Pat and me commuting between Fangfoss and our old shop in HoSM, sometimes several times a day, we became increasingly convinced that the sooner we could get everything together on one site the better. One of my mantras was that we'd make everything we could in our own workshops, so we'd be less dependent on outside suppliers and more flexible in response to our customers' requirements. The development at Fangfoss made that possible.

Half of the extended new workshop would be our woodwork shop, with timber storage, machining, preparation and woodcarving, and a paint shop in one corner. The other half became our leather workshop, with areas for tacking up and finishing our rocking-horses, and for packing parcels of accessories ready for posting. All under one roof. The metalwork went into one of the empty stables and our plan-printing equipment into the old granary, our office. The cart shed's arched doorways, formerly open to the elements, now sported smart new varnished timber and glass frontages we'd made; it became our showroom. We hired a contractor to lay paving slabs in front of the showroom and workshop, and to resurface the whole yard. Mud disappeared under tarmac and paving; the right-hand side of our yard was transformed.

A major outstanding problem was electric power. The supply to the new workshop needed to be 3-phase (ie 450 volts) to run our big woodworking machines and leather presses, and I wanted a mains supply. But Yorkshire Electricity, the local monopoly, took months to come through with a quote for its installation and when it did the figure was ten times what I'd expected.

'Seventeen and a half thousand pounds to dig a trench and put a wire in it?' I said to the YE manager. 'It's completely outrageous. Why, I could employ a good man for a year and a half for that kind of money. How can you possibly justify it?'

'I don't need to justify it,' he said, folding his arms and looking at the sky. 'That's our price. If you don't like it, go and buy your electricity somewhere else.'

So I bought a generator and installed it in a small extension Dennis built for the purpose on the end of the new workshop, and our electrician wired in a changeover switch. Every morning I turned on the generator, switched off the mains and the whole site, house as well as workshop, ran on our own power supply. The running costs were more but the installation cost about a quarter YE's quote, and I was pleased to give them the finger and be self sufficient.

We needed to heat the premises. By good fortune we found an old-school boilermaker named Ian McEwen, a brilliant engineer who'd spent most of his life building large industrial boilers. That market was drying up and he was moving into making smaller domestic boilers. Straw burners were becoming popular among farmers and he hoped it would be a profitable diversification for him. He designed and built us a boiler that looked like Thomas the Tank Engine, a real engineering beauty. Its combustion chamber held up to six bales of straw and burned wood as well. In a corner of one of the stables we excavated a metre square and deep hole, filled it with concrete and set into it a huge iron hoop with about twenty bolts sticking up, to which the chimney would be secured.

McEwen sent me off to Huddersfield to look at the chimney on a mill being demolished. The mill's boiler-house was on the fourth floor and the huge steel chimney towered up another eighty feet. As far as I could see it looked all right so I told the demolition contractor I'd like to buy it. He said it would be £200 cash. I paid him and asked his crane driver to put the chimney on the ground for me. McEwen carted it away, cut it to the right length, modified it to suit our boiler and fitted an insulated sleeve. We had to take the stable roof off and hire a crane to get the new boiler and chimney in, but it looked marvellous and worked brilliantly. A key motivation in going for this boiler was the almost free fuel we'd have. We'd store all the burnable waste out of our woodwork shop through the summer to keep us warm in winter. And, come the harvest of our wheat crop, we'd have a plentiful supply of straw, free but for the cost of baling.

We hired a field walker to tell us what to do with our twenty-five acres of wheat. He advised spraying it with fertilisers, insecticides, herbicides and stalk-stiffeners. We didn't like the idea of all those sprays but without them, he said, the grain wouldn't thrive and we wouldn't make any profit, so we followed his advice. He also suggested we forward sell our crop on the grain market ahead of harvest, which we did. It was good advice, the price was high. After the grain was harvested a friendly farmer named Carter (whose land was next to ours) baled the straw for us and loaned us a trailer to haul it up to the yard using an ancient Massey 65 tractor we'd bought, and we built a straw stack in the barn. Our children and several new friends from the village helped and it was all very exciting, with kids laughing and tumbling down the stack and adults hefting up bales and piling them high, like we were proper farmers.

We weren't proper farmers though, we were only playing at it. The wheat crop had been an enjoyable but time-consuming distraction from rocking-horses and when I added up all we'd spent on the field walker and the chemicals, the contractors to spray and combine it, the 'tidy profit' we'd made was pitiful. We had the straw for fuel, but even so I decided we'd be wiser spending our time on what we did best, so we sold the twenty-five acre field to Mr Carter. We still had twenty-two acres, one

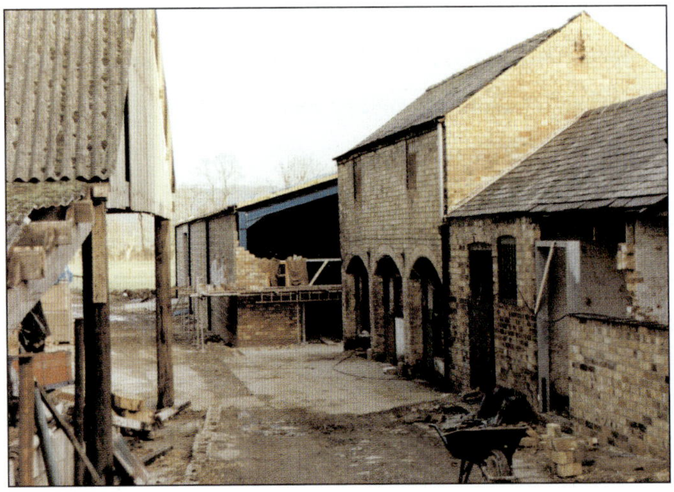
*Rocking Horse Yard, 1993. Building the new workshop is underway & new door casings, doors & windows are being made & fitted. The old foldyard (on the left in the picture) still dominates the yard.*

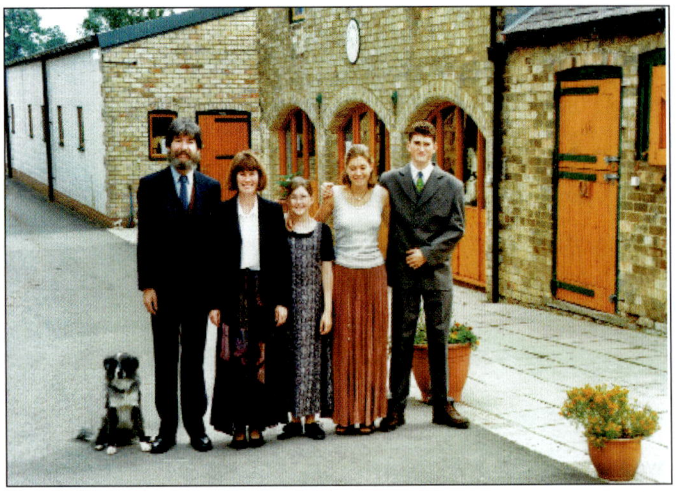
*Rocking Horse Yard, 1995. The new workshop is in use,& the old cart-shed is now our showroom. In this picture the Dew family must have been going to a wedding - from the left Josie the dog, AD, Pat, Lynn, Kate & Sam.*

heck of a big back garden.

In the future we'd have to buy in straw to burn but for now we had two and a half thousand bales, enough to last one winter at least. Every cold morning I raked out the ash, filled the boiler with straw and wood waste and lit it. It needed stoking two or three times but kept the workshop nice and warm all day and the house all evening. During the night the boiler fire died and I'd start over next morning. We had to fend off complaints about acrid smoke blowing in her direction from Mrs Meg who lived the far side of the church. I didn't want to annoy anyone but a neighbour told me Mrs Meg was the kind of woman who bought a house next to a church then complained about the bells, so I didn't take too much notice of her, and once I got the hang of the boiler it didn't smoke. Well, not much.

In the spring of 1994 we moved out of our old shop and workshop, gave up the industrial unit we'd been renting, and shifted The Rocking Horse Shop entirely to Fangfoss. I was glad we no longer wasted hours commuting every day, and now that it wasn't needed we put the HoSM property up for sale, intending to put the money we'd get for it into development at the farm.

It took more than a year to sell which was frustrating, but gave us time to get the necessary planning approvals in place for the next phase of building at the farm, and to keep The Rocking Horse Shop business forging ahead. We'd made remarkable progress but the struggle was far from over.

# 17

We moved The Rocking Horse Shop to Fangfoss with minimal disruption, at least to our customers. A few visitors showed up disgruntled, having gone to the old shop and been redirected, but our mail-order customers probably didn't even notice. We still thoughtt of ourselves as a small, friendly rural enterprise but we now had a splendid new workshop and ten full-time employees - which presented fresh challenges. It gave us the opportunity to organise everything efficiently and introduce systems to enhance the way we worked. Thus each employee had their own area of expertise and was expected to turn out the best possible work, but also be able to help elsewhere whenever the need arose, such as filling in for an absent colleague or answering the phone. If they needed extra training, we'd provide it.

When they finished making something, each worker packed it and filled in and signed a sticker with our logo on which read: 'This item was made/prepared for you by ...' This was intended to engender a sense of pride in the individual's work because they'd made something for a valued customer, not merely to satisfy me or an overseer. It worked; with each person acting as their own quality controller we didn't need supervisors. And, of course, it let us know who was responsible when problems or complaints occurred, which happened sometimes.

If we could do without supervisors, Pat and I

concluded, we could also do without a manager. Although Phil had been immensely helpful throughout the year we'd been preparing to move, and during the move itself, we worried that he wasn't entirely on top of the manager's job. I'd noticed, for example, that the leather-workers were stockpiling large quantities of finished saddles in sizes and colours we rarely sold. Phil admitted that unnecessary stock was being made and suggested a reason: we were overstaffed. He agreed the solution, that somebody would have to go, but he clearly hadn't realised we were intending it to be him, so it was a difficult conversation. He accepted what we were saying though, and agreed to go, adding bitterly that it wasn't unexpected and that Pat and I were such a tight team we were impossible to work for anyway. He collected his things together and left.

With hindsight letting Phil go was probably one of the worst decisions we made. Pat and I were a formidable team, but without a manager there was nobody to relieve the intense pressure on us. Oddly, not long after Phil left we discovered that far from being over-stocked we were so short of some leather items we were struggling to fulfil immediate orders. The correct levels of the many hundreds of stock items we now carried would always be difficult to manage and Phil might have sorted it out for us, but he'd gone.

Not long before our move to Fangfoss, rocking-horse maker and restorer Clive Green, a customer and friend who lived on the south coast near Brighton, wrote to tell me he was writing a how-to-do-it book entitled *Restoring Rocking Horses*. It sounded like a sort of companion volume to my *Making Rocking Horses*, but he was talking to a different publisher and was on the verge of signing a contract with them. I felt put out, thinking that if anyone was to write a book on restoring rocking-horses it ought to be me, especially as I knew Clive had only got interested in rocking-horses in the first place as a result of reading *Making Rocking Horses*. But he was a friend, and when he told me he felt he didn't know enough about restoration to write the book on his own and would I co-write it with him, I said yes.

Clive was a delightful ex-colonial gentleman (not unlike my Dad) and we got on very well. We realised that writing a full-length book together could be fraught with difficulty and argument, so after tossing a coin to see who'd write the first chapter, we wrote alternate ones and supplied the accompanying photographs all the way through. We didn't criticise each other's efforts (much) and if one of us wanted to cut something the other had written, we'd simply cut it, no argument. Clive persuaded the publisher to pay for illustrations and we contacted Stuart and Pam McPherson of APES, highly experienced rocking-horse specialists, lovely people and artists. We visited them in their remote workshop in the mountains of North Wales, and Pam agreed to make dozens of superbly accurate drawings to illustrate each chapter of our book.

*Restoring Rocking Horses* was published in 1992. It was generally well received and, remarkably, Clive and I completed the project without major disagreement and remained friends. *Making Rocking Horses* and *Restoring Rocking Horses* were the first book-length treatments of the subject and became the two standard reference works, for a while. *Making Rocking Horses* had sold well from the start; my publisher kept reprinting and it ran to a dozen impressions. I'd been nagging them about doing an updated version and around the time *Restoring Rocking Horses* was published, perhaps recognising the growing interest in the craft, they agreed.

The new book would include new plans for a twelfth scale doll-house size version of my large rocking-horse, carved with a scalpel and very fiddly to make. And for ambitious woodcarvers, a Carousel-style horse in which the mane, bridle and saddlery were carved instead of being made of hair and leather and fixed on later. There would be nine different rocking-horse designs plus three hobby-horses on sticks and a chapter on restoration. It would have a larger format than *Making Rocking Horses*, be completely rewritten, have new photographs, many in full colour, and be called *The Rocking Horse Maker*. When it was published in 1994 it gave the craft, and The Rocking Horse Shop, another huge boost.

The book contained scale drawings but boosted

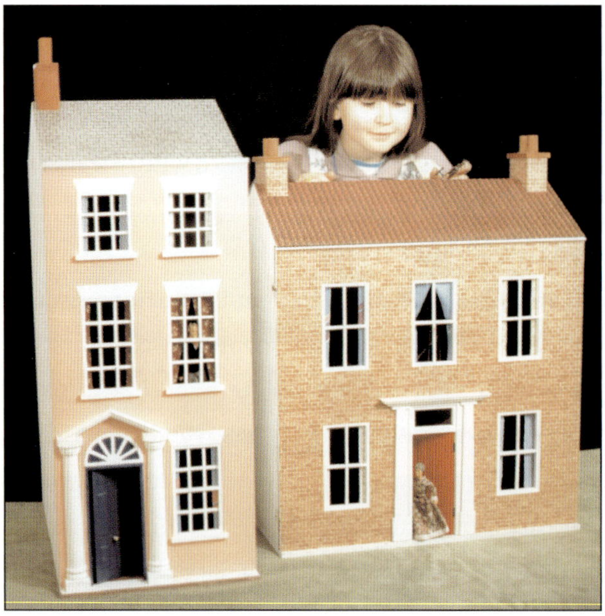

sales of our actual size plans (which saved people the trouble of scaling them up) and of all the associated timber packs and accessories. Our mail order catalogue, by now a full colour production, also offered a number of designs (with accessories) that didn't appear in the book. Rocking-horses remained the core of our enterprise but, feeling a need to diversify a little, I developed plans for Georgian and Victorian doll houses and two child's ride-in sports cars.

One car was pedal-powered, bright red and named Poppy. The other, British racing green, had a 12-volt electric motor, rack and pinion steering, electronic speed controller, hand and foot brakes, forward and reverse gears and working headlamps. I'd actually started work on the electric car long before we moved to the farm, after I bought a plan intending to make a car as a fourth birthday present for daughter Lynn. But as soon as I looked at the plan I'd bought I decided I could do better and began work on my own. Designing a car from scratch proved a bit complicated and I could only work on it intermittently because other things got in the way (like making rocking-horses and moving house and workshop) so Lynn had to settle for something else for her fourth birthday. And the next three. I finally completed the car in time for her eighth birthday and had to make it quite a bit longer than originally intended because she'd grown so much.

My first electric car was for Lynn and I knew how tall she was. But I intended publishing the car plans in our Designs for Woodworkers series and wanted to ensure that any driver from four to eight years old (who come in lots of different sizes) would be able to reach the pedals. I phoned the headmistress of Fangfoss village school and asked her if I could come in and measure some of her children's legs while they sat in a pretend driving position. When I tell people about this they invariably say, 'You wouldn't get away with that now!' It was a bizarre request even then, but the headmistress knew us and was happy to let me into school with my tape measure and do what I needed to do.

Finding a name for a new design was always difficult. Our first choice for the electric car was Merlin, but when we found there was already a sports car with that name we changed it to Dewlin, which pleased my daughter. The bodywork of both the Dewlin and Poppy cars was thin plywood bent over thicker ply bulkheads, with the curved mudguards laminated from layers of thin plywood. This made for a strong yet lightweight construction and both cars worked really well. We sold plans for them with instructions and all the metal fittings including wheels, running gear, motors and so on, and cast chrome plated bonnet mascots in the shape of (what else?) horse's heads. Both cars were fitted with smart leather-covered seats that slid forward and back according to the drivers' size.

One of our first customers for the Dewlin told me he was an aerodynamics engineer who worked for the McLaren Formula 1 racing team.

'Oh dear,' I said. 'I'm afraid you'll find this car terribly basic after what you're used to.'

'That's exactly what I like,' he said. 'I spend my working hours staring at a computer screen calculating the minutest percentages of airflow over our car's fuselage, and it's so cerebral. This is real!'

Another customer made a Dewlin for his four daughters and gave it the number plate '4 GIRLS'. He told me they went round their village taking it in turns to ride their bikes or drive the car and waving to everyone they met, and they loved it. The Dewlin was by far the most complex design I'd developed but it was still very

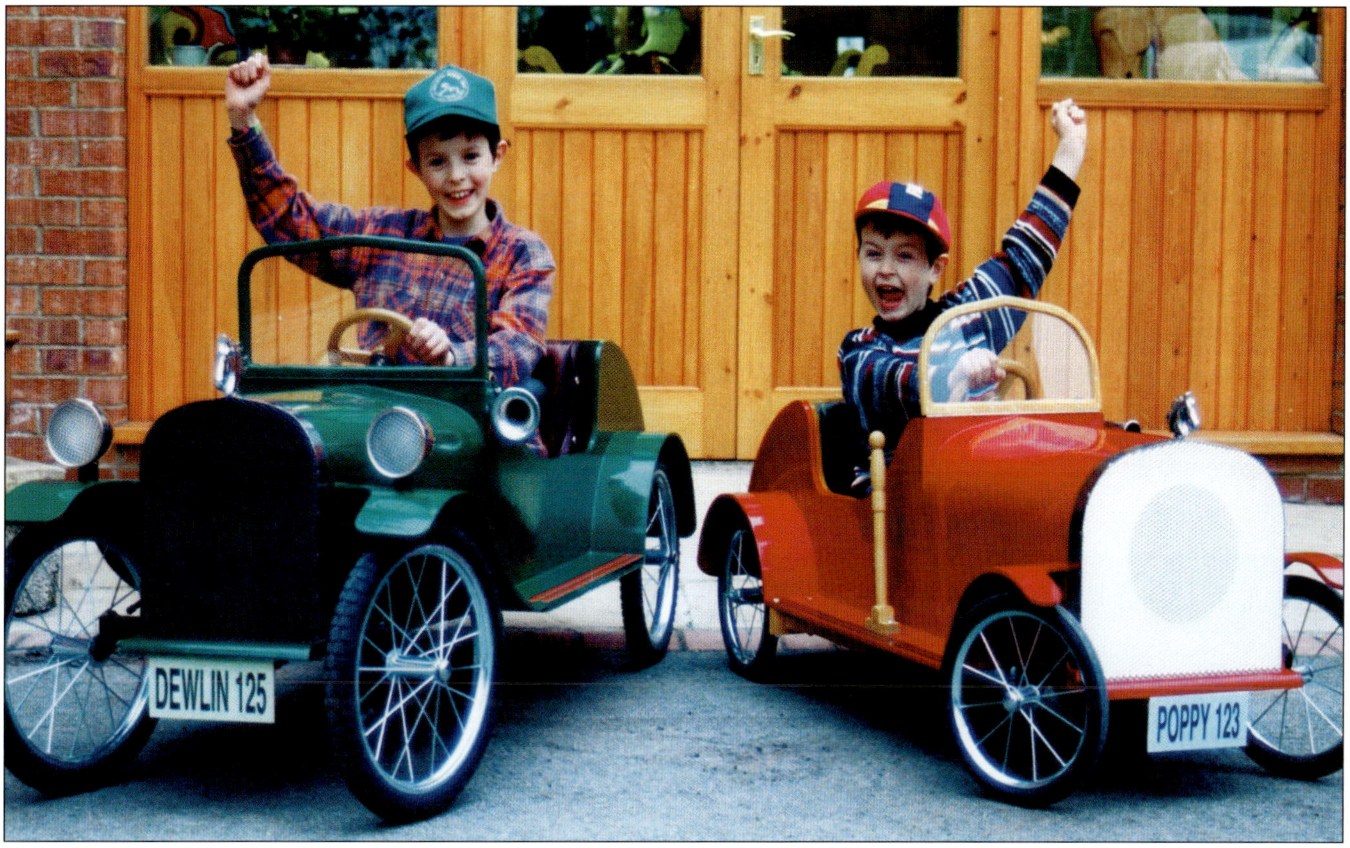

*The electric Dewlin & the pedal-powered Poppy sports cars being driven by young friends Jacob & Matt.*

simple by automotive standards. The biggest challenge in designing it was solving the many technical problems that arose in the very simplest ways possible. That was the part of the process I enjoyed most.

I'd made a pair of Large Special rocking-horses and before they were sold I wanted good photographs of them, with a rider, for our catalogue. I arranged for friend and photographer David Golledge to come, and another friend, Pauline, to bring her small daughter to model. But then Pauline said she couldn't make it. I didn't want to cancel David but was stuck without a model. Next morning, while waiting to buy a newspaper in a shop in town, an attractive little girl being carried by her Mum in the queue ahead gave me a big beaming smile and I thought, 'She'd be perfect.' I followed them out and down the street, tapped the Mum on her shoulder and asked if she'd ever considered photographic modelling. She shook her head and looked round for a way to escape.

'It's not you, actually,' I said. 'I'm more interested in your daughter.'

The Mum looked aghast. I said, 'Please wait while I explain.'

Fortunately she'd heard of The Rocking Horse Shop, her fearful expression changed to a smile and she agreed to come. The little girl was, as I'd hoped, perfect. But an eighteen-month-old has an extremely short attention span and David had a hard time getting shots in which the lighting, backdrop, setting, horse position and camera angle were all just right at the same moment as our model chose to give us one of her incandescent but extremely brief smiles. We hadn't gone digital then and David shot five rolls of film without being at all sure he'd captured the desired images. However, when I collected the results from the film processors I was delighted to find two shots out of the hundreds David had taken, one for each horse, that was exactly what I wanted.

'You needn't have worried,' the man said. 'If your model didn't have the right expression we could easily have swapped her face for a better one. These days much of our work is swapping heads, on wedding photos mostly.'

I'd read that digitised photographic images could be manipulated but this surprised me. It also put paid to any lingering belief I'd held that the camera never lies. It always does.

By the mid 90s we were sending out dozens of plans and parcels of timber and accessories every day, to addresses worldwide. We were also working on old rocking-horses that came in for renovation, several every week, and building new ones. I reckoned to start making at least one new rocking-horse every week, but I hated doing the same thing over and over (something of a handicap for a craftsman) and tried to make each one unique by adding small (and sometimes not so small) modifications. A better shaped rump, more carved muscling on the neck, improved leather saddlery, new designs for stand posts and so on. All these improvements added up to an ongoing sense of evolution which kept me motivated. I also tackled completely new designs on spec, like an Extra Large Special model which would be bigger and much more shapely than anything I'd made before, carved in solid mahogany with a lacquered natural wood finish, mounted on a massive oak stand.

As well as my own designs we published plans for a hammered dulcimer and a bowed psaltery, simple musical instruments that were straightforward to make and easy to play, designed by an old college friend Charlie Crabtree, now a teacher of craft and music. There was an energetic vibe around the workshop and I enjoyed that. When I look back on those first few years at Fangfoss I am amazed at how much we achieved, although at the time I was always dissatisfied and periodically became oppressed and depressed by the weight of so many things demanding my attention all the time, and my perceived lack of sufficient progress. Pat was managing the showroom and office full-time and looking after all our customers. Inevitably she saw more of me in my depressed state than anyone else.

Orders for our new rocking-horses stretched more than a year ahead and promised (I almost wrote threatened) to keep increasing. It was good to be in demand and have a full order book, but clearly customers wouldn't wait too long for something that was essentially a plaything, however beautiful it was and however much promise it held of becoming a valuable family heirloom. Their children weren't going to stop growing while we got our act together. I did what I could to increase production but refused to compromise on quality. So rather than have an empty showroom and a frustratingly long order book we started buying in rocking-horses from other makers, to sell on. Some were made using my designs and our accessories and fittings, some were from makers with their own unique take on the craft, but we chose only the best and all were hand-made in Great Britain.

Sam Glass was a very tall, very skinny, slow talking Scot who came to The Rocking Horse Shop two or three times a year to deliver rocking-horses he'd made. He told me that years ago, when he lived in London, he'd read my book and decided to quit his boring office job

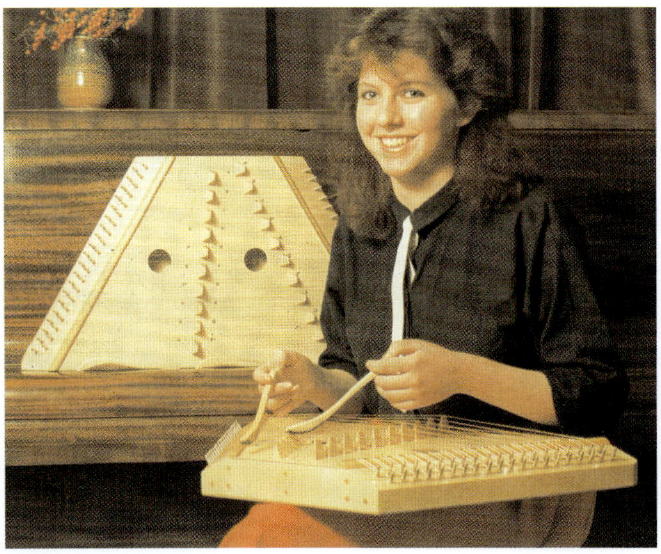

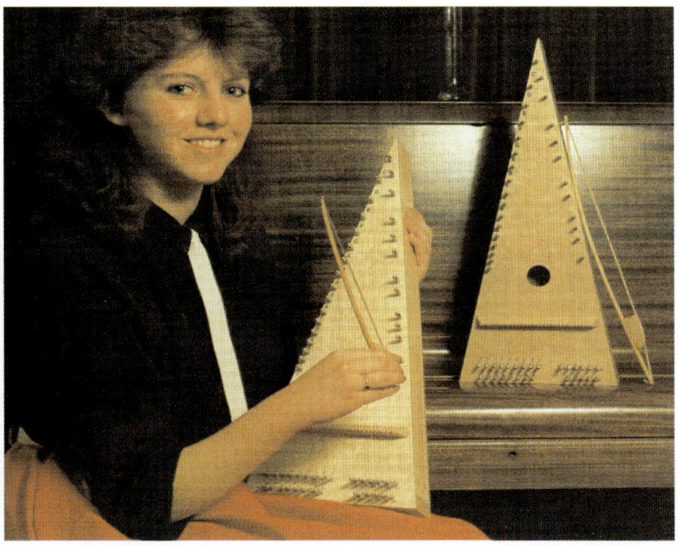

*Dulcimer & psaltery being played by our friend Dr Allan Robson's beautiful daughter.*

and become a rocking-horse maker and restorer. With his wife and two small daughters he'd driven north-west out of London in search of a house with outbuildings he could use as a workshop. When they finally found a suitable property, that they could afford, they were on the island of Anglesey, about two hundred and fifty miles from London. He said they hadn't realised quite how far they'd driven but they bought the place anyway and he got his workshop going there.

Over the years he'd turned himself into an excellent craftsman with his own distinctive style and his rocking-horses were very good indeed. But making fine rocking-horses is one thing, making a decent living selling them is something else. There weren't many rocking-horse makers but there weren't many customers either; competition was fierce. Living and working as far out as he did, Sam had had to spend an awful lot of his scarce resources trying to put his horses in front of potential customers at shows and exhibitions. It hadn't been easy.

'No, well it hasn't been easy for us either, Sam,' I said. 'But now we're on a roll and I can't make horses fast enough. I reckon there are maybe five or six people in the country who can make a really top quality rocking-horse and you're one of them. I'd love to have someone with your skill and commitment to the craft working here.'

'Are you offering me a job?'

'Yes.'

'Well you know Tony, the girls are growing up, my marriage is falling apart and my business isn't great. I'd like to take you up on that offer.'

With Sam Glass carving new horses every day in the woodwork shop, I no longer needed to. Our joiner Billy machined timber and prepared the wooden parts for Sam to assemble and carve, and for Timber Packs. Now that we had good, hardworking, competent people in every area, Pat and I no longer needed to be quite so fully 'hands-on' all the time, although we remained highly committed to the enterprise.

When we'd first moved into Manor House Farm and it was still a mess, a woman who'd lived locally for many years had made Pat laugh by observing, 'I knew this house when a real lady lived here.' Now we'd given the house a complete makeover from sewers to chimney pots. It had been re-plumbed, re-wired and re-decorated throughout, including a new light-coloured solid oak kitchen, specially designed leaded stained glass in some of the windows, a wonderful new encaustic patterned tiled hallway and a sauna in one of the smaller bedrooms. We'd got rid of our tattier possessions, bought various items of new furniture and were living in relative luxury.

Outside, we were about to start another major new project. We'd befriended a delightful young shepherd named Chris Henshaw who was busy developing his own farm not far away and looking for buildings. I said, 'You can have the old fold-yard here for nothing Chris, so long as you take it all away, including the asbestos roof.'

He took it down carefully and re-erected it in his own farmyard. The fold-yard's removal transformed our outlook by opening up the yard and giving us a view from the house across the fields and trees to the low hills of the Wolds beyond. On the site of the old foldyard, but to the left so as not to block the view, Dennis would build us a two storey L-shaped building to house a show-room for our new rocking-horses and all our Designs for Woodworkers, a reception area for visitors, a museum for our expanding collection of antique horses and offices for me, Pat and the company secretary.

I made a sketch of what I wanted and called in Rod Mill, a brilliant and very reasonably priced architect (a description almost as unlikely as 'cheap and honest lawyer', but true of Rod) who worked my sketches into plans the local authority would approve, with sufficient detail for the builder. It was a concrete block industrial building but, as with the new workshop, faced with brick to complement the brickwork of the house. It had three doorways with brick arches mirroring the arches of the old cart-shed across the yard, and although it could have had a cheap industrial profiled steel roof, for appearance's sake we chose black tiles. As always I worried about cost and didn't put a toilet in the building (staff and visitors would have to use the one at the top of the yard beside the house) and we made all the joinery in our own work-

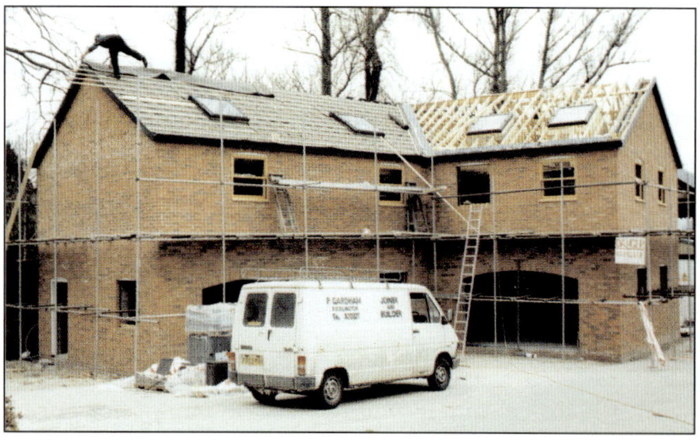

*Building our new showroom, offices & rocking-horse museum.*

shop. Even so the new building was a huge investment for us. But by '94 The Rocking Horse Shop was doing so well that we paid for it entirely out of trading profits and didn't have to borrow a penny.

The old dairy building at the top of the yard was slowly falling into total dereliction and we let it be. One day, I thought, if everything pans out, we'll demolish it and build a house there, big enough to accommodate all three of our children, perhaps even their partners and their children as well. Idle speculation of course, who can foresee the future? But thus far hadn't I been able to make our dreams come true? Some of them anyway.

# 18

In the winter of '93-94 in the far corner of our holding we began what came to be the most fulfilling and significant of all the projects we undertook at Manor House Farm. People asked if I was planting timber for the next generation's rocking-horses, but no, we planted trees for no reason other than it was a good thing to do. The wood arrived in three bin bags; eleven hundred whips thinner than kebab skewers with tiny clumps of root at one end. English oaks, beeches, silver birches, horse and sweet chestnuts - eighteen species altogether. Pat arranged for the planting to be done by students from a College of Agriculture not far away. They fenced off a couple of acres and measured out carefully to space the fragile saplings evenly. All had plastic tree-guards to protect them and stakes to keep them straight. I recall it took a week to plant them all and that the stakes and tree-guards cost four times as much as the trees themselves, which seemed wrong. To give them a good chance of survival we weeded round the saplings for the first few years then let nature take its course. From first planting I imagined a future in which the laughter of our grandchildren would echo through the woodland as they played.

We couldn't have a farm without animals. Kate looked after her sweet little grey merle bitch called Josie and, with Pat, a cute white pony named Simon. Lynn had her guinea pigs and then a puppy named Rip, a sheepdog who looked like an Alsatian but was soft-natured and a great character. Rip was supposed to guard the yard but he cried pitifully when we left him outside in the kennel we'd built specially for him, so I relented and he slept in the house porch.

When Sam was asked if he'd like an animal of his own he opted for a pig (anticipating making loads of money selling the piglets, which didn't happen). Pat found a young Gloucester Old Spot sow and we named her Bessie. She was quite a character too, for a pig. When Sam scratched her back with a garden rake she'd close her eyes, wriggle with pleasure and make low sensual noises like she was saying, 'Mmmmm, yeah.' I looked at Bessie and wondered which was better, to be happy and contented like her, or perpetually dissatisfied, like me.

There were always chickens pecking about in the yard, descendants of those Farmer B left behind. The shed where they lived had been demolished to make way for the new workshop so for a long time, until I got round to building them a new run, they were homeless and had to fend for themselves. The feral hen population fluctuated, sometimes reducing by natural wastage - I once actually saw a dog fox run off with a big black hen in his mouth, in broad daylight too - but sometimes increasing. They laid lots of eggs and, given the chance, had lots of chicks.

The fowls lived in different parts of the yard in small flocks, each led by a cockerel. When the chicks grew and too many were cockerels, they fought each other. Cockerels are viciously determined when they fight. Although I'd try to pull them apart they'd keep at it, not until one was defeated, but until one was dead. The hens took no notice of these cock-fights but disappeared from time to time to brood, then reappeared followed by a line of new baby chicks. We'd started with about a dozen but at one point counted over sixty chickens in the yard.

We always loved having eggs from our own free-range hens but while they were feral we'd have to search for them in the hedgerows and behind the straw-stack, and some might have been there for weeks. One afternoon Lynn went on an egg hunt with her schoolfriend Miriam and found fifty-four. They also came across a couple of hens sitting on clutches of eggs and as they watched four tiny chicks pecked their way out. A fifth, with a little help, hatched out in my hand. Amazing.

Chris the shepherd ran some of his sheep in our fields and gave us several orphan lambs to rear, along with his two rules of shepherding: 1. Don't be upset when they die; 2. Don't call the vet (they're not worth it). Having only ever seen them in pictures or from a distance, it surprised me that a lamb's woolly coat is not soft as I'd imagined, but hard and bristly to the touch. Bottle feeding them was a delight though; so was seeing them gambolling around in the paddock if they thrived. But Chris was right, many didn't respond to even our tenderest care.

Our old friends Porter and Linda came over from Bradford one weekend and for Sunday dinner Pat roasted a leg of lamb and potatoes in the Aga's top oven for us all. Meanwhile an ailing baby lamb lay in the lower, warming oven (with the door open) in the hope that the warmth might revive it. Porter, nodding meaningfully at the baby in the oven, asked if I'd thought about making a rocking lamb. I said I had but Linda shushed us.

Part-way through dinner Kate noticed that the lamb had died. We adjourned the meal, took out the body and placed the leg of lamb where it had been, in the warming oven (with the door closed). The seven of us then processed down the yard to the garden carrying the tiny corpse. I fetched a spade and buried it, said a few words, then we all trooped back to the kitchen, retrieved the leg of lamb and continued with dinner. It was all done quietly and without fuss or upset but Linda was shocked.

'What's happened to you people?' she cried. 'You're so hard.'

'We aren't hard-hearted,' Pat said simply. 'This is life in the country.'

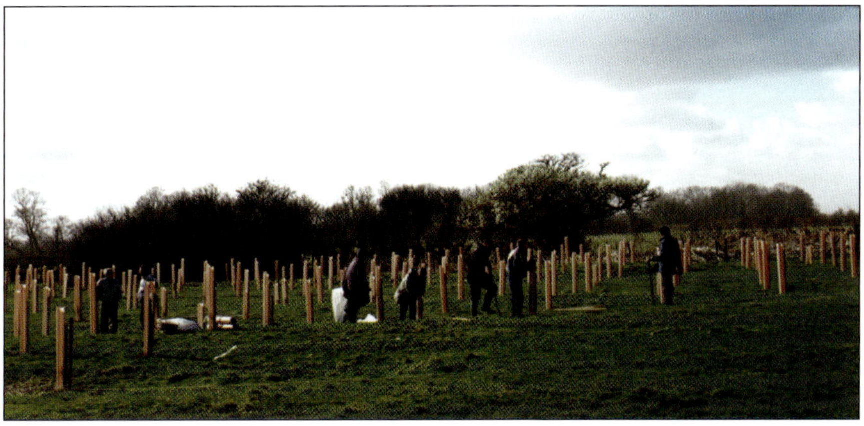

*Plasnting the wood.*

And death. Many times the yard cats left mutilated rabbits or smaller animals in the yard and I put them out of their misery. I bought a .22 Winchester rifle and Sam and I shot vermin, mostly rooks. Sam became a very good shot and in one session killed six. But however many rooks we eradicated there were always plenty more circling high, cawing loudly and splattering the yard below. We got used to death being a normal part of life on the farm, but it was never easy.

One day I noticed Simon the pony standing awkwardly in the paddock. On closer examination I realised he must have put his hoof down a rabbit hole and broken a leg. The knacker-man came within the hour and I held Simon's halter and stroked his neck while the man killed him. He then put a wire round his neck and, with a little electric winch, hauled the corpse up into his trailer, bumping it over the bodies of several cows and sheep already in there, leaving a large black stain on the grass. While this was going on Pat, Kate and Lynn stayed in the house crying. It was by far the worst day of their whole lives, they said.

For twenty years I'd had neither the inclination nor time to devote to anything much except rocking-horses, Pat and our children, the workshop, our home, and latterly the farm (in roughly that order). Periodically Pat chided me about working all the time and paying more attention to my rocking-horses than to my children.

I was offended, 'You make me sound like an absentee Dad, which I'm not. I work at home and I'm always here.'

She was right, I did tend to fit everything else, including the children, around work. But when they came in from school they'd often walk down to see me in the workshop and I was usually happy to chat while I carried on working. One afternoon Lynn, 9, was sitting on my work-bench while I carved the head of a large rocking-horse.

'Dad?'

'Yes?'

'I've been thinking.'

'Yes, Lynn?'

'When I grow up, I want to make rocking-horses too.'

'Do you Lynn? That's good.'

'Then I can look after you and Mum when you get old.'

'That's very good, Lynn.'

'But Dad?'

'Yes, Lynn?'

'I've been thinking.'

'Yes, Lynn?'

'What if you get old before I grow up?'

I dined out on that little exchange for weeks.

I'd never played a sport or had a hobby, never had time for one. But one evening whilst chatting with Harry Postill over a beer in our village pub, The Carpenter's Arms, he mentioned that he was learning to fly a paraglider.

'I saw one once,' I said. 'And it looked amazing. I'd love to try it.'

'Come with us then,' he said. 'You're more than welcome.'

This was typical Harry, friendly and welcoming, even to someone he barely knew. Harry was a cabinet maker with a long-established workshop in the village so we were in a similar way of business ('I'm a wood-butcher too,' he'd say) but I didn't know him very well then, since I was totally bound up with work and he wasn't. He specialised in making beds and as we travelled round the county to flying sites he'd often point out the homes of people he'd made beds for. It seemed to me like half the population of Yorkshire must be sleeping on his beds. He was always good company and never at a loss for words, but his conversation was rarely about work. We formed a lasting friendship.

Learning to fly a paraglider is largely about learning to control an enormous kite close above your head, a kite that's big enough to support your weight and carry you, when you get to be a good enough pilot, to the clouds. The basic training in the Yorkshire Dales required only eight days, but took us nine months. Many times we drove to the hills only to find it was too windy, or not windy enough, or the air was too turbulent or for some other reason the instructor decided we'd be safest on the ground. Valuing our lives, we obeyed. We stuck at it but there was so much waiting around I was uncertain whether I'd carry on until one fine autumn day at the head of a beautiful dale near Hawes.

I took off, made some height above the hill-top, circled a few times and found myself two hundred feet up facing the breeze. Looking down I spotted a hawk hovering right below me, fluttering his wing-tips and staring down intently at the heather below, looking for a mouse or shrew presumably. The hawk was totally unperturbed by the huge 'bird' above him and for maybe a minute we hung there as I savoured the extraordinary serenity of the moment. Then the bird wheeled away to the left and I wheeled away to the right, circled a few more times and landed, back on top of the hill for the first time. I unclipped my harness and strode over to the instructor saying, 'Right, I'm hooked, you can sell me all the gear now.'

Harry and I became weather-watchers and sky-gazers. When I wasn't obsessing about rocking-horses I was obsessing about flying. Any day promising good conditions for para-aviation we'd load our wings in one or other of our cars and drive out in search of a suitable take-off. The rocking-horse staff carried on working, Pat looked after the shop while I was out flying and I felt guilty every time, but the pull of the sky was irresistible. Flying was a great escape, requiring total commitment and concentration. All other concerns faded and disappeared. There was a lot of waiting around for the right conditions but on a good day paragliding was simply wonderful. Rocking-horses were our livelihood and continued to be the focus of my creative efforts, but getting away from them to fly increasingly dominated my thoughts. Paragliding almost always took place in beautiful parts of the landscape, involved some hard physical exercise and it got us out in the fresh air. Every flying day was a totally refreshing holiday and I would return to the fray re-invigorated. Pat had no such outlet.

Before all this, before college, Pat, marriage, children and rocking-horses, when I was at sea, I'd known peace in my head, now and again. Countless hours spent staring at the vastness of the ocean had sometimes borne in on me a feeling of kinship to all life on Earth, with all its joys and faults. Even (when I'd once isolated myself on a remote hilltop in Panama) a sense of oneness with creation in which all separateness fled and I knew all I'd ever need to know. I longed for that peace of mind again, not to recapture some fleeting Grail moment experienced in my youth, but by dint of having grown and learned and moved towards a more permanent state of wisdom in which I could cope serenely with all life's difficulties and challenges.

For a while Pat and I enjoyed a spiritual awakening when we became students at The School of Philosophy. Having determined that it was definitely not a weird cult that would entice us in only to rob us of our autonomy and money, twice a week we joined a group of like-minded lost souls who sat in a ring and meditated. There was talk of clearing the mind of clutter and attachments, which bring only misery in this life, and such a profound and apparently unshakeable happiness emanated from our teacher that I wanted to be that way too. At times in the meditations a welcome sense of inner peace did arise, and I believe we benefitted in many practical ways from the teaching.

There was talk of pausing between actions rather than rushing from one thing to the next to the next, as we so often do, until at the end of the day we drop exhausted having gained little or no satisfaction from all our furious activity. It was said that there is pleasure and satisfaction in the least of our daily tasks and we were encouraged to alter our habits to allow that satisfaction to unfold. So, for example, when the phone rang I would pause for a few seconds to still my mind and prepare for the new experience, then answer cheerfully, giving the caller my whole attention. It was undoubtedly beneficial and I encouraged our staff to do the same.

There were many ways in which the philosophy helped us to make improvements to our lives, but some of the beliefs the School favoured were less helpful. I couldn't accept reincarnation as likely and objected to one teacher's insistence that I wear a suit and tie (I'd given up uniforms when I left the Merchant Navy). Pat refused to accept that attachments, say to one's parents or children, were not good. When her Mum died and naturally she grieved, a teacher told Pat to simply let her mother go, adding that she shouldn't have been so attached to her anyway. Pat quit the School.

Having grown up listening to stories of the adventures I'd had at sea, at seventeen our son Sam decided to leave school and follow in my footsteps. I was worried for him, doubting it was even possible to enjoy much of a career at sea since the advent of flags of convenience and huge specialised container ships, bulk carriers and super-tankers. The once great British merchant fleets had been decimated and general cargo shipping, as I'd known it, was history. Britain could hardly be called a seafaring na-

Around that time I went paragliding with Harry and two other pilot friends in the French Alps. We hadn't been flying very long so it was a huge leap (literally) from the relatively low hills of Yorkshire to seriously high mountains. As we approached the Chamonix valley and I saw the Alps for the first time in my life, I was overwhelmed by the grandeur and enormity of them. The thought that we'd actually be flying up there!

The drive to our take-off took forty minutes and the animated conversation filling the mini-bus faded to an awed and frightened silence. We walked to the edge of the plateau where the ground fell away abruptly beneath our feet, and breathed deeply. We looked down the long slope of forested mountainside that fell away below us and the villages beyond that, and the wide valley stretching towards distant mountains and Mont Blanc which capped the massif on the far side, many miles away. Behind our plateau the mountains soared above us and wispy clouds formed and reformed around the summits against the vastness of the sky.

Our guide pointed up and grinned, 'Looking good'.

I laid my wing out with great care, clipped into the harness, donned helmet and gloves and stood ready and waiting, torn between a powerful desire to do this or be safely somewhere else. Our guide stood at the edge of the abyss with his hands out as if in benediction, feeling for the wafts of breeze coming up the slope that would ease my launch. He nodded. I took a step back, powered forward, boots scrabbling in the gravel, and felt my body checked as the great wing rose slowly behind me and settled overhead. I leaned forward against the weight of it and ran until there was nothing beneath me but two thousand feet of air as the wing carried my weight away from the clutches of Earth and I was free of it, albeit with pounding heart and every muscle taut. Relax!

A twenty minute ride, heart bursting with the extraordinary thrill of floating through the air suspended under a cloth wing, feet dangling and the cool breeze in my face, and I landed grinning like an idiot and packed up to go again.

'By the end of the week you'll be getting really high,' our guide promised.

In the evening, exhausted and buoyed by the intensity of our effort and emotion, we ate and chattered over the day's revelations. There was much talk of active piloting and finding thermals, those invisible bubbles of air warmed by the sun that form and grow on the earth's surface until they detach from it and float up to form clouds. If we could fly into a thermal and circle in the rising air at its core it would carry us to cloud-base and we'd touch the hand of God.

At the end of the week I came home anxious to share talk of my new-found experiences with Pat, and to see how things lay between her and me. Her welcome was cool, distant. She listened politely.

'And how have you been?' I asked at last.

'Nothing's changed,' she said.

I wanted her to try to understand the extraordinary exhilaration of flying a paraglider, maybe try it herself. In particular I wanted to share with her an incident that had occurred on our third day when I'd lost control of my wing and crashed. It had been a close call and Harry, who'd been flying further along the ridge, immediately decided he wasn't coming home because he couldn't face telling Pat I'd died out there. Harry didn't know quite how difficult relations between Pat and me had become, but even so.

She didn't seem interested and I couldn't tell what she was thinking anymore, so I didn't tell her about my fall until one evening over dinner a couple of weeks later. I told her I'd overdone a hard turn into a powerful thermal and the glider spun. I was too inexperienced to counter the spin and before I knew what was happening the lines that supported me, that ran from harness to wing, twisted up into a tight rope. The reduced wing fluttered uselessly and I plummeted. I'd been flying well and was way higher than the take-off but the sudden heart-stopping lurch into a spin was totally disorientating. My mind blurred. The wing wants to fly - we'd been told that in training - and all I could think was that if I simply let go of the controls it would. I let go and sure enough the spinning slowed, then stopped. I began to spin back the other way, slowly at first then faster until with a crack like a gunshot the wing snapped open and I was flying again, safe. But only for a millisecond. I was spinning so fast the lines spun up the other way and the wing above my head compressed and disappeared. Again I plummeted. The ground was rushing toward me at such speed there was no way to avoid it. This is it, I thought, I am going to die now.

Pat looked at me across the table. 'Why didn't you tell me?' she said.

I went on with my story. I'd been flying above a disused quarry where, the guide had told us, the sun heating the bare rock would create powerful thermals. There were rocks everywhere and had I hit one I'd surely have been killed. But, at the precise spot where I fell, thick shrub and bushes filled with leaves covered an area of steep mountainside where there were no rocks at all. I piled into this huge natural mattress, slid a hundred yards or so on my back and stopped. I couldn't believe, when I opened my eyes, that I was seeing the same bright sunshine in the same valley I'd looked out over only a few seconds before. Death had been so certain it took my addled brain a minute to appreciate I was still alive. Tentatively I moved my arms and legs, flexed fingers and toes, wriggled my back. Nothing hurt. I glanced over my shoulder. My glider had slowed my slide and was now stretched up the slope behind me in a tangled mass of twigs, leaves and branches. The wing was a mess but I didn't have a scratch. I heard a voice on my radio. It was our guide, repeatedly asking me to respond. I fumbled my radio from its pocket and pressed the button to talk.

'I'm absolutely fine,' I said. 'Soon as I can get myself together I'll pack up my wing and walk out of here.'

I was staggering about, trying to keep balance while drawing the wing towards me, when some French pilots came clambering up the slope to help. They were young, fit and cheerful and quickly stuffed my glider into the backpack. Their van was parked on a forest track a few hundred feet down and one of them carried my glider while another held my arm as we descended. I'd started to shake and was glad of their help. I kept muttering mercy, mercy.

We spread the glider out on some grass and untangled the lines and pulled out all the twigs and debris. It was surprisingly undamaged, a few small rips was all. If you fall off a horse everyone says you should get straight back on and ride. I stitched patches over the tears and the next morning took my glider up the mountain again and flew. The week went really well from then on.

'Why didn't you tell me?' Pat said.

'I'm telling you now.'

I'd hoped the shock of having nearly lost me altogether might somehow bring her back closer. I was wrong, again. The only reaction I could see was annoyance that I hadn't mentioned it sooner, as if that proved I didn't care for her.

Some say that when you're about to die a great white light appears and you're drawn towards it. Like God welcoming you, or the devil maybe. Or your whole life flickers before you, or you see all the ones you love and you reach out to them. It seems there are all manner of possible visions in those last moments before you die. But when I was falling (and it took quite a few seconds because later, when we measured it, we found I'd plummeted some 1500 feet before I hit the ground) nothing like that occurred. I saw no visions of God, Pat, my children or anybody. Rocking-horses never crossed my mind. I didn't even wonder if there was anything I might do to avert the inevitable. All I had was the blunt, matter-of-fact knowledge that I was going to die and that would be the end of me.

Pat moved out of Manor House farm to a flat in York. A few days later she wrote to me saying she'd like to come back, but only to collect a few things. She knocked on the door of our house and waited for me to let her in.

'Take whatever you want,' I said. 'Anything, everything.'

'Just a few things,' she said.

I sat on a chair and watched her. I asked her two or three times to come back to me.

'No. I can't. No. Don't ask me again.'

'Have you got someone else?'

I thought it wouldn't be so bad if she had a lover.

At least I'd have someone else to blame.

'No.'

I said, 'What are you doing where you live now that you couldn't do if you lived here with me?'

'I don't know,' she said. 'I just can't do it with you anymore.'

She kept coming back to work though. She arrived each morning, parked in the yard out-side, walked to her office, worked, drove away each afternoon. We couldn't help brushing past each other sometimes, and sometimes we talked about rocking-horses but that was all, nothing else. It was intolerable. I felt nothing but despair, the air round us thick with it. I watched her and hated her. She was leaving me for nothing. I didn't want to hate her.

She said, 'You don't have to make this so difficult.'

I said, 'I'm not, I do, it is.'

She said our separation was a trial, as if there was a possibility of resuming our marriage sometime. But everything had changed. She didn't like the person I'd become and I understood that. But I couldn't become a different person, not for her or anybody. One day I asked her if she still loved me.

'No,' she said. 'You've killed it.'

There could be no going back for us. No way forward either. She hired a divorce lawyer who advised her to keep on working, I supposed to give her more leverage in the financial settlement that was looming.

I said, 'If we're going to split, let's do it equably. We're equal, right? We started with nothing and everything we've got is equally yours and mine. We can't be chopping everything in half so let's do it like this. Let's have a balance, like weighing scales. On one side of the balance we put our house, the workshop, all the buildings and everything in them - our furniture, the machinery, the tools, the stocks of raw materials, all the rocking-horses, old, new and part-made, the tractor, the van, the car, our land, the animals - everything we have including The Rocking Horse Shop business. On the other side we put money. We make the balance even, right? On one side stuff, on the other money. That would be equable wouldn't it?'

She shrugged and nodded without looking at me. I started making a list of everything we'd accumulated and its monetary value. It frightened me.

Perhaps it frightened Pat too because she toned down some of the demands her lawyer was pushing her to make. And since she clearly found coming to work as intolerable as I did, against her lawyer's advice she stopped coming. I didn't know which was worse, seeing her or not seeing her. But it was horrifying how fast all our points of connection were severing. I kept remembering more stuff we had and piling it on the scales, adding more money on the other side to balance it. I thought if we were equal the choice could go either way. She'd take the money or I'd take it. She'd take the rocking-horses and all our assets or I would. I thought maybe we could flip a coin.

'How about it?' I said. 'Let's flip a coin.'

I was entertaining the idea that if I got the money I'd go away somewhere and live another life, not this one, in some other place, not here, with some other woman, not her. This marvellous rocking-horse enterprise Pat and I had built together wouldn't die because she'd carry it on without me. She'd be running it and perhaps I'd even be able to help. From a distance at first but then, who knows? She'd find it hard, running this lot all on her own. Maybe she'd ask for my help. I'd give it, naturally, and maybe…

But Pat refused to flip a coin or any nonsense like that. She'd take the money. She wasn't interested in any of our stuff. It seemed I had no choice but to be left alone with The Rocking Horse Shop, the farm, the house, the buildings and everything in them (excepting a few choice items she'd keep). And a mountain of debt. I thought, so be it.

For years I'd disappointed our bank manager by refusing to borrow a penny. I'd been so proud to tell him, 'We don't need the bank's money. Anything we want we'll pay for.'

Now I phoned him and said, 'How would you like to lend me half a million?'

He came at once and a bank loan was soon

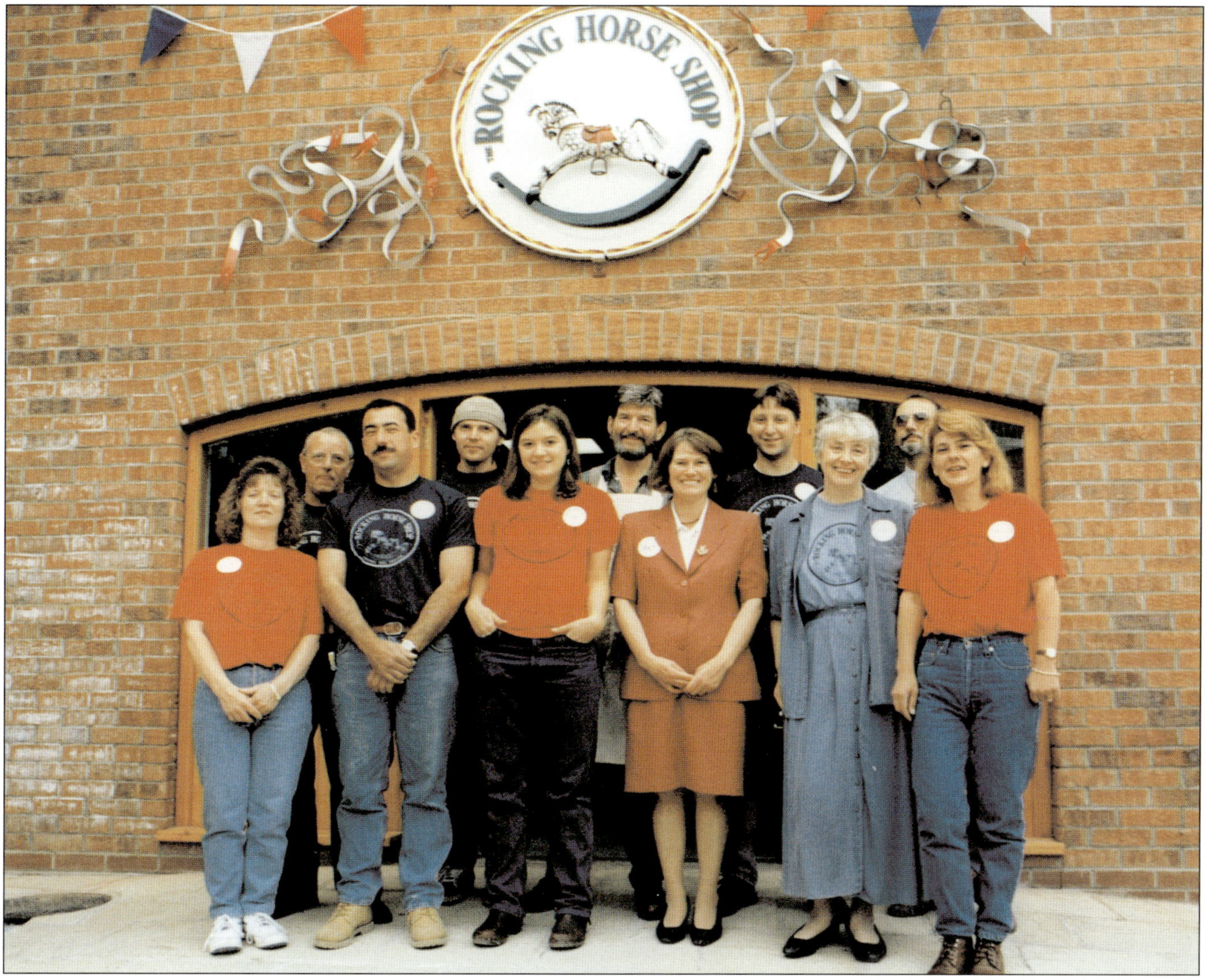


*Happy days. This must have been taken sometime before Pat left.*

arranged. It was hedged around with so many conditions to guarantee they'd get their money back it made me laugh. I recall, 'neither death nor insanity nor any other cause shall prevent the repayment of this loan in full'. I did get them to agree a clause allowing me to repay the debt at any time without penalty. I intended to get out from under this burden as soon as I possibly could.

I yearned to be free, free of melancholy certainly, but debt-free had to be part of it. It would clearly take an immense amount of work but with the help of rocking-horses I'd do it. Before, Pat's biggest complaint was that I was so consumed with rocking-horse work it was all I did. Now, to pay off this massive debt, created by her leaving, I'd have little time for anything *but* rocking-horse work for the foreseeable future. It was laughable really.

I've often thought I should have quit rocking-horses when Pat left, but I couldn't do it. We'd built a wonderful thing together and I couldn't bring myself to lose that as well as her.

Pat had gone. The children would leave too. They'd go out into the world and find their own ways. They might or might not come back. More likely not, not now our family'd been fractured. I'd be alone with my daemons and my rocking-horses but I'd keep going. What else could I do?

I should be grateful I had something to hold onto. In any case since none of my children could relieve my despair, they'd be better off out of it. I'd always be their Dad and I'd always love them, in my way. They'd have their own lives and I'd carry on without Pat and our children being around if I had to. I'd have to.

# Part Five

## 20

*I guess it doesn't matter anyway.*

When we were still together, back in '94, Pat and I held our first Open Day at The Rocking Horse Shop. Before that we'd attended shows and exhibitions which were always very expensive, sales were meagre to non-existant and we frequently came away disappointed. We'd had a stand at a 'Great Northern Woodworking Show' which was anything but great, and started thinking about holding our own show

An exhibition on our own premises would be easier to prepare for and set up, and cheaper since there'd be no stand fees or hotel bills. We'd be able to show visitors our whole enterprise, not just the small selection of our work we could fit in the van, and we could set our own agenda. We'd have free entry and give visitors free tea and coffee (instead of making them pay through the nose for a polystyrene cup of lukewarm muddy water) so they wouldn't feel ripped off. We'd make them feel welcome, entertain them. It'd be fun.

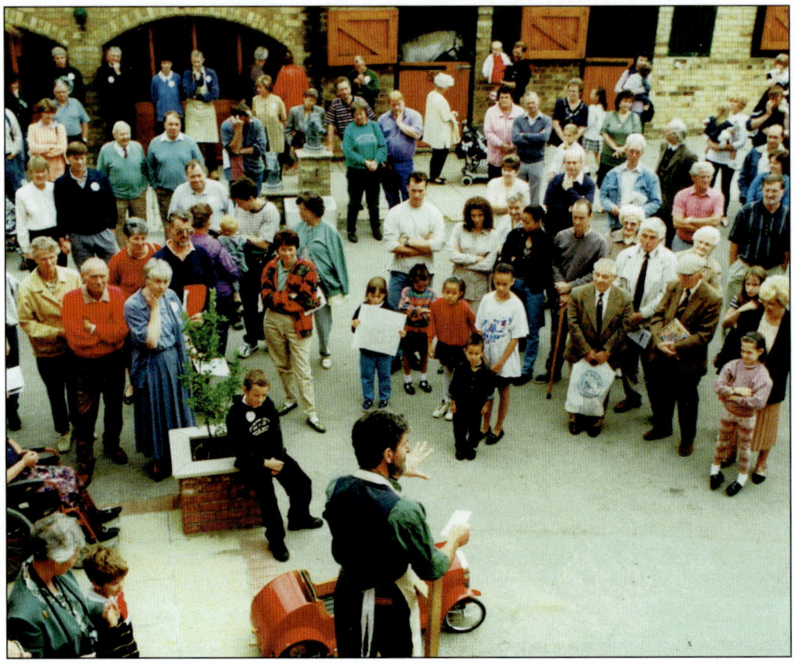

The highlights of our first Open Day were the launch of the Dewlin electric sports car and the official opening of our new workshop by a visiting celebrity. Nicholas Owen was a regular newscaster on national UK television and about the only real-life celebrity I knew. Nick and his Dad had lived with us for a while after his Mum died when we were kids (in his autobiography Nick had kindly written, 'the Dews were our saviours'). My Mum loved him like the other son she'd never had and I'd always thought of him as the brother I never had. He readily agreed to come with his wife Brenda, make a speech and cut a ribbon.

On the day we hung out bunting (made in our leather shop) and Lynn drove round the yard in the new Dewlin car waving a flag. Nick's presence brought in the crowds and, smiling and likeable chap that he is, he did the honours perfectly. Visitors wandered through the workshop while our people demonstrated carving, making bridles and dappling techniques. We had lots of 'today only special offers' on our plans and accessories and a rejects and seconds stall which was very popular. It was quiet at first and we worried nobody would come, but late morning people started pouring in, hundreds of them, and we were run off our feet. Our takings at the end of the day came to over £7000, the most we'd ever taken in a single day. Our decision to have free entry and give away refreshments was vindicated.

Naturally we wanted to do it again, make it an annual event. We chose the first Saturday in September because it was near the end of the summer holidays when, with luck, the weather would still be good. Most people wouldn't be thinking about Christmas yet but we toymakers were, and maybe we could encourage customers to order early and help spread the load in what was always our busiest time of year. Entry and drinks would again be free but we'd ask visitors to donate to our chosen charities - the NSPCC or The Leprosy Mission.

The formula worked well and each year our Open Days got bigger and better. We invited artists and craftspeople to display and sell their wares and I was so confident (or arrogant) I invited other rocking-horse makers and restorers, never mind the competition. They came, professionals as well as a growing army of amateur enthusiasts. Where ordinary folk carry in their wallets pictures of their kids and grandkids to show you, these people produced photographs of their rocking-horses.

Each year we started planning earlier and earlier for what we hoped would be a great trading day and fun. It was, although the '97 Open Day coincided with the funeral of Princess Diana. We fielded many phone calls asking if we were going ahead with our event. We'd publicised it so widely we couldn't cancel, but put aside a room with a TV where people could go and quietly watch the funeral if they wished. Quite a few did, then came out and enjoyed the rest of the day, which turned out to be highly successful for us.

At the '98 Open Day over a thousand people came; the day was absolutely manic and we took over £16,000. Afterwards Gerry and Lyn Grant, the friendly couple who ran Fangfoss Pottery (just across the village green), came round to ask if they could join in the fun next year. It had been such a madly concentrated day I was already thinking of making it a two-day show to spread things out a bit. If the pottery got involved, and the pub and maybe some of the other local businesses and organisations, it could become a village-wide event. I said I'd give it some thought.

Every week for years we'd received letters from home woodworkers enclosing photographs of the rocking-horses they'd made, telling us about their sometimes quite remarkable circumstances. One maker, who lived in a high-rise flat in London and had no workshop, described how he rolled the carpet back in his living room, set up his workbench in a corner and carved his horse in the evenings after work while the rest of his family sat watching TV. Another told how after his wife died he'd gone into a deep depression and sat in his chair doing nothing for months, until he started making a rocking-horse for his grandchildren. He said he'd become so enthralled by the project it revived his will to live. A young man, paralysed from the waist down, explained how he'd managed to make his horse while sitting in his wheelchair. A retired headmistress told us she'd never done any woodwork or carving in her life but wanted to make a large fully carved rocking-horse. I suggested she start with one of our simpler designs before tackling the more ambitious project but she wouldn't be dissuaded, and the photos she sent of her finished rocking-horse showed what an absolutely splendid job she'd made of it. And so on, hundreds of letters and photos.

It was clear that for every maker, whatever their story, the project was a major effort and achievement. We'd acknowledged the letters of course, but now I started toying with a couple of ideas that would give all these people more recognition and at the same time spread the word about our remarkable craft. I wanted to start a Guild of Rocking Horse Makers and publish a full colour quarterly called The Rocking Horse Magazine. In '99 with Pat gone I let these new projects fill my thoughts and my time.

The stated purpose of the Guild of Rocking Horse Makers would be 'to promote and encourage the craft'. I hoped it would lead to a useful exchange of ideas and information on all matters rocking-horse, be a forum for the growing number of enthusiasts, and (incidentally) enhance The Rocking Horse Shop's reputation as world leaders in this fascinating if footling field. Ahead of its launch I invited all the best rocking-horse makers and restorers I knew to become honorary members. It cost them nothing and gained them a little kudos so they did, almost without exception.

I was lucky to have befriended a commercial artist named John Gledhill who handled the design and layout of the magazine and drew many of the cartoons for it. Working with John was one of the few times I've worked successfully in close creative collaboration with somebody else. To start with I wanted an easily recognisable logo for the new Guild of Rocking Horse Makers, featuring a rocking-horse that would be appealing but neither too cartoonish nor too staid, and quite distinct from The Rocking Horse Shop's. I sketched an idea on paper, John added his ideas and sent it back, and it to-ed and fro-ed until we had a design that fitted the specification. John then transferred it to his computer, firmed up the final version and added colour.

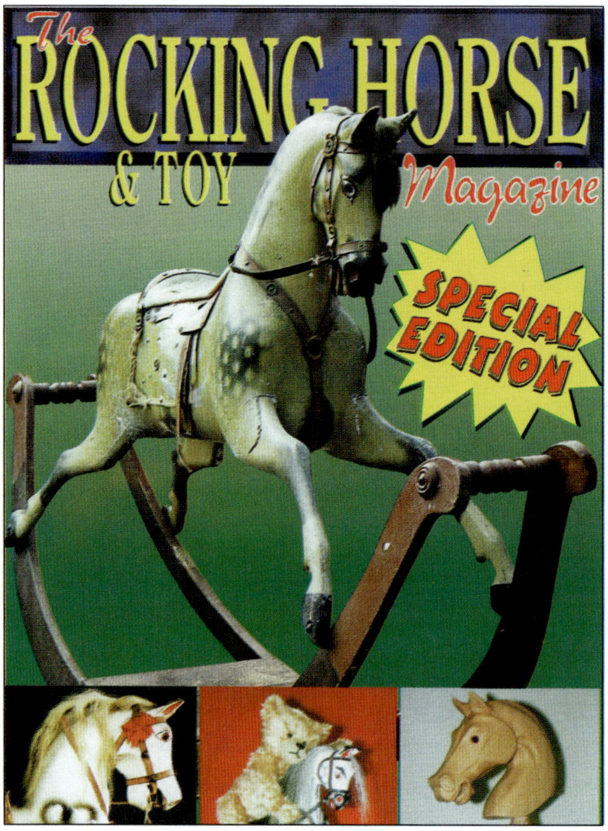


It was a fruitful way to work and I often drove to John's house near Hull, to sit beside him making suggestions as he worked on a design or a layout on his computer. He always welcomed my input, or said he did, and John's wife Kwan always stood behind us saying, 'Don't do that John,' 'Not good John,' 'That not working John,' 'No, no, John.' John never seemed to mind; he quietly and cheerfully got on with the work.

A central feature of The Rocking Horse Magazine would be two double-page spreads with a selection of the pictures and stories DIY rocking-horse makers sent in. It would also contain in-depth articles about historic rocking-horse makers, profiles of the best contemporary makers and restorers, tips and hints, a letters page and a simple toy project for readers to make with their children or grandchildren. We had cartoons and a spoof agony column written by 'Auntie Jacky' for whom the answer to every human problem and affliction was 'make a rocking-horse, dear'. I persuaded Robert Nathan, a fine toymaker, great character and manager of the British Toymakers Guild, to write a regular column. I had some other contributors including Dorothy, who worked in our shop and had a big interest in the history of rocking-horses, and Pam McPherson of APES, but inevitably wrote the bulk of the magazine's thirty-six pages myself, a challenge I welcomed. I intended filling my days so completely I wouldn't have time to be depressed.

As well as working at a furious pace I was actively trying to find a new partner who would not also be a business partner (I wouldn't make that mistake again). I didn't mind being on my own as much as I hated sleeping alone, but I wasn't interested in one night stands. I longed to find a woman agreeable enough to share my bed and ultimately my life. In short, a wife. Not long after Pat had left, Nick Owen phoned to commiserate, as he'd been married, divorced and was now married again to the lovely Brenda.

He said, 'I know exactly what you're going through, Tony. Divorce is horrible. It took me seven years to fully get over it and be ready to marry again.'

'Seven years! My God Nick, I hope it doesn't take me that long. I've got a date tonight.'

My date was Lynn, referred to as Big Lynn to distinguish

her from my daughter Lynn, who became Little Lynn. Big Lynn was a speech therapist with the most beautiful Edinburgh accent, two young daughters, a great deal of style and personality and large appetites in everything. Her husband Roger, a vicar, had left her for a woman in his congregation amid much hurt and public embarrassment. Big Lynn had suspected the affair but when pictures of him and his lover cavorting in bed were splashed across The News of the World, a salacious Sunday newspaper, she openly challenged him.

He responded by saying, 'It's not me.'

To which Big Lynn replied, 'Don't be ridiculous Roger, I'd recognise that spotty arse of yours anywhere.'

They were heading for divorce and Big Lynn, her self-esteem severely battered, needed to prove to herself that she was attractive to other men. She was to me. Our first date went well, we arranged to meet again and soon became an item (as the word was then).

Pat and I were heading for divorce too. The life we'd shared, that had totally occupied us for so many years, had ended. It had worked remarkably well and successfully when we were together but now we weren't. There would have to be major changes for both our personal lives and The Rocking Horse Shop. Friends commented that it looked like we were managing our separation amicably, but it never seemed very amicable to me. We disagreed over almost everything and the only positive was that we never argued about the children.

At fifteen Little Lynn wasn't so little anymore. She opted to continue going to school in nearby Pocklington and live with me during the week, and with her Mum in York at weekends and for half the holidays. She wrote a schedule so that she and we would know exactly where she should be, and who with, on any given day. While she was with me, once or twice each week we'd drive to the Leeds Wall and spend the evening climbing. It was a great workout and a lovely way to spend quality time with my daughter because climbing requires total trust in your partner.

Sam and Kate both loved climbing too, encouraged by their uncle Dave and cousin David, committed rock climbers both. When Sam was home on leave they often went climbing together and Sam spent almost all his spare time exercising to improve his strength and grip. He'd become a fine, handsome young man with a ready smile and pleasing manner. Kate, now nineteen, had been accepted at Manchester University but then decided to go travelling, to India, Bali, Australia and New Zealand. Initially she was with a friend called Andrea Shirt, but after they went separate ways Kate acquired a boyfriend, an Irishman named Pat (another Pat) and went with him. I had a world map pinned up on the wall in my kitchen, on which I plotted Sam and Kate's travels.

During his apprenticeship, Trinity House placed Sam on several different types of ship trading worldwide. He gained his Second Mate's ticket and became a junior officer, so was doing well. He'd been brought up hearing my sea stories but seafaring had changed out of all recognition. Now ships were far bigger but far fewer men worked them, mostly older than him and not British, so not many for him to socialise with. He went around the world several times (and even round Cape Horn, which I never had) but saw little of it except sea. One trip, on a huge tanker trading between the Persian Gulf and the Philippines, Sam was away five months and in all that time stepped ashore only once for a few short hours. I completely understood when he said that he intended leaving the sea to go travelling, like Kate, and experience some of the real world.

Whenever they were at home and not engaged in other activities, I'd get the three kids to help out in The Rocking Horse Shop. Sam would work with me in the woodwork shop and Kate enjoyed helping to make bridles and saddles in the leather shop. Kate was also good in the office and had a confident yet relaxed manner with customers; they always took to her as they had Pat. I'd get Lynn, four years younger, to make dappling pads or count nuts and bolts into little poly bags. Mindless tasks but they had to be done right or a whole rocking-horse project could be stalled and a customer frustrated. Lynn was very bright, capable of so much more, but she did this mundane work cheerfully and took it very seriously.

In May I drove Sam to Manchester airport for him to board a plane for Australia. Lynn came with us and on the way we called in to see our old friends Porter and Linda. Pat joined us for a meal and I was struck by what a beautiful person she was. I asked her yet again to come back to me and yet again she said no, nothing had changed, meaning I hadn't. Aside from that it was good to be with friends and family, and Sam was bubbling with excitement over his trip. Kate would meet him in Oz and they were going to Arapiles, about a four hour drive from Melbourne, a rock-climbers' paradise apparently, where there were many brilliant crags. Sam had his tent with him and as much climbing equipment as he could carry.

I was working hard, playing hard, drinking hard, not sleeping much. One morning when I went to the bathroom I pissed blood. The doctor took a sample and sent me off to hospital for some tests. The consultant said she couldn't see any obvious cause and asked me how long I'd had one kidney. I told her it was news to me, I thought I had two like everyone else. She said everybody does have two but my spare was all shrivelled up. The other one was very enlarged, doing the work of two. I asked her if I'd have to change my diet or stop drinking.

'You're generally healthy,' she said. 'So if it's not causing you any problems there's no reason to change your lifestyle.'

'Thank you so much. I'll carry on as I am then.'

On my way out of the hospital I bumped into Mike Jones, who'd encouraged us not to quit The Rocking Horse Shop back in '89. He joined me for lunch and over a pint told me he'd just received the all-clear from the hospital after a minor operation. His consultancy business wasn't going well though, he'd had to give up his office and was now working on his own from home. My ears pricked up. He asked how I was managing.

I said, 'Managing? I'm not. I've got no manager and no Pat either. The business has taken a nose-dive. I'm working hard and we're paying the wages, just about, but it's not what it was. Not what it could be. Listen Mike, you know more than most what The Rocking Horse Shop is all about. How would you like to be General Manager? You can have a free hand to run the show while I get on with what I do best. I've got some new designs I'd like to develop, and I'm starting a rocking-horse magazine and a Guild. How about it?'

Mike came over to look at the current set-up in Fangfoss and, after agreeing the details, said he'd give me five years because he'd promised his wife Judith he would definitely retire at sixty-five. He had a very practical, hands-on approach to management. First off he built himself an office at one end of the big workshop, with glass walls so he could see what was going on but have private conversations on the phone or in person. He bought new racking for timber and leather and re-organised all of our stock storage.

Pat and I had had a rather informal (ie confused) way of giving regular customers discounts based on how much we liked them. Mike introduced a tiered system of trade discounts based on how much a customer spent with us. Much more businesslike. He introduced an improved system for packing and despatching parcels and bought two jack-leg cabins, one a canteen for the staff (they shouldn't have to eat lunch at their work-benches, he said), the other a decent toilet and wash place for staff and visitors. Within a couple of weeks of him starting, everywhere I looked something was happening and there was a renewed air of vitality about the place.

Mike could be a little abrasive and not everybody appreciated the changes he was introducing, but I thought they were exactly what The Rocking Horse Shop needed. Making the enterprise operate in a more businesslike manner would make it less dependent on the individual running it. We also incorporated, and becoming The Rocking Horse Shop *Ltd*, meant that the business could be regarded as an entity separate from me. I would continue to be intimately involved and it would always need to be guided and steered, but not necessarily by me

I'd always thought of The Rocking Horse Shop as a family enterprise involving me, Pat and our children. I still hoped that one day Sam would come back and take it over, maybe Kate and Lynn too, but now Pat was gone and the children were growing up and away, the possibility of a different future was unfolding. For the time being however, with Mike the manager's help, I had to keep running the show.

# 21

*You can't go back and you can't stand still.*

Our rocking-horses were all hand-crafted in the traditional manner using blocks of solid timber band-sawn to shape, glued together and carved. That was the technique I knew and to which I was beholden, but I was always interested in alternative materials and methods. Some years earlier I'd designed a rocking-horse in plywood, constructed round a hollow box body. I'd never completed it and the parts had lain on a shelf for years gathering dust, waiting to be revisited. There were several active makers of laminated plywood horses around the country: Relko made very striking and rather expensive-looking rocking-horses on sweeping bows; Ian Armstrong made quirky but appealing and relatively inexpensive rocking-horses (which we sold in our shop); and then there was Judy Fergusson.

I met Judy when we both had stands at a British Toymakers Guild show in London. She was an energetic and highly intelligent woman with a friendly smile and I liked her. I liked her rocking-horses too, and the fact that almost everything about her approach to the craft was different from mine. Her rocking-horses had features I'd intended for my plywood one (had it worked) and since I had no wish to copy her, asked if she'd consider us publishing a couple of her designs under our Designs for Woodworkers banner. She said she'd think about it.

I arranged to visit Judy to look at her set-up and discuss the possibilities of collaboration. She lived on the Isle of Wight at Small Horse Farm, where she kept Shetland ponies and had her rocking-horse workshops. She showed me how she cut out the plywood parts, mostly with a hand-held jig-saw, glued them together, then shaped them. Her 'carving' was done with power sanders and her favourite tool was a narrow belt sander she could poke into all the awkward concavities, like under the chin. She reckoned to burn out at least one power sander every horse she made. I was a proud traditional mallet-and-gouge carver and rather sniffy about carving by sanding. Still, I thought, there's skill in wielding any tool and 'hand-crafted' doesn't have to mean everything is done with the sort of tools Noah used.

Judy was adept with her sander and knew her product. To create a smooth curve over the rump, for example, she simply sanded away the small steps formed during the assembly of the plywood parts. As she sanded, the laminations revealed a pattern of dark curving glue-lines which not only looked very attractive but acted as a shaping guide. It was terribly dusty so we worked outside in an open-sided shed. I was cold and the dust itched its way into every orifice. I decided I'd be happy to sell plans for other people to make these plywood horses of Judy's, but I wouldn't want to make them myself.

At the end of a long day working and talking rocking-horses with Judy, I met her husband Pat (yet another Pat) and we wound up drinking whisky all evening. He was older than Judy and retired, but had been a racing car driver and soldier in his time. During the war he was captured by the Nazis and sent to the famous Colditz prison. He hadn't personally tried to escape, he told me, but every prisoner in the camp was involved in helping those who were, by finding or stealing anything that might be useful to the escapees, and for other purposes. Pat had built a still out of bits of old hose and drain pipe and the prisoners stole potato and vegetable peelings from the cookhouse which Pat distilled into hard liquor, thus helping to keep their spirits up.

I told him about my paragliding and he told me about the glider the prisoners built in the attic at Colditz. The plan was that a section of roof would be lifted clear and the glider, made from wood and cloth, would slide down a launch ramp, take to the air and fly over the perimeter fence to freedom. Dust and spider webs were collected by Pat and the other prisoners and festooned around trapdoors leading to the roof space, so when the guards made their regular inspections that was what they saw and never looked further. Colditiz was liberated by the Americans before the glider was ready to fly so it was never tested, but when the camp Commandant was taken to see it he simply couldn't believe that the prisoners had built a 40-foot wingspan aircraft in the attic without him or his men having the faintest inkling.

Judy agreed to provide full-size drawings and

construction notes in return for royalty payments on plans sold. We'd publish two of her rocking-horse designs: a cute Half Size table-top model on bows for beginners, and a medium size version modified to be mounted on a stand (unlike her usual ones on bow rockers) and so that all our regular medium accessories would fit. She came to Yorkshire and stayed at Manor House Farm for a week while she made the two rocking-horses. I photographed the whole process for the step-by-step instructions and we paid her for these two rocking-horses so we could keep them to help publicise her plans. These laminated rocking-horses had a novel and appealing appearance and home woodworkers clearly saw them as a less intimidating and much cheaper alternative to the traditional solid wood method. They sold really well.

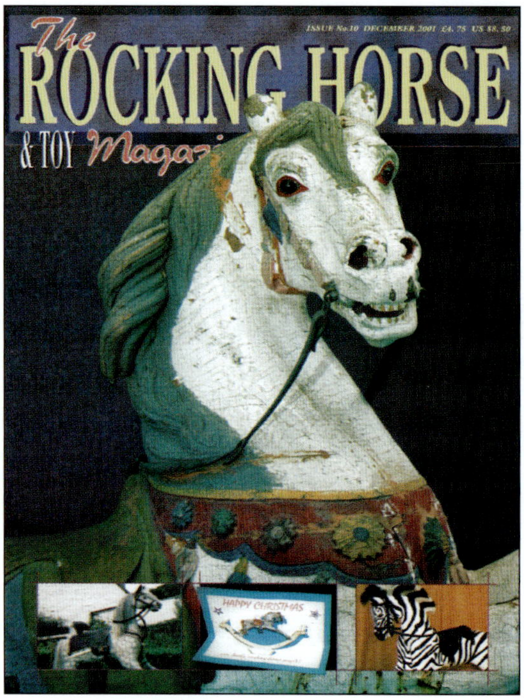

*The Bayol carousel horse appeared on the cover of The Rocking Horse & Toy Magazine.*

Joe Carr, from a travelling family, was an engaging antique dealer who was almost as crazy about rocking-horses as I was, but as a dealer, not a maker, and he had his own excellent collection.

One day he called in to see me and said, 'I have something in my van you will buy.'

'Oh yeah?' I said, steeling myself against temptation. 'OK Joe, let's have a look.'

On previous visits Joe had sold me a beautiful extra-carved large Ayres with broken ears and leg, horribly over-painted by someone with no idea how to dapple; an extremely rare Leach with a finely carved head but so hideously cracked and worn the poor thing cried out for tlc; and a highly unusual early 18th Century horse on finely shaped bow rockers who'd been painted all-over grey and had congealed paint all down his neck where someone had tipped a pot of white gloss over him. Only rocking-horses that had been very well cared for and retained their original paint and tack in near pristine condition made it into Joe's own superb collection, so he sold me his rejects. But he knew what I liked and that I had a soft spot for the very old and beautiful, never mind if they were extremely battered or even falling apart. He also knew I could fix them if I wanted to, although in practice I often left them as they were, warts and all. I liked the marks of use and misuse, they showed what the horse had been through, its character. No need to airbrush their history, let them be what they are.

Joe opened the back of his van and with a dramatic flourish pulled off a dust sheet to reveal a magnificent carousel horse prancing on its hind legs. He'd been made around 1880 by French carver Gustave Bayol, a true master of his craft famous for making exquisite carousel animals. This horse's massive and handsome head twisted dramatically to the right (looking out since, unlike British ones, French roundabouts go counter-clockwise). His joints were wobbly and much of the detail of the carving on the mane and tail was obliterated under a great many coats of paint, but he was a real beauty. I longed to attain such feeling and vitality in my own carving. Joe was right, there was no way I was not going to buy this marvellous beast. After some obligatory haggling he joined my collection. Madness, I already had nearly a hundred wooden horses and really hadn't room for another.

I'd always referred to rocking-horses as 'him' although the sex of a rocking-horse is somewhat indeterminate. In the case of the Bayol and many merry-go-round horses they were stallions and had genitalia (sometimes cast iron) to prove it. But the vast majority of rocking-horses had nothing underneath and were therefore geldings or mares. Owners would often give their rocking-horses the names of famous horses, horses they'd owned, members of their family, pet names, sometimes female. I never commented, it was a minor matter and after all, what's in a name?

One afternoon an extremely excited lady with purple hair stormed into the shop and informed us she was a pregnant grandmother.

'Not me,' she shrieked. 'I'm past all that. It's my daughter that's pregnant. We're all so thrilled.'

The baby wasn't due for many months but she wanted to get her rocking-horse ordered and the deposit paid in plenty of time. She'd clearly been planning for the event and told us exactly what colours and finish she wanted for the horse, and we were to put a brass plaque on the stand, engraved 'FOR DORIS'.

'A girl then, you know that already?'

'A girl, yes! It hasn't been confirmed yet but the foetus's name is Doris. Isn't it lovely?'

I took down the details of her order and the lady paid a deposit. Several months later she came back, even more exuberant than on her first visit, to tell us the baby had arrived. She was ready for her rocking-horse to be delivered and wanted to pay the outstanding balance..

'Mother and baby are both doing fine,' she announced. 'We're all absolutely delighted. The baby's name is Tom.'

'That's wonderful news and your horse is all ready for you. The only thing is, we've fixed on the 'FOR DORIS' plate you ordered.'

'Oh that's perfectly fine Mr Dew, I want that name to stay on the horse. The foetus's name is still Doris you see, even though the baby's male and his name is Tom.' That sounded to me like a recipe for one very confused little boy.

Among her effusions, the FOR DORIS lady had said, 'Your rocking-horses, they're magical!'

No magic here, I thought, nothing but hard graft tempered with a high level of care. That's not magic. These rocking-horses, they're no more than bits of wood cobbled together, anyone can see that. Anyone can do this, anyone prepared (or foolish enough) to put in the effort required. No, it's not magic. But then again…

I couldn't resist adding to my collection and bought a rocking-horse at Christies auction house in London. He was so big we couldn't fit him in the car so he came home lashed to the roof. Quite a sight bowling at speed up the motorway with kids ogling and taking photos. He was a big old thing with huge glass eyes and almost all his paint missing and a great rusty nail sticking an inch out of his neck. Stand and leg joints were loose and what was left of the gesso dirty and faded, worn down to the bare yellow pine in places.

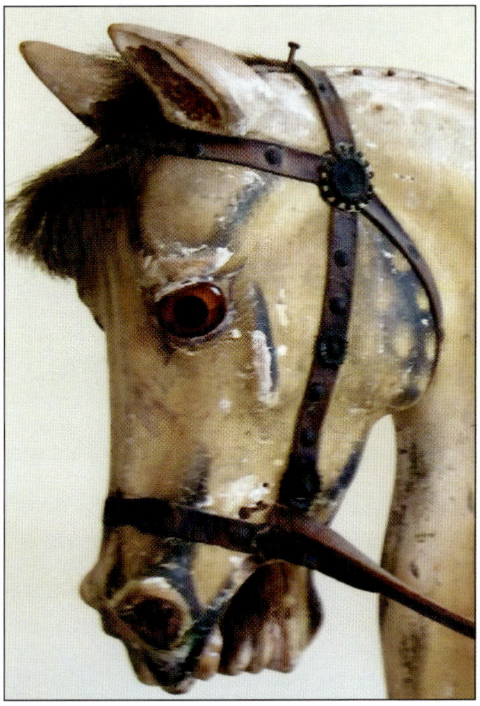

*Fine old Ayres rocking- horse - my favourite!*

But to my eyes that horse had something, something special. He was the same size and make as one I'd bought from Joe Carr, also in a poor state, so I now had two large extra-carved rocking-horses of similar vintage out of F. H. Ayres workshop, yet they were as different one from the other as a living creature from an effigy. Not that the Carr horse was bad, he was a fine example of the breed, and after the sympathetic repaint and restoration I'd lavished on him he was a shining star of my fine and expanding collection.

Yet there was something alive about the Christies horse that got to me, that made me shun any thought of doing anything with him for fear of spoiling that subtle, indefinable quality that made him altogether uniquely lovable in spite of, or perhaps as a result of, the years of neglect and abuse he'd endured. (Lord Grantley's exquisite 1650 rocking-horse had, at some point, been removed from Woburn Abbey. The next time I saw it, in a photograph, it had been repainted and, in my opinion, completely ruined in precisely this way.) I didn't even want to yank out that rusty nail, not even when moving the horse from place to place, as we frequently did, it gored my arm for the umpteenth time. I knew it was ludicrous to even think of 'life' in a wooden rocking-horse. I couldn't define it but nevertheless knew it when I saw it, and it was that I sought to capture in the best of my own work. Now and then I'd get it, and it gave me a quiet sense of fulfilment. Most customers or visitors never saw it, and of course rocking-horse making is a vernacular craft, a world away from fine art. Yet occasionally someone would say something to indicate they'd recognised that special quality, and those few words of encouragement helped me to know that all my years of assiduous practice had been worthwhile. I'd never be cash rich, but I was surely on the right track.

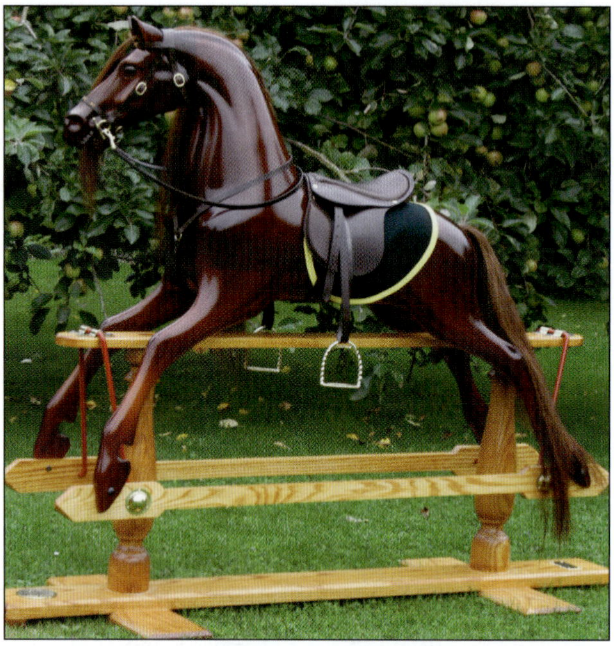

I bought a big old Collinson from a school in York, got it for a giveaway price, but it was a sad purchase. Collinson rocking-horses were basic and never possessed the qualities of a fine Ayres (or Dew!), but this one had served his riders well for many years. A young girl had fallen off and broken her arm so the school, in the interest of Health and Safety, and in spite of the fact that the rocking-horse had never caused accident or complaint before, decided to sell.

'But you can't blame the rocking-horse for that,' I said. 'The kid could've broken her arm falling off a desk or downstairs or tripped over her own feet. She could've done it anywhere. It's an accident. It's not the rocking-horse's fault, or the school's.'

'I know,' the headteacher said. 'But the inspector said we must consider this: if another child should fall off the rocking-horse and injure herself and we've done nothing after this incident… I'm sure you understand.'

'Good God, are children to be swathed in cotton wool? Risk is there, of course it is, but it's minimal, surely, against all the joy this old horse has given, and ought to keep on giving. Oh dear, it makes me so…'

'I know,' the headteacher said, shaking her head. 'But there it is. We daren't risk it.'

In the ten years I'd lived in Fangfoss the village had more than doubled in size. The old bus depot and yard, the brickworks site, big gardens and gaps between houses, corners of fields, even Craven's delightful meadow near the crossroads, had disappeared under houses and tarmac. A few years before, Farmer Craven had walked to his meadow every morning with a milk churn on a sack cart, to milk his cow by hand for the family. I recalled him confiding, 'A village needs a meadow, Tony.'

But now the old barn and meadow had gone, replaced by eighteen houses and a tarmac road. The annual village barn dance was no more and I assumed Mrs Craven now bought her milk in plastic containers from the supermarket like everyone else.

Few villagers welcomed all the new houses, except for the people who bought them and now lived in them, and then they were always the most vocal in demanding no more building. Fangfoss didn't have a village hall or a shop, let alone a doctor's surgery, and just before I applied to demolish the old dairy in Rocking Horse Yard and rebuild it as a house, East Riding Council declared the village unsustainable. No further development would be allowed and my application was bound to fail. I argued that since the village had been here a thousand years and had always been smaller than it is now, Fangfoss could hardly be deemed 'unsustainable', and that small-scale developments are a good thing because they keep the village alive by helping to keep the pub, school and church open. But my application was rejected, dashing my hopes of raising a substantial amount of money to pay off some of my debt mountain.

On top of the divorce settlement a huge unexpected income tax demand had landed on my desk and had to be paid immediately. I sacked my accountant ('You should have warned me,' I told him) and sold whatever tools and furniture I could spare to raise some money, and several of my more valuable rocking-horses. Unfortunately, since I loved him, my big Bayol carousel horse would have to go too. Dad, who'd long since retired as an accountant but came each week to check our books, offered to buy him.

'That would be wonderful, Dad. But you don't want a great big horse like that. What would you do with him?'

'Keep him here. I'll pay you for him then lend him to you for your museum. When you get the money you can buy him back from me.' I almost burst into tears.

In July '99 as a reward for doing well in her GCSE exams - she hadn't got her results yet but she was such a clever swot we knew they'd be good - Pat (now living in a house she'd bought in York) and I gave our daughter Lynn a return ticket to Australia so she could spend a few weeks with her brother and sister. Sam and Kate met her in Sydney, and Hannah joined them. Hannah was the daughter of my friends Alan and Lynne Shone. I'd got to know Alan well when we'd sailed together thirty years before and he and Lynne had lived in New Zealand twenty-five. I'd never been there but we'd kept in touch intermittently over the years and they'd once visited us in Fangfoss.

They were my oldest friends and we'd been very close, so I'd told Sam and Kate that if ever they made it to New Zealand they must look them up. The previous year, when Sam was Third Mate on a P & O container ship which put into Auckland, Kate flew across from Australia to see him and they met Alan and Lynne (after whom my Lynn was named) and Hannah, their only daughter. Hannah and Sam hit it off and she was now joining them in Oz.

They travelled in an old camper van Sam had bought and for a month the three siblings and Hannah were together going up the East Coast to Queensland, having adventures and enjoying themselves. Later, we would come to appreciate what a very special, unrepeatable time this was for them. Sam's relationship with Hannah didn't last but still, it pleased me no end that for a while my son had partnered the daughter of my oldest friends. At the end of their tour they took Lynn back to Sydney for her flight home, Hannah returned to New Zealand and Kate and Sam went their separate ways. Kate rejoined her Irish boyfriend Pat, and Sam went on alone, staying in Townsville and Cairns then hitch-hiking across country to Alice Springs and Ayers Rock (which, after much deliberation, he climbed). He was now strong and thoughtful, yet outgoing and humorous, growing up to be a better man than I'd ever be.

In November Pat sent me the divorce papers. I'd been so sure this would never happen, I was floored. Shrug and move on, is that what I had to do? As Christmas approached Sam wrote to me, *'I realise that splitting up with Mum has been a low point but… the more I spend time thinking of the path I would like my own life to take the more I am amazed at how your life seems to be the embodiment of success… I know I may seem to be bumming around as it were, but I like to think I'm concreting some of the thoughts so I can take proper action when I get home… I would like to educate myself a bit more and I'm not sure whether I can do that now or if I'll want to travel more, which would undoubtedly be more fun and it does allow you to play through the various characters you think, or I might think, I might be.'*

He was essentially on his own, looking for an answer to the question 'what do I want to do with my life?' at the same time always hoping to find someone special to love and be loved by, to share his life with. I knew how that felt. But I was beginning to feel old. If Sam decided he'd like to come and work with me at The Rocking Horse Shop, eventually to take over, that would be as good as it could get.

# 22

Through the Summer of '99 we held regular meetings to plan the new village-wide show, set for the first weekend in September. 'Fangfest - the Fangfoss Festival of the Practical Arts' - would focus on art and crafts, its stated purpose to benefit local businesses and organisations as well as charities. We wanted to attract as many people as possible to the village and provide, as our flyer declared, 'a fun-packed weekend for all the family'. The Rocking Horse Shop was the principal attraction and we expected to make some money.

We had a huge blue and white striped marquee erected in my paddock and sold space in it to craftspeople and artists, at a nominal charge to cover the cost of the tent. Behind the marquee was a funfair with swing-boats, hook-a-duck and a kiddies roundabout for the younger children, archery for the older ones. An ice-cream maker came, and a mobile kitchen set up in the barn to provide hot lunches or sandwiches and cakes. My sisters Pat and Jacky looked after tea, coffee and biscuits which we gave away, with visitors encouraged to put a donation in one of our charity boxes. Most did, and generously. Entry to Fangfest was free but brother-in-law Bryn stood at the gate counting the visitors as they came in and selling them a programme of events at £1 each.

At Fangfoss Pottery Gerry and Lyn put on demonstrations of raku firing with lots of smoke and flames, and Harry did well with his beds even though he was a walk away from the village epi-centre. Harry'd found a man with a pony and trap to ply from his workshop to Rocking Horse Yard and back all day, so a good number of people made it there and enjoyed the ride. The school or-ganised craft competitions for children and provided extra parking space, and the pub had a hog roast and live band.

On Saturday evening the caterers laid on a meal in our barn for Guild of Rocking Horse Makers members and about forty came, including locals and my girlfriend, Big Lynn. The weather had been perfect all day and it was a warm evening. We wound up drinking on the patio until very late. I tried to forget about Pat and feel pleased with how my revised rocking-horse world was turn-ing out.

Sunday was a repeat of Saturday but, after a slow start, even busier. In our workshop the staff again demonstrated various aspects of the rocking-horses maker's craft including dappling, gesso and carving. We had lots of special show offers and the shop was kept busy selling plans, accessories, hand and power tools. Upstairs in the cleared-out office I gave talks in which I outlined the history of the rocking-horse and introduced our new Guild of Rocking Horse Makers and The Rocking Horse Magazine to packed audiences.

The sole criteria to become a member of the Guild was that you had to have made a rocking-horse. It didn't matter what size or style and we didn't judge quality or value (customers would do that, if the horse was for sale) but you had to have made it substantially yourself. At Fangfest we signed up dozens of new members who all received a signed Certificate of Achievement and True Craftsmanship, a copy of Issue 1 of the magazine and an enamel badge bearing the Guild logo. By the end of the day Bryn had counted in almost 2000 visitors, our takings were a record high at £25,660 and we were all utterly exhausted.

The successful launch of the Guild of Rocking Horse Makers and The Rocking Horse Magazine brought The Rocking Horse Shop valuable publicity and we featured in many newspapers and periodicals. One review in Traditional Woodworking, a national mag for woodworkers, pleased me immensely: 'The Rocking Horse Magazine's depth of expert interest certainly can't be questioned… an odd combination of almost fanzine-style production and extraordinarily high quality paper and printing… you'd probably be willing to pay ten times (the cover price) for so much good, relevant material'. The magazine also featured on a TV programme called Have I Got News for You and led to me doing two television programmes about making and restoring rocking-horses, being interviewed for several TV and radio shows and for newspapers and magazines. Fangfest weekend marked the start of our busy run-up to Christmas, as I'd hoped it would, and all through autumn we were flat-out in the workshop.

Kate came home from Australia at the end of October and I gave her a job at The Rocking Horse Shop. She had a place (deferred when she'd missed the start of term) the next January at Manchester University, but was unsettled after her travels and talked incessantly about flying back out to Oz when she'd earned enough for the fare. We had dozens of new horses to finish and get safely to their destinations before Christmas and I asked Kate to organise the deliveries. Rocking-horses for abroad had to be shipped first, those for nearer home could go last, leaving eleven to be taken by us to addresses scattered round England. Kate worked out a route and phoned the customers to let them know roughly when to expect us (and with no sat-nav then, this was quite a task). We loaded two horses in the back of my big Volvo estate and nine more into our rocking-horse box (actually a modified cow trailer with a lockable rear door and no ventilation holes, built for us by local engineer Graham Edwards) towed behind. Kate and I took it in turns to drive, and once the back of the car was empty one of us could stretch out there to rest.

Our first delivery was in rural Lincolnshire and we were driving along very narrow lanes with high hedges either side, unable to see much.

'So what's the name of this place we're going to, Kate?'

'I don't know, the lady didn't say.'

'OK, so what's the name of the house?'

'Manor Farm, but she says the name isn't on it.'

'OK, where is it near?'

'She says it's on its own, not near a village.'

'OK, any landmarks?'

'No, she says it's flat and featureless round here.'

'Hmm. So how are we going to recognise this house?'

'She said the house is very big and very dirty.'

'OK, a big dirty house. Anything else?'

'I asked her that and she said no, but then as an afterthought mentioned that she has an aeroplane in the front garden.'

'You're joking.'

'That's what she said.'

'OK. So we're looking for a dirty big house with no name and we don't know where, but it has an aeroplane in the garden. Brilliant!'

'Sorry Dad. That's all I've got.'

I was still shaking my head and thinking we'd never find it when we rounded a bend and there before us was a large and extremely filthy farmhouse with an RAF jet fighter aircraft on the front lawn. The lady of the house was lovely and welcoming, delighted with the rocking-horse we carried in. Her house was filled with fine antique furniture and fascinating artefacts and she was happy to show us round. She gave us tea and biscuits and I was so engrossed in our conversation and looking at everything, I completely forgot to ask her how the jet aircraft came to be in her front garden, it clearly hadn't landed there. But we had to get on.

Our route zig-zagged down through Suffolk and Essex, over the Thames into Kent, across Surrey, Sussex and Hampshire and it was midnight by the time we made it to a village in the west of Dorset for our final delivery. The people had told Kate their house was lit up and we couldn't miss it. We spotted it a mile away in a row of houses set back from the main road, incandescent with thousands of coloured flashing lights. A large family had congregated for Christmas in this small house, brightly illuminated inside as well as out, and one of the young men helped us wrestle the large rocking-horse into the narrow hallway and up the stairs. He was fresh home from Australia and he and Kate were soon in deep conversation about Oz. He showed us some of the didgeridoos he'd been making since his return to the UK, hoping to sell them. A niche business with an even narrower market than ours! The didgeridoos were very well made and beautifully decorated in the aboriginal style, so when the Mum brought us coffee and cake and Kate was busy talking to her, I quietly bought one as my Christmas present for Kate and hid it in a corner of the horse-box.

I liked doing our deliveries in person and customers were invariably delighted with the long-awaited rocking-horse we brought them. At the same time I was always anxious in case they didn't like him or he got damaged in transit. So I was relieved to get the last one delivered and head home. We finally got back around five in the morning having driven over seven hundred and fifty miles. I love Kate dearly, always have, but my relationship with her had never been quite as easy as with Sam or Lynn - middle child syndrome perhaps - and over the years we'd had some furious rows. Sam had often acted as peacemaker when Kate and I were at loggerheads. So it was good, now that he was away, to enjoy this quality time with her and hear all about her climbing exploits with Sam and what a great time they'd had together in Oz. After all Kate's talk of going back out there I was pleased when she told me she'd gone off the idea and would be starting at Manchester University in the New Year.

Sam was still in Oz where he was enjoying himself and had given us no indication of when he might be coming home. I hoped it would be soon. He emailed his grandparents that he'd been staying, *'at Moonarie at the Southern tip of the Flinders Ranges … as it is the best climbing spot in South Australia … a huge bay of cliffs perched on top of a steep valley. It was in a cave at the bot-tom of one of these cliffs where my blanket unrolled and I built my wood fires for ten days, juggling, reading and rock climbing … I am now in Adelaide checking out a few crags before heading East to Arapiles …'* where he'd be spending Christmas and the New Year, camping and climbing. He continued, *'It is summer now so with its natural swimming holes, incredible cliff faces and smiling faces, I intend to pass into the new millennium in Eden …'*

Deliveries all done, the Christmas parcels sent and a last-minute rocking-horse sold on the 22nd December to cap a highly successful and profitable year for The Rocking Horse Shop. On the 23rd the staff and I had a final tidy-up of the premises, then a meal and pub crawl round Pocklington. After that we wished each other slightly drunken Happy Christmases, kissing and hugging all round, and finished for a week's holiday. Christmas would be the usual round of visits to friends and family and much eating and drinking, the one big difference for me this year being the absence of Pat. Every New Year's Eve since we'd lived in Fangfoss we'd had a party and I decided to go ahead and have one this year anyway. Although Sam wouldn't be at home, Kate and Lynn would, and maybe thirty people would come, including Big Lynn. After breakfast on the 31st we were busy tidying up the house in preparation for the party when the phone rang.

'Mr Dew? Mr Anthony Dew?'

'That's me.'

'My name is Dr Peter Bristow. I am in charge of the trauma unit here at Alfred Hospital in Melbourne, Australia. I am afraid I have to tell you that your son in my care. He has had a fall and sustained a serious head injury. He is receiving the best possible treatment and his condition is stable. Let me put it like this, your son's condition is serious but not life-threatening. We have him on life support systems to allow his body to keep functioning whilst putting the minimum of pressure on his brain. I am discussing with the brain surgeons the possibility of operating on him to relieve this pressure. We are continually monitoring his condition. A nurse is with him constantly. We are doing everything we possibly can for him.'

'Serious but not life-threatening?'

'Yes. I realise this must be a shock for you, Mr Dew. Do you have family there?'

'Yes. We're getting ready for a party. My daughters are here. My wife, Sam's mother, she's elsewhere. We must find her.'

'Yes. May I suggest you talk to your family and call me back in a couple of hours. It must be late morning there. It's eleven in the evening here now. You will be aware of the press speculation about the Millennium Bug. I shall be staying on here until two in the morning or so, to make sure everything goes smoothly through the transition into the new century. I don't anticipate our computers will be affected but we have back-up systems just in case. If you call me back in a couple of hours I'll still be here, and I'll be able to update you.'

'Thank you.'

'I'm afraid that is all I can tell you now, Mr Dew. Please call me in a couple of hours.'

'I will, thank you.'

The line goes dead and I slowly put down the handset. I call out, 'Kate, Lynn,' and they must hear the urgency in my voice because they come quickly, faces alight with concern. I slowly repeat to them what the doctor has told me, trying to repeat his words exactly.

'We must find Mum. She may be out walking. Or at the stables. Phone first. See if you can reach her. Take the van. Find her. Get her to come here as soon as you can.'

Friends Gerry and Lyn are nearby and have been invited to our New Year's Eve do, so I phone them and explain that I cannot face a party. They say they understand and will take over and divert all the guests to Fangfoss Pottery. I phone Big Lynn and tell her the party's cancelled. She says she'd like to come anyway, to be with me, but I say no, please don't. It is Pat who must be here. Kate and Lynn locate Pat and bring her home. We sit round the kitchen table and the three of them watch, not moving or blinking, as I dial the long number. Even their skin has become stiff, like wax. The doctor answers immediately.

'Mr Dew? Good. I've been waiting for you to call before I go home. There have been no ill effects from the Millennium Bug. The scare stories in the media seem to have been unfounded. Our systems have worked right through without a hitch.'

'Good. How is Sam?'

'Your son's condition remains as it was when I spoke to you earlier. It has not changed. His injuries are very serious. I believe I told you of the possibility of an operation to relieve the pressure on his brain, but I am afraid the brain surgeons are of the opinion that they cannot operate on him, that the nature of his injury is just too serious. An operation would be futile. We continue to monitor him and do everything we can to keep him comfortable. He remains on life support.'

I hold the phone tight and listen intently to the calm voice that floats into my ear, trying to take in every nuance.

'What you said before doctor, serious but not life-threatening?'

'That is correct. Your son's condition is stable.'

'We, that is, Sam's mother and I, we are thinking of flying out to be with him.'

'I think that would be a very good idea.'

He says this quickly, 'I-think-that-would-be-a-very-good-idea.'

The words terrify me. You don't suggest a person fly half way round the world unless… If only he'd said, 'No hurry old man. Come if you like but the boy will be right as rain in a week or two. Don't you go getting yourself all ...'

'Mr Dew? Are you still there?'

'Yes. We, that is Sam's Mum and I, we'll get a flight as soon as we can.'

'Good. Stay in touch. Myself or one of my staff will let you know of any changes in your son's condition.'

'Thank you,' I said, and put the phone down.

'We must go to him.'

# Part Six

## 23

*Don't it always seem to go…*

For months we've been hearing that computers are designed to run only to midnight on 31st De-cember 1999, then they'll stop. Much of our world, so dependent on them, will abruptly cease to function. There will be chaos. Many of these stories have been put about by people profiting from Millennium Bug cures and fears are likely overblown. But there is genuine concern too: nobody knows for certain how or if the world's computers will cope. In the event, electronic clocks will keep going and aircraft will not fall out of the sky. To be on the safe side though, many airlines have grounded their fleets. January 1st 2000 is not a good day to fly.

Nevertheless Kate manages to get us on one of the first flights out of London to Sydney. Pat's brother-in-law Big Dave drives us to Heathrow and her sister stays at the farm with Kate and Lynn. Pat and I sit in the dark near the back of the aircraft, staring at our reflections in the window. In my pocket are the divorce papers the

arranged a tandem flight for Hannah which she loved. But mostly I wandered alone and they let me be, to think and grieve. I stayed a month.

Back home I immersed myself in dealing with the unceasing demands of The Rocking Horse Shop. Work would be my solace. I'd lost count of the people who'd told me how wonderfully therapeutic my craft was. If that was so, I thought, I must be the most contented of men, which didn't seem likely. Still, joy might be found for a while, if I pushed aside the futility of it all. Sam was constantly with me, and the knowledge that I would never say, 'My son,' again about a living being. But alone, while carving or at my desk, his absence was as if he was travelling still. Except that the criss-cross of lines on the world map on the kitchen wall stopped at Melbourne. They would never go further.

The day after I got back from New Zealand I was having lunch in the kitchen of Manor House Farm, from where I had a good view across the yard to the shop, when I saw a young man run out. Chilled out and jet-lagged still, I said to myself, 'That guy's in a hurry,' and thought no more of it until Sheila, our office administrator, phoned to tell me our money box with about £750 in cash had been stolen. He'd gone in the back door of the shop, up the stairs and into Sheila's office, found the box in a drawer of her desk - all without being seen - and legged it. A combination of coincidences had given the thief his chance to steal so much 'petty' cash: I'd left the back door open when I'd walked Rip earlier; the bank had started charging us for cash deposits so instead of banking it Sheila kept it in the cash box thinking we'd spend it but we hadn't; nobody was in the office because I was at lunch and both Sheila and Mike were busy with customers in the shop downstairs.

The thief and his two accomplices, who'd been waiting for him in a car outside, were soon caught. They drove to a Designer Outlet near York and chose some fancy £150 shirts. But when it came to pay using notes and coins from our cash box the suspicious shopkeeper called the police and they were arrested. The ringleader eventually went to prison. Good outcome, except we

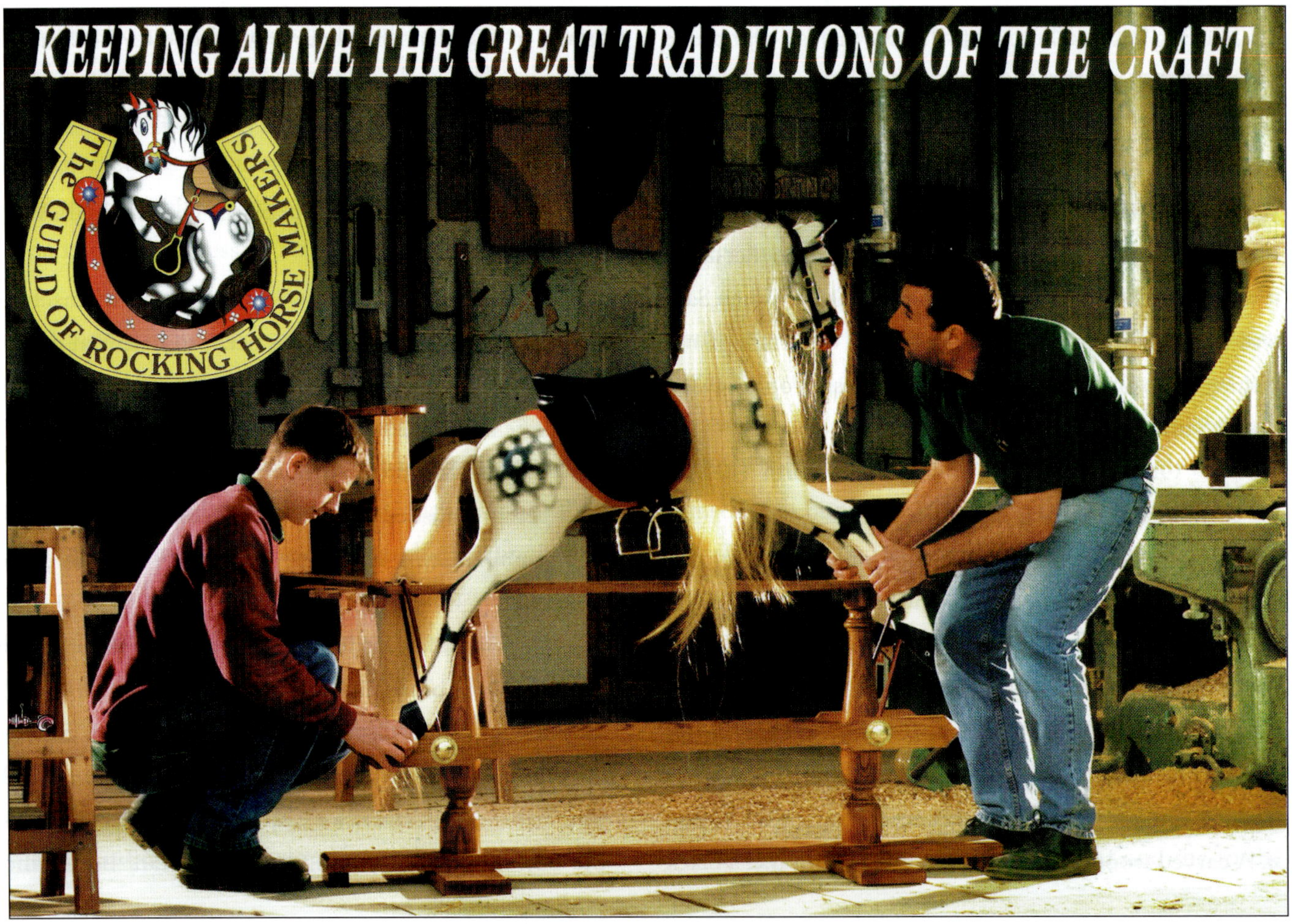

never got our money back.

I volunteered to do a charity bungee jump from a tall crane in the village school playground.

'Sure, I'll do it. I'm a paraglider pilot. How hard can it be?'

I climbed to the launch platform knowing that as soon as the bungees were strapped on I should leap. But as I stood up there peering at the concrete ground sixty feet below, I hesitated. Jumping would be madness. I was surprised by how much I wanted to live.

I could hear impatient murmurings from the crowd below and the organiser asked, 'You want to do it the easy way?'

'There's an easy way?'

'Close your eyes and I'll give you a shove.'

'No,' I said. 'I'm going to do this but I must have my eyes open.'

The crowd started chanting, '10. 9. 8…'

When they reached, '1' I had to jump. It was easy and I walked away grinning. I'd been wondering 'what-if' the bungee didn't work but of course it did. Paragliding, I'd fallen fifteen hundred feet, hit the ground and didn't have a scratch. My Sam fell thirty feet. He could have taken a fall like that a thousand times and it wouldn't have been fatal. I'd give anything to change places with him but my prayers haven't been answered. How easy it is to relinquish life, how hard sometimes. Shit happens.

Mike the manager had looked after The Rocking Horse Shop while I was away. He mostly ran the show and I let him get on with it. One morning he came into my office to tell me a leak had flooded the storage racks and several boxes of accessories and books had been ruined.

I shrugged, 'Clean it up then.'

Mike told me he'd started to make a rocking-horse for his own grandchildren. He said it would give him a better understanding of the craft. I was pleased he had such enthusiasm and dedication since I'd lost mine.

'It's not technically difficult,' he said. 'But the carving is much harder than I'd expected, I mean to get a really good-looking shape.'

'Yes,' I said. 'It is.'

'I'm struggling with the contours of the body,' he went on. 'It would help if you drew up some profiles. They could be included with the plan and would help amateur makers such as myself.'

'Good idea, Mike. I'll see to it.'

I knew I had to drag myself out of the bubble of careless despair miring me.

Mike told me he'd interviewed a new trainee to work with Sam Glass in the woodwork shop.

'He's a good lad, very keen, and I'd like to take him on,' Mike said. 'Only thing is, his name is Sam.'

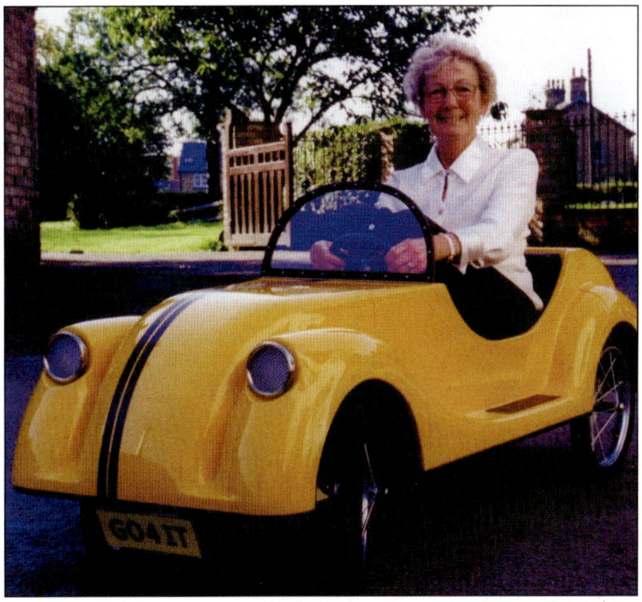


*Mike's Jaglin electric car was intended for 4 to 8 year-olds. But our lovely 70-year-old neighbour Wyn could fit in the seat & she test drove it for us.*

'Another one? Still, can't blame him for his name. If you think he'll be right for us Mike, hire him. We'll call him Young Sam and Sam Glass Old Sam.'

With his engineering background Mike had taken a big interest in the cars and started working on a prefabricated fibre-glass body to bolt onto the same chassis as the electric Dewlin. Mike's sports car, which we named the Jaglin, had a sleeker, more contemporary appearance than the classic vintage look of the Dewlin. The body shell parts were bright yellow with black go-faster stripes. It looked good and would be a relatively straightforward project to build which we hoped would appeal to car enthusiasts as well as home woodworkers, so we hoped to sell lots. We didn't.

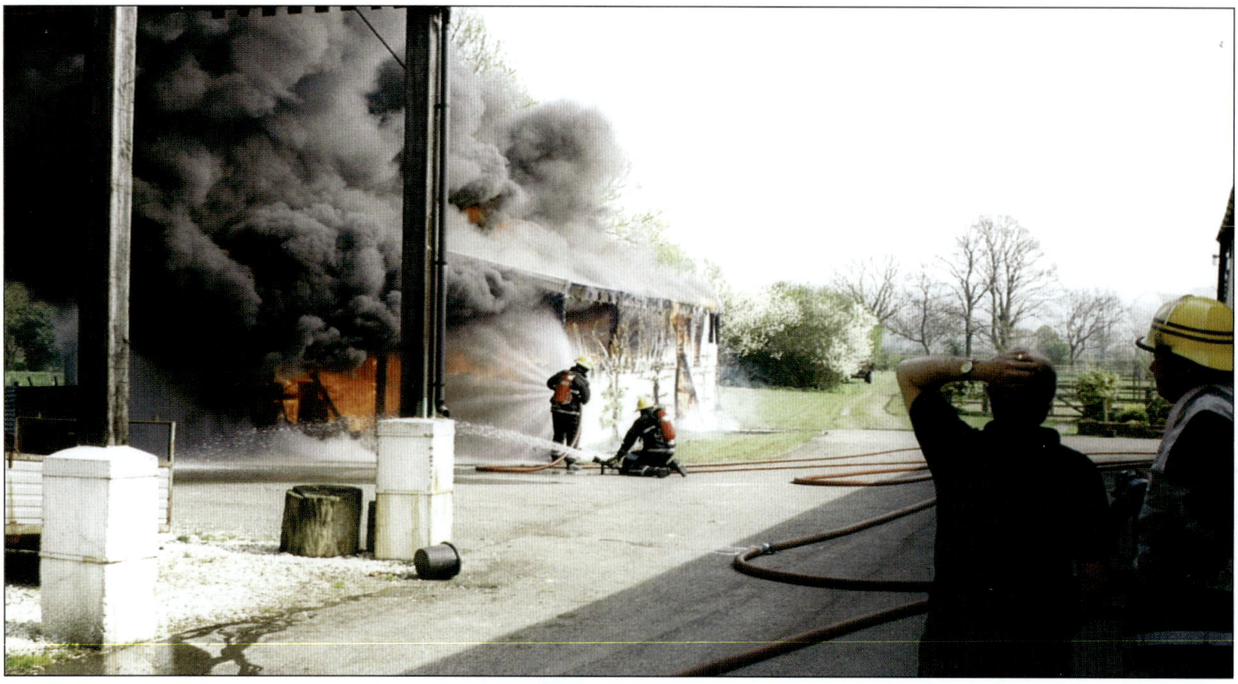

While Mike took care of day-to-day business and built his car and rocking-horse, I stayed in my office working on the magazine. I'd get so immersed in it that for a while I could forget everything else. For the third issue I changed its name to The Rocking Horse & Toy Magazine to broaden its appeal. I had visions of sales in the thousands, the magazine finding a place alongside other specialist publications on newsagents shelves across the country. That didn't happen.

The trees Pat and I had planted were now up to four metres tall. I hired a bulldozer to flatten a ride and create a circle with a mound in the centre on which we planted an English oak. Friends and relations came with more trees to plant in a circle round the oak and along the ride. Henceforth, each June around the date of Sam's birthday, we'd have a gathering of friends and relations. We'd eat sandwiches, drink wine or cordial, catch up on our news and play rounders. Sam's Picnic in what we now called Sam's Wood. It would become a happy event tinged with sadness for those no longer with us.

Slowly both Guild and Magazine numbers grew. Neither was doing as well as I'd hoped but we won special supplements in two magazines, Craftsman and Traditional Woodworking, which helped spread the word. The magazine alone was almost my full time job but it was creative work I enjoyed. I particularly liked writing the agony column as Aunty Jacky, a ludicrously obsessive rocking-horse fanatic given to suggestive sexual references.

'Like you, really,' daughter Kate said, which I thought was a little unfair.

In one issue I included a letter about an English rocking-horse making company who were said to be importing the rocking-horses they were selling from the Far East. I'd heard this from several people and believed my information was sound, but neglected to check with the company concerned. Soon after publication I took a furious phone call from them, shouting down the phone that it was all lies. I apologised and said I'd be happy to print a retraction in the next issue. I pointed out that these rumours were rife among rocking-horse people and if they were untrue this would be a good opportunity to refute them and offered to run a double page spread in the magazine about the company. I printed the retraction but didn't hear anything more from them about the two-page spread. A storm in a teacup, I assumed.

One morning I went to York on an errand and on the way back flicked on the car's CD player. Grateful Dead (who've provided the soundtrack to my life ever since Porter introduced me to them back in '71) had a version of Smokestack Lightning that ran seventeen minutes, the exact time it would take me to drive home. I had the volume high when I saw a tall plume of black smoke in the distance. I thought, that looks dangerously close to home.

But the road meandered, the smoke appeared first on one side, then on the other. I was thinking, it's my place, no it's not, it is, maybe it's only a straw fire in a field. But the song ended as I drove into Rocking Horse Yard and saw it was my carving studio burning, great gouts of orange flame leaping from the windows and a pall of smoke shutting out the sun.

My people stood along the wall of the main workshop watching, except for Mike who'd gone to switch off the power to the burning building. The fire brigade had been called but hadn't yet arrived. Julie told me Young Sam had lit the boiler in the studio, as I'd asked him to before I left, but when he went back to check it fifteen minutes later and opened the door, the building was full of smoke. He closed the door and ran to raise the alarm.

'He did the right thing,' I said.

Julie said, 'The chickens were trapped in their run behind the building. Young Sam rescued them. His motorbike was in the shed but he saved the hens before he went for his bike.'

'That says a lot about the lad.'

'I know. I hope you're not too angry with him. It wasn't his fault.'

'No,' I said, staring at the flames. 'I'm not angry with Young Sam.'

In the shed and carving studio there'd been maybe ten rocking-horses under construction, a monumental horse's head I'd been working on intermittently for months, a stack of part-made projects, my massive workbench and antique cast iron vice with the lion on it that I'd had since the beginning, masses of equipment and almost all my carving tools accumulated over thirty years as a rocking-horse maker.

One in particular, a wide shallow gouge I'd had a long time, was my favourite. Nothing special, except it fitted into my palm like an extension of me and it was the tool I reached for ahead of any other. Losing that was like losing a hand.

Also crippled by the fire were two fruit trees I'd planted intending them to serve, in due course, as goal posts in the football games I'd play with my anticipated grandchildren.

Julie said, 'I don't know what to say. You've lost everything. You must feel terrible.'

'I don't feel anything,' I said.

# 24

*It's not over 'til it's over and you throw away the key..*

With my carving studio reduced to a misshapen steel skeleton over a smouldering heap, the fire-fighters relaxed and stood around drinking from their flasks.

'It's good to be called to fight a real fire for once,' one said.

Then they rolled up their hoses and left, taking

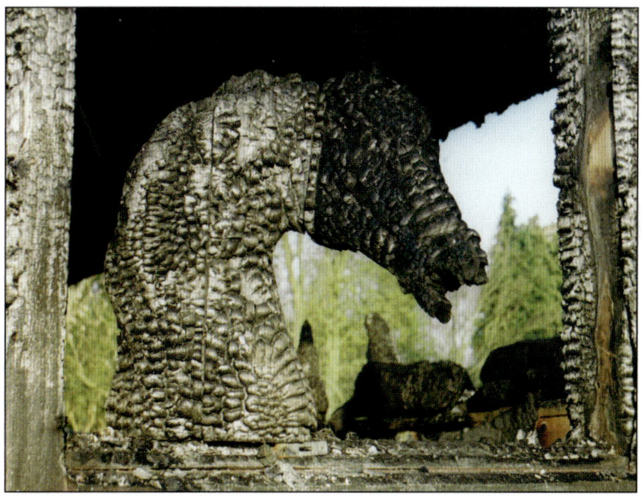

with them a few trophies including a charred yet still recognisable wooden horse's head and a fire extinguisher that had exploded leaving a jag-ged hole in its steel casing. All that remained of my carving studio was my monumental head and a small herd of rocking-horses reduced to charcoal, my heat-ruined carving tools buried beneath heaps of ash, and the building's steel frame buckled beyond repair. The firemen had doused the buildings nearby to prevent the fire from spreading so The Rocking Horse Shop continued to function as if nothing had happened and our customers were unaffected.

The main workshop suffered no more than some twisted plastic guttering and a few heat-cracked windows which, to this day, I can see from my window as I write.

Several times a day I walked with Rip past the burned-out wreck of my carving studio and the stink of soot so depressed me (even more than usual) that I phoned a demolition contractor to come and take it all away. After that nothing remained but a blackened concrete pad, the building's footprint. I started sketching a replacement and filled my waking hours with rocking-horse work, my ongoing search for love and attempts to reach a higher plane of existence, literally, by flying my paraglider at every opportunity.

A month after the fire I went with Harry and some other flying friends on what had become our annual pilgrimage to the French Alps. A wonderful escape. Later in the year we travelled abroad again to paraglide, this time to Greece. Chris Dawes, our paragliding guide there, gave us his three rules for survival: 1. Relax, 2. Look ahead, 3. Steer gently in the direction you want to go. OK I thought, I'll do that then.

My affair with Big Lynn having ended when Sam died, I was now with Janet, a spectacularly intelligent woman with a wonderful plummy accent. She was loving company and a great cook, and delighted me by producing exquisite dinners with fine wine any evening of the week, such that every night we spent together was a special occasion. She had a son named Robbie aged eight and I became very fond of him. Robbie was part of Janet's attraction, although of course nobody could replace my Sam, nor Pat for that matter. Janet agreed to model for some of our rocking-horse merchandise - T-shirts and baseball caps with our logo on - but otherwise I took care not to involve her in The Rocking Horse Shop. She fascinated me though, and the more I knew her the more I loved her.

Returning to Rocking Horse Yard after an outing to the coast with Janet and Rip one Sunday, where we'd walked the dog to the end of Filey Brig and back, we found three men waiting on my doorstep. Chinese, all three wore business suits, two were late thirties, the third older, around 52, my age. One of the younger men spoke English and did all the talking. He said they represented a hand wood-carving company near Shanghai which among other things made rocking-horses, and they'd heard of me and my famous Rocking Horse Shop. The older man was an experienced woodcarver and the third man was an executive or manager in the company, although he spoke not at all and I suspected he was a Chinese Communist Party apparatchik sent along to watch the other two and report back.

I pricked up my ears at the mention of Shanghai, recalling an impromptu trial on the Shanghai waterfront I'd witnessed back in 1964 at the height of Mao's cultural revolution. On a Swedish ship moored ahead of ours a dock worker was accused of stealing a pair of worn-out shoes from a trash bin, thrown out by a seaman. He'd taken the shoes because he had none, but it took the Red Guards less than twenty minutes to find him guilty of theft, sentence and condemn him. He was executed, shot dead, right there on the quay. Justice Chinese style, swift and vicious. China's fortunes had skyrocketed dramatically since the death of that hideous monstrosity Mao, and China's policies regarding the outside world had transformed, but the CCP's savage control hadn't lessened.

I might have told them right away to get lost, but I didn't. I liked the look of the old fellow-carver and saw no good reason to disrespect these three individuals despite what they represented - cheap imports designed to undermine home-grown makers such as myself. Also, I was intrigued. I'd always believed our sort of small-scale batch and one-off production model, dependent on old-world hand-craft skills and with an extremely limited market, was simply too small and too specialised for potential competitors from Asia to bother with. Obviously I'd been wrong yet again.

The trend was for Western businesses to outsource their manufacturing abroad, to countries where labour was cheaper and more docile and regulatory controls less onerous. We'd always gone against that trend and been proud of it, but the message from every bureaucrat I'd ever encountered was one of discouragement. Maybe it would be sensible to accept the real world as it is instead of continually and futilely kicking against the pricks. It might make life easier, simpler.

I showed them round the workshop and showroom and they showed me photographs of what they were making. I ignored their (probably unconscious) disrespect to me and my craft in assuming they could pass off a Made-in-China version of such a quintessentially English artefact as a rocking-horse as acceptable. On the whole their rocking-horses, carved in a deep brown hardwood, looked pretty good to me. What's more, the translator assured me, they could be made and finished to my specification, packed, transported and delivered to my door, ready to sell, at one sixth the cost of mine. I couldn't even buy my raw materials for the cost of one of their finished rocking-horses shipped half way round the world.

It was tempting. Quality control would clearly be an issue and I'd have to visit their factory to see their operation and give some hands-on instruction. But I'd welcome that opportunity. From what I'd read Shanghai had expanded and changed out of all recognition from the drab impoverished city I'd visited at the height of Mao's disastrous Cultural Revolution back in the 60s. It would be fascinating to go again now. So I considered their proposals seriously for a while before rejecting them.

Almost a year had passed and I'd totally forgotten about the angry response to my letter in The Rocking Horse & Toy Magazine when a writ for defamation landed on my doormat. The claim was for over £100,000 damages plus legal costs. At the time I'd understood the anger a but this was so belated and so outrageous I laughed. I'd have to fight them though.

I'd had a couple of brushes with the law before. A few years earlier we'd met a fellow maker at a show and admired his rocking-horses, carved in mahogany and finished with a beautiful deep French polish, distinctive and very striking. He appeared to be doing well with them and we assumed he was a friendly rival. But his solicitor's letter declared that we were infringing his Design Registration and we must cease production forthwith or legal action would ensue. We were shocked. I'd been making natural wood finish rocking-horses for years. Surely he didn't think he could have Design Registration protection over the pattern of wood grain? Whether he succeeded in scaring off some of his competitors I don't know, but we'd ignored the legal threat and heard no more about it.

Around the same time (when we were just getting nicely established in The Rocking Horse Shop in HoSM) an old friend and customer I'll call C opened a shop not fifty miles away, called The Rocking Horse Shop. He was selling finished rocking-horses as well as plans and accessories and doing restorations. He'd bought accessories from us many times and appeared to have copied some of them. He'd even used the same border design as ours on his price list.

'It's a clear case of 'passing-off', my solicitor said. 'We'll send C a letter giving him twenty-one days to change his trading name and everything else he's doing that could confuse his shop with yours in the public's mind, or we'll take him to the High Court.'

'Won't that be terribly expensive?'

'Yes. But he won't risk it. He'll concede.' Which he did.

About six months later I met C at a show and he said, 'I think you went right over the top Tony, threatening me the way you did.'

'Did you?' I said. 'Well I thought you were a friend, but if you imagined I'd sit here and do nothing while you ripped me off you were sadly mistaken.' The matter was ended and I never saw him again.

This writ was potentially a lot more serious. My accusers refused to meet to settle the argument so I had to respond through the law. Fortunately I knew a friendly, clever and extremely clear-thinking solicitor named Drum. For months Drum countered the avalanches of accusatory documents that came with brilliantly brief and pithy responses. Eventually, for a hearing in London's High Court of Justice, we were obliged to hire a barrister at a fearful hourly rate. Drum and I travelled down by train to meet him in his London chambers, a scene straight out of a TV sit-com.

'I won't argue your fee,' I told the barrister. 'But

I hope you understand that what I'm paying you to defend me is more than ten times the hourly rate of the highest paid person in my company. And that's not me.'

'Defamation is the playground of the rich and famous,' he said.

'That's not me either,' I said. 'I'm only a rocking-horse maker. But so are they. Their claim is ridiculous. I'll happily see them in court.'

'You won't though, Mr Dew, not happily. Your legal costs are already high, the cost of a full trial will be astronomic and will likely bankrupt you. You don't want that. But then again, neither do they. I know this is hard, because your livelihood is at stake, but try to treat this as a game. It's a game of intimidation. Their claim, ridiculous though it may be, is intended to force you to settle high. You want to settle low. Ultimately you will have to settle, but we must persuade them to believe that you're prepared to fight them all the way.'

I said, 'They don't frighten me.'

'No? Good. They may not scare you but the cost might. The question is, how much are you prepared to pay them to get them off your back?'

We made an offer which they rejected, then there was an inconclusive but costly High Court hearing, followed by more letters and threats and another hearing. In court my barrister wiped the floor with our opponent's and I was glad he was on my side, but even so the costs kept mounting. Eventually, after two gruelling years, an offer was accepted, I paid, and the case came to an end. Mike, God bless him, kept The Rocking Horse Shop afloat throughout that period, but I was foundering. I had to get away.

I flew out to New Zealand again to stay with old friends Alan and Lynne. This time, as well as spending time with them at their lovely house on Waiheke Island, we toured the South Island, saw whales and glaciers, walked the Milford Track, a most beautiful and spectacular three-day trek, and I went paragliding in Queenstown. Back on Waiheke Island near the end of my stay I was buying souvenirs to bring home when the woman in the gift shop asked if I was an islander.

'No,' I said. 'I've been here a month but I've got to go back to England, unfortunately.'

'Is that right?' she said. 'You look so laid back and happy I thought you must be an islander. I guess Waiheke's worked its magic on you, hey?'

'You're absolutely right,' I said.

I came home and told Mike I wanted to sell up and move to New Zealand.

'I thought you might. I'll start putting out feelers.'

We knew a number of rocking-horse people who might be interested in buying me out, including Jimi, a fine musician, artist and craftsman. Jimi was an ex-employee of ours who'd left to set up Wensleydale Rocking Horses in the Yorkshire Dales. Mike found several other possible buyers including a bright and friendly young couple who sounded extremely keen to be rocking-horse people. The problem was The Rocking Horse Shop was such a specialised yet broad-ranging business it was hard to find anyone both willing and capable of taking it on. Also, Manor House Farm was now a valuable property but couldn't easily be separated from the business in the back yard. It all became very complicated. After high initial interest none of the prospective buyers came to anything, although talks with the keen young couple dragged on for months before collapsing.

Mike and the staff of The Rocking Horse Shop were working well and the orders kept coming in, but not enough of them. Two years had passed without a single new design from me, although we did publish two marionette plans, for a man (pierrot) and a mouse, designed by a highly imaginative puppeteer named Mal Trott. The puppet plans were very appealing and we sold quite a few, but they were never going to make much money. At the same time as our income was flatlining the cost of raw materials was spiralling, my old machines kept breaking down and it seemed that almost every week the government or EU introduced new rules and regulations, always incredibly complicated, which massively increased our administrative burden. We became embroiled in a protracted battle with the VAT regime over some bureaucratic mix-up, and another with East Riding Council over the level of commercial rates they demanded. We kept hearing of small businesses failing under the strain and I thought we might be next.

By early 2002 The Rocking Horse Shop was employing fifteen people and we were haemorrhaging money. I called a staff meeting to explain the situation.

'The problem is simple: too much money going out, not enough coming in. The Rocking Horse Shop is sinking. We must look hard at every aspect of our work. Where can we make economies? How can we reduce wastage? Can we cut costs without sacrificing quality? What can we do to bring in new customers? Can we work harder? Our wage bill is our single biggest outgoing. I'm asking each of you this, what can you do to help the enterprise survive and prosper? I don't want to lose anybody but some of you may have to leave altogether. Some of you may offer to work fewer hours, or even take a lower wage. This affects all of us, believe me. We have to act and act soon. If we don't, we'll all be out of work.'

There were murmurs of understanding, agreement or incredulity. After the meeting I called each employee in turn to my office. When Julie came in she said, 'I'll work harder, take a pay cut, work fewer hours, whatever is needed. I love this job, Tony.'

'Thank you, Julie,' I said. 'I really appreciate that.'

Most of the others said something similar, if not quite so wholeheartedly. Two part-timers agreed to leave altogether. Sam Glass told me he was thinking of leaving anyway.

'I wasn't expecting that, Sam. As our carver you're a key person. I thought you liked it here.'

'I do. But I liked being my own boss too and I don't want to do anything but carve rocking-horses. If I stay you'll want me to carve less and do other work around the workshop.'

'Well, that's true, Sam. There aren't enough orders for finished rocking-horses coming in to keep you employed here doing nothing but carve, not with Billy and Young Sam preparing the timber and restorations.'

'I know. But Jimi wants me to make rocking-horses for him, so does the guy from that new rocking-horse company in Sheffield, and I can make them for other people too. I could still supply carved horses to you, but from my own workshop. I fancy being a jobbing rocking-horse maker and I reckon I can make a go of it on my own.'

I said, 'I wouldn't want The Rocking Horse Shop to lose you altogether Sam, but I understand what you're saying.'

When Greta came in she said, 'I can't do anything more than I do already. I work hard. I never make unnecessary waste. I don't want to drop my hours. I don't think you pay me enough anyway.'

'That is all true, Greta. But The Rocking Horse Shop's in a bad place. Everybody's making a contribution. We can't have a situation where you're the only one not making some sort of sacrifice.'

'Does that mean you're firing me?'

'I don't want to lose you Greta, but…'

Mike said that since his retirement was coming up soon anyway he'd be happy to work four days or even three and take a pro-rata pay cut. I told Mike not to overdo it, The Rocking Horse Shop needed him and so did I. I said it wasn't going to be good not having Old Sam carving in our workshop but I could do more in there, and if he'd supply us with bare carved horses to finish, we'd manage. I'd take a lower salary and almost all the other employees had agreed to work fewer hours, at least until trade picked up again. The exception was Greta.

I remembered when Greta came for her interview for the leatherworker's job. An immigrant from Eastern Europe, she was worried I wouldn't understand her thick accent and that she wouldn't be up to the job. But she was keen to try and said she knew how to work a sewing machine, so I took her on. She soon settled in and learned all she needed to know to be a first-class rocking-horse saddle and bridle maker. She was liked, most of the time, although she turned out to be a larger, louder and far more forceful personality than any of the others. Julie, who worked alongside her, was a total contrast. Petite and unassuming, Julie was Greta's equal as a craftswoman and they were paid the same, but Greta

of. Ultimately, after many months, the proposal was dropped. We breathed a huge sigh of relief but it had been another terribly time-consuming distraction. Our constant refrain was, 'Haven't these people got anything better to do?'

The perennial answer was, 'No'.

In 2003 Mike the manager reached sixty-five and retired, as he'd said he would. Mike had been my anchor and support and I knew I'd struggle on my own. I needed a new manager but couldn't bring myself to do anything about it. Then out of the blue I came across D, who told me he'd owned a small company specialising in restoring and selling classic cars.

He'd done very well, D told me, but when his principal customer died, the mainstay of his business, his work dried up. He didn't have the heart to start building it all up again from scratch but he was still young and hoped to put his experience and management skills to good use in some other venture. He told me our work at The Rocking Horse Shop fascinated him and he'd love to be my manager. He was a practical young man with a very pleasant manner and I liked him. I said I'd let him know in a few days.

I was pleased and excited, D would be absolutely ideal. My only hesitation was that when I'd asked him for references he'd waffled about how with his one and only customer now sadly deceased there really wasn't anyone else he could ask. That was plausible, but I felt I should have a second opinion. I remembered that Stuart, a former neighbour and friend, worked for Brookes, the car auctioneers, so I gave him a ring.

I explained the situation and said, 'It occurs to me Stuart, that like rocking-horse people, you classic car dealers are a fairly small community, so I wondered if you'd ever come across this guy D. I'm not asking you for a formal reference, just your impression. Do you know him?'

Stuart paused and I heard him breathing.

At last he said, 'I know him all right, Tony. The man's a crook. I wouldn't touch him with a barge-pole.'

# 26

*I want more, and more, and then some.*

Jane Cook was a small woman with long blonde hair and an outgoing personality. If she was pleased with something you said or did she was quite likely to throw her arms round you and give you a hug, even if you didn't know her very well. Not very British, but endearing. She had three young children and a husband who was 'in computers' and they'd recently moved back to Fangfoss after living and working in the USA for several years. A neighbour told me Jane's work had involved troubleshooting problems in small franchise businesses so she knew a lot about small business management, and with her cheery manner would be the perfect person to help me run The Rocking Horse Shop.

In the mélée of the school yard I spotted her right away, laughing and chatting whilst waiting for her kids. I introduced myself and said I'd heard that she was looking for a job. She laughed and said she'd love to have a job but she'd three children to look after. I said I was sure we'd be able to fit the work round her family arrangements and maybe she could start on a part-time basis. She agreed to come to The Rocking Horse Shop next morning after she'd dropped the kids off at school, when I'd show her round and tell her what the job involved.

She was delighted with everything she saw in the showroom and the workshop - which didn't surprise me, everyone was - and said she was astounded by the scale of the business, there was a great deal more to it than she'd imagined.

'Yes, not just a shed in the back garden,' I said. 'That's why I need a manager.'

Jane started work almost immediately and was so full of energy that her part-time was the equivalent of most people's full time. We held regular Management Meetings, just her and me, and she wrote up the minutes. Beside each item on the agenda she'd write 'Action' and then 'JC', or 'AD' if it was something I had to do. By our

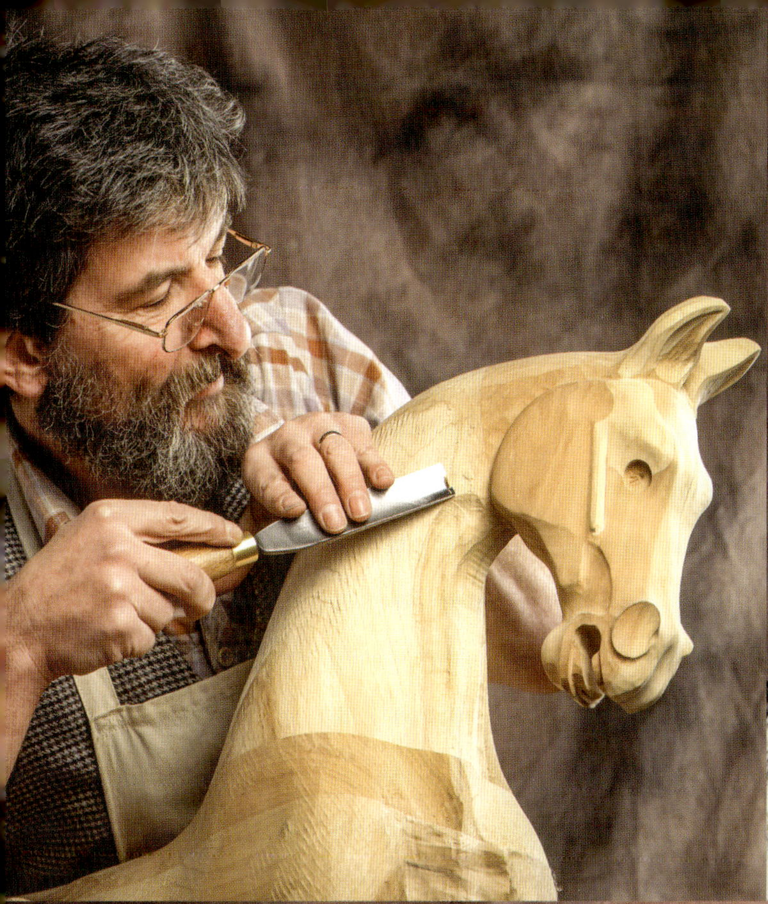

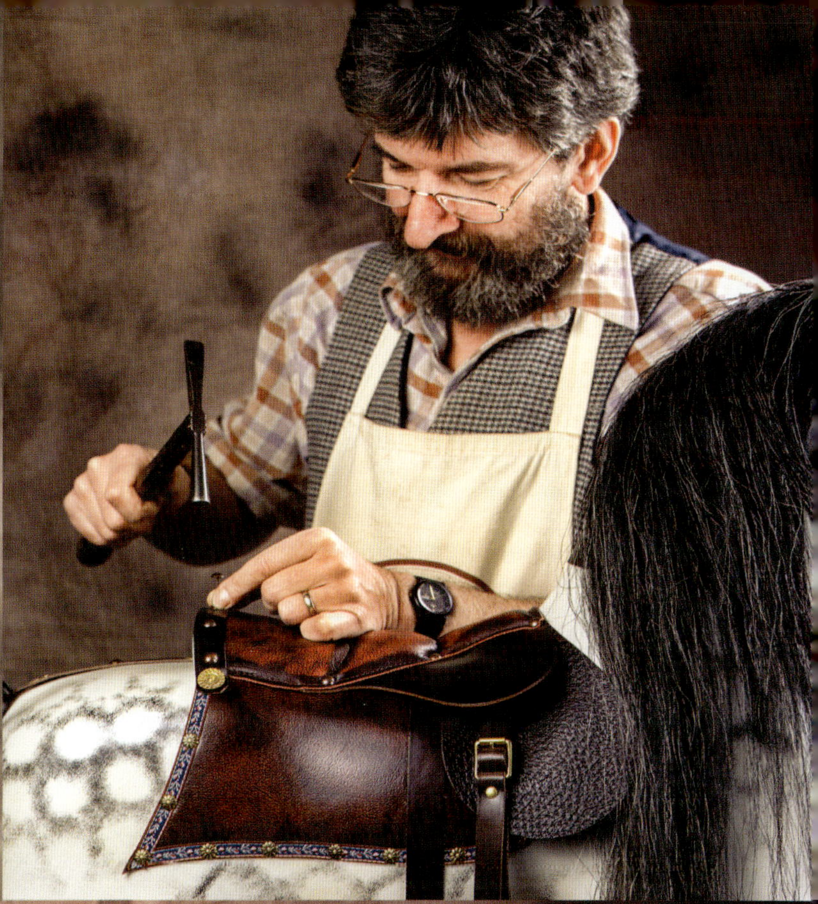

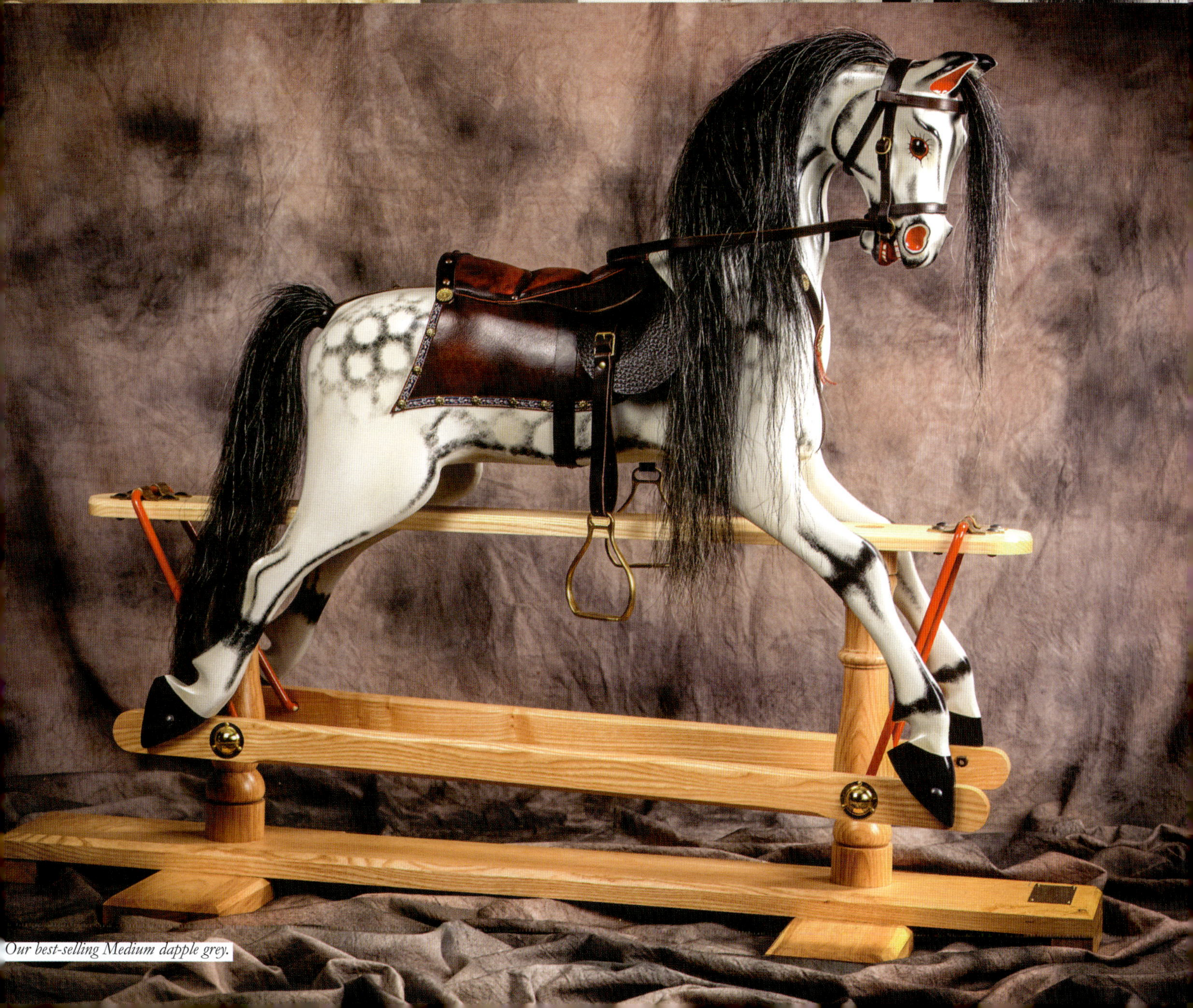

*Our best-selling Medium dapple grey.*

next meeting she'd always done all the things she said she'd do, which was a lot. I was very impressed and felt lucky to have found her, and almost on my doorstep. The staff and customers took to her and with Jane looking after business on a day-to-day basis, I could devote myself to writing The Complete Rocking Horse Maker and my other projects. She also helped me to feel less guilty about taking time out to go paragliding whenever the weather suited.

The insurance company's payout after the carving studio burned down wasn very fair, but not enough to build a replacement. I had a choice: put up a smaller building I could afford, or go for a more ambitious project altogether. I revived my abandoned plan for the old dairy and sketched a two storey building with carving studio, museum and shop on the ground floor, holiday accommodation above. Architect Rod Mill said we sound out the East Riding's planners to see if they'd be agreeable in principle to such a development before I got involved in spending a lot of money I didn't have (but hoped to make). It took nine months to get a response out of a planning officer, but when it came it was positive. Rod got on with drawing and submitting detailed plans.

Daughter Kate, after a less than happy year in Manchester, had transferred to York University and was living with her Mum, so I saw her more frequently. Daughter Lynn had gone to Sheffield University and was studying French and Spanish, coming home for the holidays but spending half of them with her Mum. For a while my sister Jacky lived with me after she'd split up from her husband, and I liked her being around, but now she'd found a place of her own and moved out. Janet and I had been going strong and there was no shortage of love between us. But, fearful that maybe we wouldn't be able to live happily together for the rest of our lives, I baulked at the prospect of marriage and we sadly parted. So I was rattling round Manor House Farm on my own. One morning on the library carpet I found a pile of congealed cat shit sprouting mould.

Most days I went from the kitchen to my bedroom and back, with forays into the living room to eat my ready-meals whilst watching TV, and I hadn't been in that room for weeks. The rest of the house was dormant too. I no longer believed Manor House Farm would ever be a family home again, not for me and mine.

One day, having lunch with Jane in the kitchen, as we often did, she was standing at the window sipping her tea, staring down the yard.

'You know Tony,' she said. 'This is absolutely my dream house.'

'Is that right, Jane?' I said, 'In that case you'd better buy it from me right now, because I don't want to live here any more.'

Jane and her husband put their house up for sale. It took a while - these things never happen as quickly as you hope they will - but when the sale went through I moved out of Manor House Farm and they moved in with their family. I rented the top floor of Fangfoss Hall next door, a Grade 1 listed building and the grandest property in the village, at least from the outside (it's since been fabulously done up by the owner and I was lucky that at that time he let me live there as a sort of low rent caretaker). From its window I could watch the progress of Rocking House, the building that was underway to replace my old carving studio. The money from the sale of the farmhouse paid for it and I was able to pay off the rest of the money I owed, to my great relief. I was debt-free at last, but still single.

I wasn't seeing Pat much but whenever we did meet I was overwhelmed by a sense of what we'd lost. I kept pushing thoughts of her away but they kept resurfacing, like a madness that came over me every full moon. For several years running I'd taken a stand at a three-day show at Westonburt Arboretum near Bath in late August, in a marquee organised by the British Toymakers Guild. It was a marvellous event, held over a long bank holiday weekend, and quite a few toymakers would be there who Pat knew, so I asked her to come with me. I longed more than anything to reconnect with her but felt it wouldn't work if I tried to woo her with a fake version of myself.

To my surprise - she must have been entertaining hopes of a reunion too - she agreed to come. On the way we stayed at a smart hotel; whilst at the show we slept in a tent; on the way home we stopped at a cheap hotel. To be with her again after all these years, to replay a slice of the life we'd shared, to talk together intimately and honestly, to sleep together and make love again… We went with great hopes, we came home disillusioned.

'Nothing's changed,' she said sadly. Our final attempt to get back together had failed. I dropped her off near her house and we said goodbye very softly, knowing this was the end. I watched her walk away but it was me getting smaller in the distance.

I went back to work on *The Complete Rocking Horse Maker* determined that it should be at least as good as a high-quality book from an established publisher. We bought up-to-the-minute publishing software and daughter Lynn got her young head round the complexities of it, and showed me. Lynn was brilliant working on the book's layout, especially the scale plan drawings, some of which had half a dozen overlays. We used the same software to design our catalogues and flyers, and the instruction booklets that went with each of our Designs for Woodworkers.

By this time we owned the equipment to do most of our leaflet printing in-house, although producing a full-length book was be-yond us. Through a paragliding colleague, Ian Currer, who'd written and self-published Touching Cloudbase, a standard handbook on free-flying, I found a printer who was both excellent and inexpensive. I'd hoped to publish the book by Fangfest at the start of September, but in spite of working all hours and dropping everything else, including my annual paragliding holiday in the high Alps, it wasn't finished in time. It was finally completed and away to the printers in mid September. I slumped with relief.

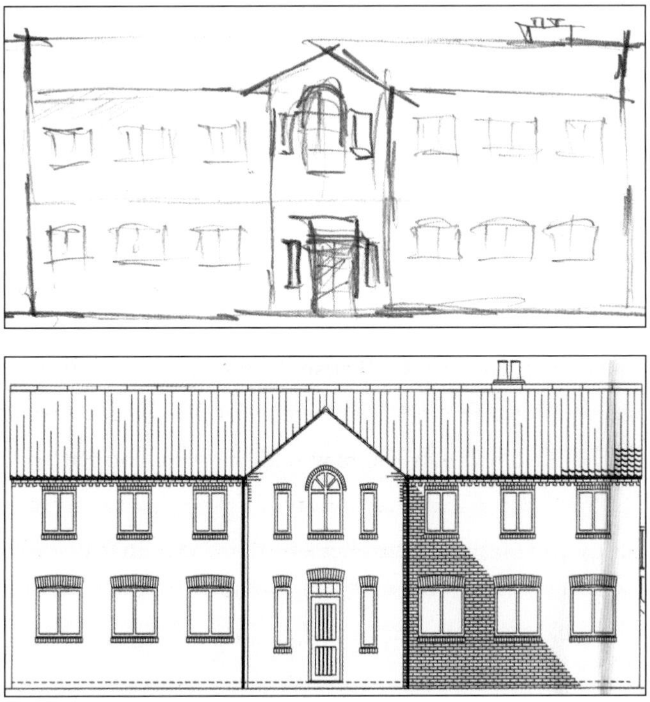

*AD's sketch for Rocking House & the architect's drawing.*

Jane said, 'Why don't you go paragliding now, you've earned it. I'll book you a flight to Geneva and a hire car. I can take care of business here while you're away.'

It isn't wise to go paragliding without a buddy but I went anyway, driving south from Geneva and staying in a hotel not far from St Hilaire du Touvet where there was a huge annual free-flying festival. Thousands of visitors as well as hang- and paragliding pilots would be there, and a big attraction was a fancy-dress fly-down, when pilots dressed as dinosaurs, steam trains, Christ on the cross, you name it, flew from a high mountain plateau to the valley below. The atmosphere was electric and convivial. I was able to fly high above the masquerade fliers, floating to and fro in the sunshine looking down on a bizarre array of costumes launching and flying. I could relax and appreciate the rare experience of simply being alone and at ease, with nothing to do but enjoy myself.

On my last day at the festival I flew in the morning then went back up the mountain on the funicular railway to enjoy a picnic lunch on the grassy plateau next to a launch site while watching the flying displays. Eventually it was time to go and I gathered my stuff together. As I made my way through the crowds of people sitting and standing on the mountain slope, I became aware of something special happening. I turned to watch a hang-glider, high above the crowd, performing a series of vertical loops, an extremely dangerous and very fast manoeuvre.

At the same time several paragliders were flying horizontally and slowly in front of the ridge. As the hang-glider looped he got lower and lower and suddenly, travelling at tremendous speed, he smacked into a paraglider.

The two aircraft jerked apart and the paraglider pilot was hurled violently to one side then swung back under her wing which, remarkably, kept flying. Several lines were broken and streaming out but the paraglider limped away and she landed safely. The hang-glider, however, broke its back. Its two wings folded up, clapped together with a crack like a pistol shot, and plummeted. The pilot had no time to throw his reserve parachute before he hit the ground. He died on impact. An extremely skilled and promising twenty-two year old Austrian pilot, dead. In an instant the pleasant chattery atmosphere in the crowd was replaced by a shocked silence. I came away thinking how suddenly and irrevocably everything can change in a moment, and of that young man's parents.

In early December *The Complete Rocking Horse Maker* arrived from the printer and was everything I'd hoped it would be. I relished knowing that the result justified the tremendous effort we'd put in. We had a stack of pre-publication orders to send out and sold a good many copies as Christmas presents. It was never going to be Harry Potter, but if it sold steadily over a period of years, gradually spreading the word about our craft, it would be a valuable part of the enterprise. Once we'd covered the cost of printing we'd be in profit for The Rocking Horse Shop. I never counted the cost of my own work.

After many months of frustrating delays with planning, actually building Rocking House proceeded quickly. Jane's brother Mark was a first class local builder so I hired him and thoroughly enjoyed working with him to resolve the multiple problems a new build inevitably throws up. As soon as he'd got the roof on and the windows in we fitted out one of the large ground floor rooms for use as my new carving studio. It was a lovely bright room, painted white, with lots of windows and lights.

Before the fire I'd started teaching carving courses in the old studio and was keen to resume in the new one. We built a couple of sturdy wooden workbenches, made some mallets and bought an array of new, high quality carving tools for the students to use.

Carving a three-dimensional horse's head from scratch was a big challenge for most of them but I enjoyed teaching and the students, who ranged from fifteen to ninety with an equally wide range of skill and experience, were always interesting and sometimes very funny.

One student, carving what would clearly be a very good head, complained that it wasn't turning out as he wanted. To encourage him I said that the first horse I carved was a little, shall we say, idiosyncratic, but I'd loved it because it was my baby. Then I saw it was really an ugly thing and I could do a whole lot better.

'I felt exactly the same way about my first wife!' the student commented.

Some students found the experience intense and tiring. Few were used to standing all day at a bench, concentrating hard and doing physical work. I tried to keep the atmosphere light and positive whilst ensuring nobody got left behind. I didn't want to do it for them but occasionally I'd suggest I might help one of the students along by carving a little for them. 'Would you?' they'd almost always say. 'Oh yes, please.'

The carving courses were always fully booked and I looked forward to them, although I was grateful not to have to teach full-time. The students, initially doubtful and uncertain, would invariably be pleased with what they produced, surprising and even delighting themselves. I always tried to make good on the promise I made in my little speech at the start of each course: 'I guarantee you'll go home with your heads held high.'

*The Complete Rocking Horse Maker* was followed by two small books: *The BTG Book of Rocking Horses* and *The BTG Book of Toys*, to celebrate the 50th anniversary of the founding of The British Toymakers Guild (I'd been honoured to be chairman for a couple of years). After that I stalled, unable to come up with any new rocking-horse-related idea that wasn't merely a minor variation on the theme or that hadn't been done already, either by me or somebody else.

I quoted for making and fitting a new handrail on a staircase to the crypt in one of London's famous Wren churches, but when I didn't get the job I was immensely relieved. I really didn't want to have to go to work two hundred miles away from my workshop, and decided not to pursue more architectural carving commissions. But it seemed fitting, as enterprising entrepreneurs, that our ambitions for The Rocking Horse Shop need not be entirely confined to rocking-horses. Jane and I talked often about how we might 'grow the business' (the current jargon). One way would be to take over another small firm operating in a related area of craft and merge it into The Rocking Horse Shop.

An opportunity to do precisely that arose when I heard that Craftwares was for sale because Ann, the owner, was looking to retire. I'd known Ann quite well for years having been a Craftwares customer, but recently, when she heard about my Sam, she'd confided that she too had a son who'd died. I hadn't known. It was strange. There'd been a time not so long ago when I knew hardly anyone who'd been divorced or lost a child. Now I was running into divorcees and bereaved parents at almost every turn.

Craftwares sold leather and leather accessories - buckles, rivets, thread, needles, punches and so on - to hobbyists and the trade, mostly by mail order. We were already selling leather fittings to our customers who wanted to make their own rocking-horse tack, so Craftwares would enable us to reach out to home leatherworkers, a potentially interesting new niche market. The price wasn't high and with a bit of shuffling we could make space for all Craftware's stock on the racks in our leather shop. It looked like Ann's business would dovetail neatly into ours. We signed a confidentiality agreement and she gave us several years' accounts. It appeared her company was sound and modestly profitable. So far so good. But she had one customer who bought more than all the others put together. Remembering my classic car man and his tale of reliance on one customer, this made me wary, especially when we discovered that this one made bondage equipment for sex shops.

I told Jane, 'I've been around but I have to say I've no experience of bondage and I've no idea what the demand might be. Ann reckons it's huge. This guy buys a lot of stuff from her and apparently he can't make it fast enough. We could sell to him but also make that sort of stuff ourselves with the skills and equipment we've got in our leather shop. Ann says the mark-up is massive and there are no returns, no complaints from dissatisfied customers. Too embarrassed, perhaps. This could be a great business opportunity for us. But the problem is, when we speak to customers what are we going to say? 'Good morning. This is The Rocking Horse Shop. Are you interested in a toy rocking-horse or a sex toy?'

Jane smiled, then became serious and said, 'It won't work, will it? The two things don't mix. We can't risk our good name.'

'No. You're right. Pity. It's got to be a no.'

Some years later the massive sales of *Fifty Shades of Grey* confirmed what a profitable business opportunity we'd missed. But so it goes. Our plans to expand the business stalled. My personal life was stalled too. But then a couple of things happened that made the future look brighter on both fronts.

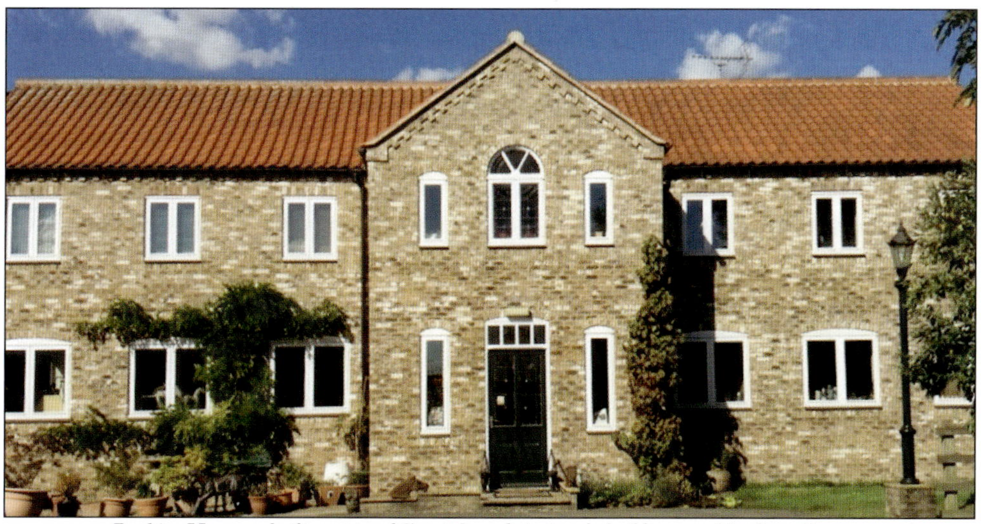

*Rocking House as built - not too different from designing & building a rocking-horse (in some ways).*

# Part Seven
## 27

*Only desire and luck will prevail in this world.*

It was seven years since we'd published Judy Fergusson's rocking-horse designs. Compared with traditional solid timber, laminated plywood construction was far cheaper and in many ways easier for home woodworkers, more accessible. Judy's designs had sold well at first but then sales gradually declined, as normally happens, and I'd accumulated quite a file of comments and criticisms from customers. Several mentioned that the components of Judy's horses slithered all over the place when they were trying to glue them together, making assembly difficult and messy. I had a solution to that problem as well as other ideas about how we might enhance and reinvigorate the designs.

The difficulty of handling large heavy sheets of plywood in our workshop meant we'd never done a timber pack for the laminated rocking-horses, but I'd met a brilliant wood technician named Mike Morton with a large CNC (computer numerically controlled) routing machine in his joinery workshop not far away.

Mike said, 'I can cut all the parts for your plywood rocking-horses in whatever quantities you want, with a higher level of accuracy than you'd ever get cutting and drilling them by hand, no problem.'

That sounded good to me. I wrote to Judy suggesting that if we made some modifications to her designs we could open them to a wider group of home woodworkers and re-launch them along-side precision-machined Timber Packs. Sales, and her royalty payments, were bound to leap up. I was taken aback when Judy replied sounding highly offended.

'Those plans are mine,' she wrote. 'I don't want you to go changing anything about them, not one thing.'

She wouldn't be persuaded so I decided that the only way forward was to work out a plywood design of my own, based on our best selling Medium traditional fully carved rocking-horse, which was quite different in appearance from Judy's. It wasn't easy to realise and I made more than half a dozen prototypes, working closely with Mike and his CNC machine, before we got it right.

A key element of the new design was that all the plywood parts had location holes and dowels so that every piece fitted exactly in the right position and stayed in place during assembly. These location dowels would radically simplify construction but would be inside the horse, so not visible. Also, Judy's plywood horses were very heavy so I made holes in some of the body pieces in mine to lighten them.

My Medium size rocking-horse was a little bigger than Judy's and the legs were longer, so I was able to do away with a rather odd-looking kink in the hoof rails which Judy's shorter-legged horse had necessitated. And I mounted the new rocking-horse on a solid timber stand (instead of Judy's plywood one) with attractive turned posts. The combination of plywood horse with its striking patterns of lamination-lines, and a varnished hardwood stand with turned posts, looked very appealing indeed.

One challenge I faced in preparing the new design - and a selling point deemed vital to its success - was to make it possible to cut all the parts of the horse from a single standard sized sheet of plywood. I spent hours on my knees shuffling my patterns around before arriving at a satisfactory solution to this jigsaw puzzle. Home woodworkers could buy a sheet of plywood, transfer the patterns onto it as explained in the instruction booklet, jig-saw out all the parts for the horse and drill the location holes themselves. Or, they could buy from us a complete set of components precision machined with all holes pre-drilled in exactly the right places and to the correct depths. I liked to be able to offer customers the choice since there are always those who like to do as much as they can themselves, but the Timber Pack certainly opened up the project to those for whom the preparation was a difficult and time-consuming preliminary and would be pleased to let us do it for them.

My original plans were done with pen and ink on paper on my drawing board. Mike scanned my plans and converted them into a computer programme linked to his routing machine, which rearranged the parts for cost-efficient cutting. We then ordered components from Mike, ten sets at a time, and all we had to do was pack them, add the instruction booklet and ship them out. The horse would be assembled and shaped by the home woodworker using hand-carving tools.

This proved to be a really fruitful and practical blending of modern high-technology with traditional hand-craft. It sat well with the general ethos of The Rocking Horse Shop where we used internet-based marketing, accounting, ordering and communication systems in the office, but basically 19th century technology in the workshop where traditional hand-skills were not only appropriate and highly satisfactory, but profitable too. The best of both worlds.

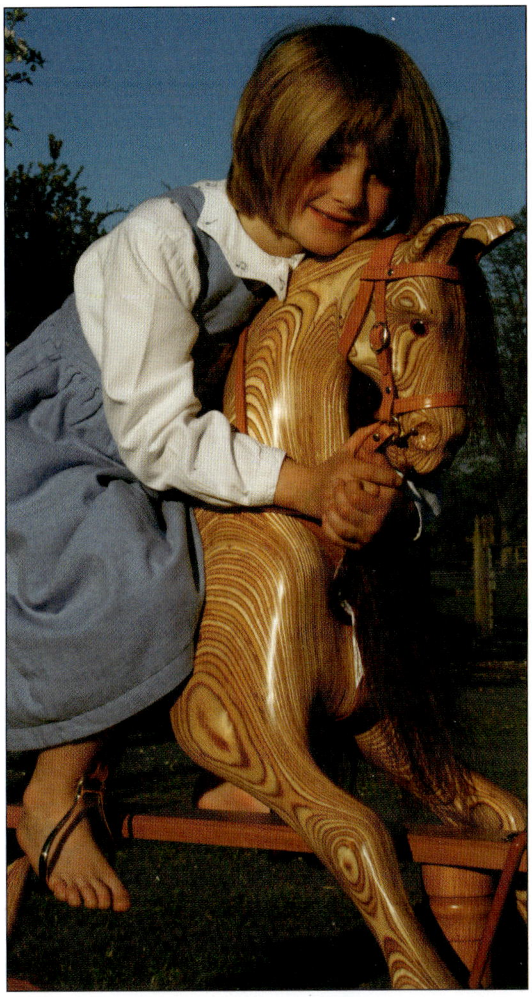

*One of the first plywood 'Rockys'.*

I'd never much cared for plywood and for a long time hung onto a purist's regard for 'proper' carving in solid timber. Now we used hand-held power-carving tools and sanders for shaping, but I found that birch plywood could be carved quite readily using the traditional mallet and gouge approach - much pleasanter than using noisy, dusty machines.

There was something very pleasing about the swirling pattern of glue-lines revealed as the carving progressed. This was a new and exciting take on a very traditional form and I was converted into an ardent fan of carved plywood. We named the new design 'Rocky' and he was an immediate hit. Not long after his launch Rocky shot to the number one slot in The Rocking Horse Shop's best-seller chart.

We regularly had visits from groups of school children, Yorkshire Countrywomen, Rotary Clubs and so on. One morning about a dozen women came. I gave them our usual guided tour, talked about the history of rocking-horses, how they were made and our own designs. I always hoped that among the group would be one or two who might be interested in buying or restoring a rocking-horse for their children or grandchildren, or if not that, making one. I finished the tour in the showroom where we gave them tea and biscuits while they admired the rocking-horses on display and we chatted. One of the group, a tall, good-looking woman in her fifties with an open, smiling face, told me she was an artist and would love to draw the rocking-horses.

'Come anytime,' I said.

A week later the woman - Shirley - showed up on her bicycle with a drawing pad in her saddle-bag and spent much of the day in the showroom sketching rocking-horses. Each time I passed we chatted. She told me she was a widow with two grown-up children and lived on her own in Pocklington, about five miles away. She came again, twice, and one evening I phoned her and asked if she'd like to come with me to see a movie. She said she'd let me know and hung up.

Half an hour later she called back and said yes, she'd like to come. In the meantime, she told me later, she'd phoned her daughter Andrea to tell her that the rocking-horse man had asked her out and she didn't know whether to go or not.

'Go, Mum,' Andrea told her. 'What's the harm? It's only a date. You're not going to marry the man.'

why it is, when so much is written about the doings of British monarchs, that their childhood, when the adult is formed, is given so little attention. It was remarkable that the rocking-horse had even survived. It was extremely battered and worn, with half its head and various other bits missing, and was surprisingly crudely constructed. But the pitted surface of the wood had a wonderful deep, dark patina caused by four hundred years of small bottoms polishing the seat, starting with Prince Charles no less, King James 1 of England's sickly heir to the British throne. What history!

'Such a shame he's been hidden away where nobody can see and appreciate him,' I said.

Bunny told me that his now very elderly owner wanted to sell. With Bunny acting as go-between there followed some interesting and intense negotiations. For a while I thought I might buy it but the asking price was astronomic. The Victoria and Albert Museum of Childhood in London wanted it but had no money (almost all their exhibits are donated). Then we heard that an Italian toy museum was about to buy it and was offering all the money. Everyone felt the rocking-horse really ought to stay in England but it looked like it might go to the highest bidder. Finally the V and A's Museum of Childhood found enough money through heritage and lottery funding and the rocking-horse went there.

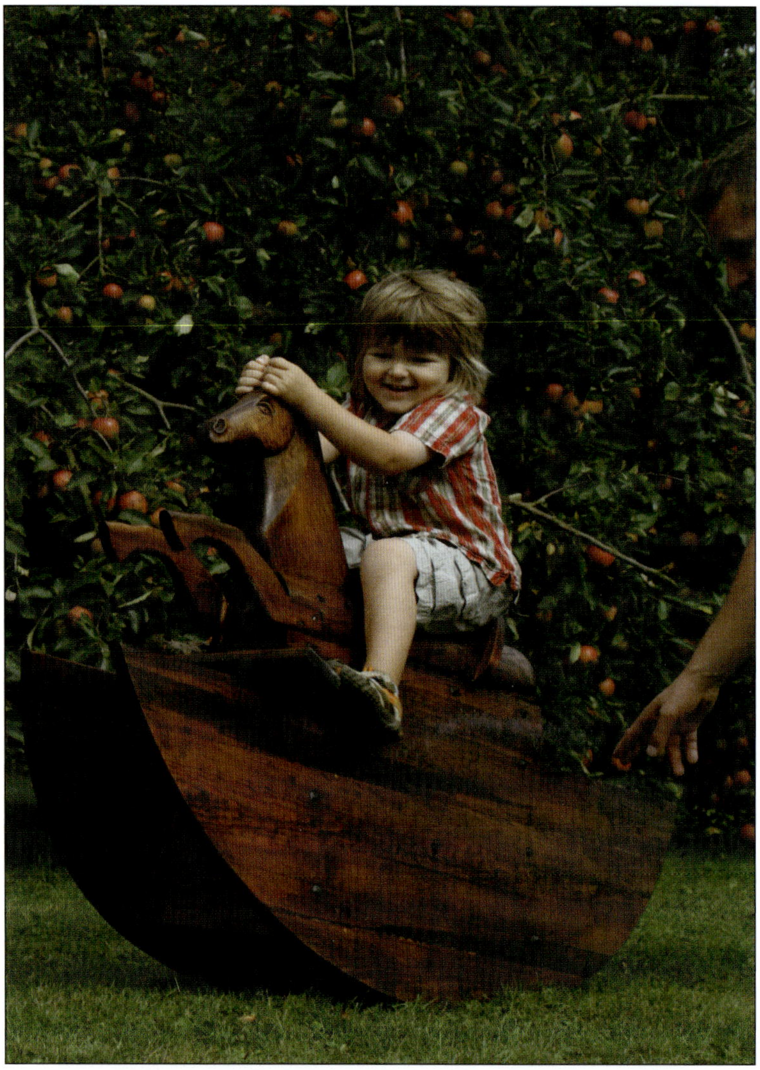

*AD's reproduction of the Prince Charles rocking-horse.*

It was the right place for it to be, and the museum's curator kindly allowed me to spend a day in the basement measuring, drawing and photographing the rocking-horse. I intended making as exact a copy as I could, using similar materials. I found some old pine for the rockers, head and other parts, and a piece of solid elm to turn for the body. I phoned my old friend the blacksmith Chris Topp, and asked him if he could forge me some early 17th Century nails.

'No problem,' he said.

The dimensions of the Prince Charles rocking-horse were all neat round numbers: 6 inch diameter body, 2 inch thick wood for the head and neck, 1 inch thick for the rest including the rockers, which had a radius of exactly 2 feet. I thought long and hard and made my best guess as to how the missing parts - legs, cantle and pommel, ears and half its head - would have been.

I felt an affinity with the original's maker and liked to think he might even have been an ancestor of mine. I imagined him thinking, 'I'll make a decent job of this but I won't waste a lot of time or good timber on a mere toy, even if it is for a prince.' The neck was morticed and pegged into the body but the rest of the parts were simply glued and nailed together. Forged tapered nails are highly effective for holding wooden pieces together and are quick and easy. The head showed evidence of some fairly detailed carving round the eyes which I tried to reproduce, and there were two odd triangular pieces that stuck up on the tops of the rockers which I puzzled over for ages before deciding they would likely have supported a simple footrest, laid across to project either side and nailed in place.

The original was very fragile and valuable, no chance of a child actually being allowed to ride it anymore. But the reproduction was as close as I could envisage to how it would have been when first made, and very sturdy. We borrowed the three-year-old son of one of Shirley's neighbours, a lad named Sam (another one) to see how it performed. The horse was very heavy but had a high centre of gravity and dynamic action, so young Sam rocked away no problem. He could easily have made it rock right over because here were no roundels on the rocker ends to stop it. I guessed that was something the maker of this first rocking-horse simply hadn't thought of, and reckoned that if it did go right over the legs and head would have been the first things to hit the ground so they must have broken very early on. Little Prince Charles wouldn't break his nose because there'd always be palace flunkies standing close by to catch him.

I liked it that we were part of a tradition stretching back four hundred years, one that (if the bureaucrats allow) will continue long after we have shuffled off. Getting as close as I had to the world's first rocking-horse confirmed a clear relationship with the past. With each generation of makers adding something of themselves to the theme, the craft and the tradition is kept alive. I loaned my reproduction to the Museum of Childhood and it went on show there for about nine months, in a glass case alongside the original. I'd have preferred it to have been ridden so that child visitors could imagine themselves as a young prince destined to be King of England, but Health and Safety considerations forbade. Nevertheless I was pleased and proud. Not many living toymakers get to have their work exhibited in London's Victoria & Albert Museum.

# 28

*Self pity is a corrupt version of honesty.*

I hated it when people said we were in the nostalgia business. I wasn't raking over the embers of some lost golden past. Rocking-horses may have been around a long time but I believed the craft, and my work at The Rocking Horse Shop, was vital and valuable now, and would continue to be into the future. That's what I told myself. But I was pushing sixty and slowing down. Who would carry the torch after me?

Even supposing one or both of my surviving children nursed a desire to one day take on The Rocking Horse Shop, because I knew how heavy the sacrifice would have to be, of their time, youth, energy and all other interests, never mind the emotional toll on their partners and children, in all love, humility and sincerity I'd advise them, don't. I still hoped the enterprise would survive and thrive though. I couldn't bear the thought it might simply end when I did.

I had planning approval for holiday accommodation upstairs at Rocking House, but I needed somewhere to live so as soon as it was habitable I moved in. If challenged by one of the council's officials I intended moving out into a tent in the garden and calling that my 'principal residence' for a few weeks, then moving back inside. Shirley and I were together but not living together. We went on dates, to art galleries, the movies and on holidays. Often, after dinner at my place or hers, we'd sit at the candlelit table drinking wine and talking long into the night before going up to bed. She had an endearing way of listening rapt to my stories of the sea and rocking-horses, sometimes shuffling her chair round to get closer so our legs and fingers intertwined. We were vastly different in so many respects, yet got on together remarkably well.

Shirley was an artist, a water-colourist; trees were her speciality. She'd always been interested in painting but only took it up seriously after her husband John died.

They were both Yorkshire people from Barnsley and had known each other since Shirley was four, married young and had two children, Andrea, and then a son, Steve. Andrea lived alone in York and she and Shirley were sometimes taken for sisters, which pleased Shirley immensely, if not Andrea. Steve lived in Sweden with his Swedish wife and two daughters in their early teens. Shirley and her husband had lived in Devon for many years but after John's cancer diagnosis he said it was his wish to die in Yorkshire. Shirley wouldn't live in Barnsley again so they drove round the county until they found a house she liked and which they could afford, in Pocklington (about five miles from The Rocking Horse Shop). They didn't know anybody in the area but bought the house anyway.

After John died (on New Year's Eve, same date as my Sam) Shirley was on her own with no friends nearby. She might have become a lonely old widow but instead started joining things, going out and meeting people: art classes (she soon ran one), a ramblers group and volunteer helper at the local Arts Centre. She also had a part-time job in a high-class gift shop and seemed to take most of her pay in designer wineglasses and lamps for her home. Several men were after her and she'd had a few propositions, one of them quite wealthy apparently. I liked Shirley being around and she was happy to join in with whatever I happened to be doing. Gradually she became an indispensible part of my landscape.

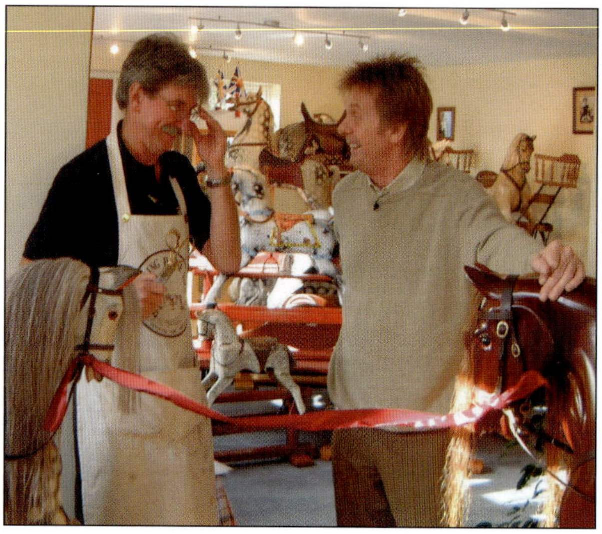

*Rock & roll musician & rocking-horse maker Joe Brown cut a ribbon to open our new showroom. The press headline was, 'Meeting of old Rockers'.*

The Rocking Horse Shop business having contracted somewhat, we no longer needed all the space we had. After we openeed our rocking-horse museum and new showroom in Rocking House the building up the yard was left empty so I changed its name to Infoss House and advertised it to let. Shirley used the space upstairs as a studio and it looked as if a specialist upholstery company might take on the ground floor and use it as workshop and showroom, which would have been ideal, but that fell through. It wasn't satisfactory having The Rocking Horse Shop's showroom and offices in Rocking House right at the end of the yard, so I moved them back to the the ground floor of Infoss House and applied for planning permission to convert the rest of the building into two apartments. This would benefit The Rocking Horse Shop in that the shop would be more visible and accessible for customers again and, looking to the future, the rent from the flats would provide me with a pension.

As usual, planning officers opposed my application and I fought them. There were many months of delay and I became thoroughly depressed. I calculated that more than a fifth of the thirty-five years I'd been in business - over seven years - had been wasted battling planning officers and awaiting their arbitrary decisions. They hadn't defeated me but they'd sapped my energy and helped create a bitter and obstinate old man. I wrote angry letters to various heads of department saying I didn't think they'd be content until they'd driven me to suicide. Who in their right mind would try to run a creative manufacturing business in this fucking country? I even started a hit list with the name of East Riding's Head of Planning at the top. I imagined mounting his severed head on a spike on top of Beverly Bar Without as a warning to other officious bureaucrats. I was a toymaker who spent his days creating beautiful artefacts and purveying innocent pleasures. Yet I dreamed of murder.

When Jane and her husband bought Manor House Farm from me we talked of it as part of a process that could eventually lead, in the absence of any other successor, to her taking over The Rocking Horse Shop altogether. In business you cannot stay still, you're either forging ahead or dying. I wanted to never stop making things but felt increasingly drained by the endless hassles running the business involved. Once upon a time I'd confronted every challenge with energy but I was wearing out. I longed for a life in which I could be the calm, creative person I'd always wanted to be.

I convinced myself that selling up wouldn't be selling out, it would ensure The Rocking Horse Shop's survival into the future. I'd step away whilst still helping and advising, I'd draw up new designs from time to time and keep an active interest in the enterprise which was, after all, my baby. I still had a head full of ideas and a wealth of experience. For her part Jane was extremely enthusiastic about taking over The Rocking Horse Shop which, she said repeatedly, she loved. Almost as much as I did, it seemed.

I said, 'I hope you understand, Jane, how exceptional this enterprise is. We're small enough to retain an intimate and caring relationship with our customers and all our staff. And with all the materials we use - no rainforest timber, no unnecessary waste, all that. To employ modern technology as we do is fine, because the speed and efficiency of communication and the opportunities it throws our way are to be welcomed. But to be able - at the sharp end - to physically and with our own hands make something beautiful and worthwhile, to be able to look after the processes involved from raw material through to end product, from first contact to end user, that's something really special for everyone involved. To be able to do all that, and be completely free of debt, and make a good living, that is so remarkable it's almost unique. There's a rare level of satisfaction here, and spiritual fulfilment too, I believe. We can truly say we are the standard-bearers for a sustainable 21st Century way of being…' And so on.

I enjoyed sounding off in this fashion, with Jane apparently entranced by my message and approving it. But all talk of her taking over came to an abrupt halt when she was diagnosed with breast cancer and started the long grim process of treatment, including surgery. She was clearly terrified. Her husband bore the brunt of her private distress but in public she kept smiling, for the most part, putting on the brave face.

Jane had some very bad days but carried on managing The Rocking Horse Shop as best she could. She said the work helped her take her mind off her body. For almost three years nothing was said about her taking over but at last she started to get better. When she was functioning again, almost as well as before, I asked her if buying me out was something she still thought about. I told her I'd understand if given what had happened she wanted to drop the whole idea, but I would like to know.

'Oh yes,' she burst out. 'It's what we've always wanted and still do, very much. I've got the all clear now, we can go ahead.'

We consulted our accountants and lawyers and Jane and her husband bought a majority shareholding. I no longer had control of The Rocking Horse Shop but retained a strong connection with it and hoped my influence and experience would continue to be valued. I imagined myself becoming a grand old man of British rocking-horse making, referred to with respect, perhaps even some affection, as a key figure in the revival of a wonderful traditional craft. After thirty-five years, half a lifetime, I could relax. I hoped.

In September 2006 Shirley came with me to the annual show at Westonbirt and helped sell our rocking-horses and plans and books on a stand in the BTG marquee. A few years back there'd been half a dozen rocking-horse makers at a BTG show but now there was only us. We were next to Monica of MonToys, one of the BTG's stalwarts, an elderly widow and maker of furry glove puppets. Monica stood in front of her display with a squirrel on her hand which talked to passing children and leapt at them. Naturally the kids wanted to stroke the cute little animals but Monica refused to let them.

'Look with your eyes, NOT your hands,' she shouted stridently, and to the parents, 'Kindly tell your child to do as it's told.' Children leapt away from her, some even started to cry.

Monica was oblivious to the offence she caused,

remaining delightfully true to her old-school ways, and she kept us laughing all weekend. The toymakers weren't all as extraordinary as Monica but they were all characters, lovely people with wonderfully imaginative creations and I'd always enjoyed being around them. I daresay Shirley being with me caused some twittering: the year but one before I'd been at the show with my girlfriend Janet, the previous year with ex-wife Pat, and now here I was with new girlfriend, Shirley. They probably thought me a regular Lothario. Or serially indecisive.

Shirley was a good companion, as happy to paint a wall as a picture and she helped me with the conversion of Infoss House. We were both workers but made a conscious decision not to work all the time, as I'd done for so many years. We took time out to go on dates and long walks, enjoy leisurely meals together and so on. By this time Shirley was with me almost every day and night but she kept her own house and wouldn't move in with me. We were heading towards decision time: all or nothing. Shirley said if she married again it would be forever. I was frightened marriage might turn out to be a bad decision. She said if we married she'd never leave me. I didn't want to commit to marriage but at the same time it was increasingly hard to imagine life without her.

Sometime in 2007 Young Sam (Old Sam's assistant in the woodwork shop) left. He was having trouble with his back and the job, which involved man-handling heavy boards off the timber delivery lorries onto the racks and then to our machines, was getting to be too much for him. He'd been working well, I liked him and was sorry to see him go, but we did need somebody who was physically capable. They should also be bright enough to learn and understand everything that went into our rocking-horse Timber Packs. It wasn't rocket science but there was a lot to it.

From time to time a large and shambling young man with red hair and a puffy face had come round asking questions about our rocking-horses and did we have any work he could do? He lived locally and said he'd worked with wood before. I hadn't taken to him and had put him off. Now, with Young Sam leaving, Jane and I agreed we'd give him a try-out. He was certainly very keen, arrived early each morning, worked hard and asked questions all the time. He was a bit slapdash in his work but I thought that with training he'd become a decent enough woodworker, if not a crafts-man. After a three month trial we confirmed his appointment, he became a regular member of the team and I trusted him with a key so he could let himself into the workshop in the morning. His name was Rob, a highly appropriate name, as it turned out.

Rob had been with us about a year and Shirley and I were out one Sunday evening when Jane phoned in a panic. I knew she'd had suspicions about Rob and had been checking up on him.

'I've found his website,' she said. 'It says they make new rocking-horses, restore old ones, and - wait for it - do plans and accessories so you can make a rocking-horse of your own.'

'They're copying us.'

'Yes. They've got a mail order service and everything. They're only a couple of miles away and they're bound to damage our business. I can't believe Rob could be so two-faced.'

'No. Right. I'm on my way home.'

The next morning as he parked his car in the yard I met Rob and told him to come to Jane's kitchen. He followed me in, slowly.

'Sit down,' I said. He sat hunched, looking up at us with a sheepish stare and his mouth hanging open.

I said, 'Your game's over Rob. I thought you were asking all those questions because you were keen, interested in your work here. But all you were doing was stealing our ideas so you could set up in competition. You've been ripping us off.'

'I'm not..'

'Yes you are, you miserable little shit. You got my workshop key?'

'Yes.'

'Give it me.'

He fumbled in his pocket, handed it over.

'You're fired. Right, let's go. I want you off these premises now.'

I kept close behind him, propelling him across the yard towards his car with a hand in the small of his back, my mouth close to his ear, talking into it, telling him exactly what I thought of him. I opened the door of his car, pushed him in and slammed it shut, watched while he fumbled his keys into the ignition and started the engine. His eyes were fixed ahead and he never once looked at me as I walked alongside, staring at him until the car pulled away and disappeared down the road. I walked back to the house where Jane was standing at the kitchen window looking out, her hands gripping the rim of the sink.

She said, 'I thought rocking-horse people were all nice.'

'Yeah, well he's one of the exceptions,' I said. I was shaking too. 'He might steal a few of our customers but don't worry about him, Jane. It won't be long before he fails.' Which it wasn't.

I came home late one evening from a writing group I'd joined and said to Shirley, 'You know Mary Ann, the poet, how adventurous she is? She's going on a trip to Angel Falls, Venezuela. A 12-day trek through the forest. She's booked already. Sounds good to me. I could go, she says. I'd love to see those falls. One of the wonders of the world.'

'Really?' Shirley said. I knew what she was thinking: is this him dumping me to go with that other woman? 'And are you going to go?'

'I'd like to,' I said. 'But I'm hesitating. Bound to be hard. Lots of younger, fitter ones. I don't want to be the old guy trailing along at the back. And then again, I'm thinking, if ever I go to that part of the world again, the place I'd really love to go is Easter Island. You know I've read just about everything that's ever been written about that island. Carving huge stone heads with harder stone, all that. I'd love to see them, stay on the island a week or so, then on to New Zealand, stay with my old friends Alan and Lynne on Waiheke Island. Haven't seen them for years but we're sure to get a good welcome. Make it a round-the-world trip. Stop off at a few other places on the way maybe. So anyway, I'm wondering if you might fancy coming along. And when we get to New Zealand, if we're still on speaking terms that is, maybe we can find a little church and get married. Would you like that?'

She looked at me for quite a long time and said, 'Is that a proposal?'

I smiled at her, 'Well yes. I suppose it is. Yes.'

'Yes.'

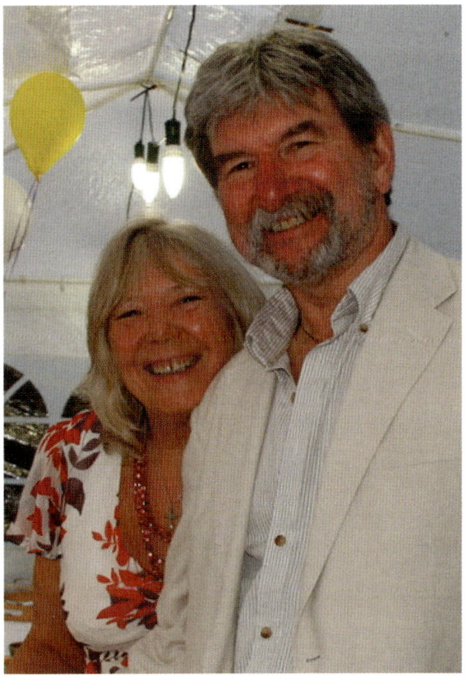

# 29

*If you can't stand the heat.*

Surprisingly, Shirley loved Easter Island as much as I did, and we had some marvellous adventures before starting our married life together, in a tiny church on Waiheke Island. A beautiful Samoan lady vicar presided, who looked to us to be about twelve years old. Alan and Lynne and their daughter Hannah and her daughter were the only other people there. It was all just lovely.

Back in Fangfoss Shirley and I got on with sorting out Rocking House and preparing the apartments over The Rocking Horse Shop's showroom ready for the first tenants to move in. Jane appeared to have settled into running the show without me. I felt put out.

'It's understandable she should want to do it her way,' Shirley said.

As well as running the business while we'd been away Jane had looked after Psips the cat. She (the cat) was the last descendant of the yard cats Pat and I had inherited when we bought the farm in Fangfoss. Underneath her long black fluffy fur Psips was a skinny little thing, almost feral and quite savage. If anyone tried to stroke her, even me she'd known and been fed by all her life, she'd lash out with her sharp claws. She caught mice, rats and baby rabbits, often leaving the half-eaten corpses on the doorstep. She never came in the house but every morning I put food for her in a bowl outside our door. That's what Jane had been doing while we'd been away, only outside her door.

I said, 'There's no need for you to keep putting food out for Psips, Jane, now we're back.'

'I don't mind.'

'I know, and it's been good of you to feed her, but you don't need to now.'

'But she's got used to coming to me.'

'I know, but if you stop feeding her she'll come to me again.'

'But she'll come crying at my door.'

'She will, but she'll soon learn to come crying at my door if she wants her food.'

'But she likes coming to me.'

'She likes it where her food is.'

'I don't mind, really.'

'I know you don't mind, but she's my cat, I should feed her.'

'But I like feeding her.'

I said to Shirley, 'She's got my house. She's got The Rocking Horse Shop. Now she wants my fucking cat as well.'

Shirley said, 'She's only trying to be helpful.'

There was still plenty of work for me to do on Rocking House and I went paragliding at every opportunity. I filled my days with other stuff because there was nothing for me at The Rocking Horse Shop anymore. If I asked Jane if I could help with anything she said no. If I went in when I knew they'd be having a meeting and all the staff were there, Julie would give me a mug of coffee but I felt awkward, unnecessary. I'd wanted to step back but I hadn't expected to be so deliberately excluded or to feel quite so bereft. I was still a Director but everything had changed, even in the yard.

I said, 'Jane, I notice you've closed all the stable doors.'

'Yes, I have.'

'But the swallows can't get to their nests.'

'I know, I can't stand them flitting past my head.'

'But those little birds fly all the way here from Africa each spring. They come back to the same nests every year. You can see them out there now, flying up and down the yard, fluttering helplessly at the closed doors. They can't get in.'

She said, with a couldn't-care-less wave of her hand, 'I know. But never mind. They'll find somewhere else.'

I'd always welcomed the swallows' annual reappearance in the yard after their incredible journey and didn't know how to react. I didn't own the yard anymore and things were bound to change. I had to change too. I turned a blind eye, or tried to. People still called me the rocking-horse man but I told them, 'I've finished with rocking-horses, now. I'm just the gnome at the end of the garden.'

It would have been easier if I hadn't had to go through Rocking Horse Yard to get to our house. It probably would have been easier for Jane too, to be free of my brooding critical presence. Apparently, since I'd told her about my earlier intention to sell up and go to New Zealand, she'd thought Shirley and I would move away once we were married. We had thought about it, but decided to stay. Rocking House was still little more than the shell of a building but it had potential and Shirley set about making it our home. I got on with life without rocking-horses. Almost.

One morning in December Jane showed me an email she'd received from someone named Marcia Farquhar, a conceptual artist who wanted a rocking-horse for a work she'd been commissioned to produce. Marcia was coming by train from London to see what we could make for her and Jane asked me if I'd meet the lady with her. The Met Office was forecasting freezing temperatures, high winds and snow on the day Marcia was due but she came anyway, accompanied by a short man she introduced as her producer, Mole. They arrived at York Station in a blizzard and had a hard time persuading a cab driver to bring them out to Fangfoss. It was a white-out when the taxi drove into Rocking Horse Yard, the snow driving horizontally, ankle-deep already and heaping against walls and doors. The driver was afraid he'd get stuck out in the sticks and said he'd give them just twenty minutes then he was heading back to York. Marcia, a middle-aged woman in a long coat and longer boa wrapped round her neck, made a spectacular entrance in a mad flurry of snow-flakes, followed by a scampering Mole.

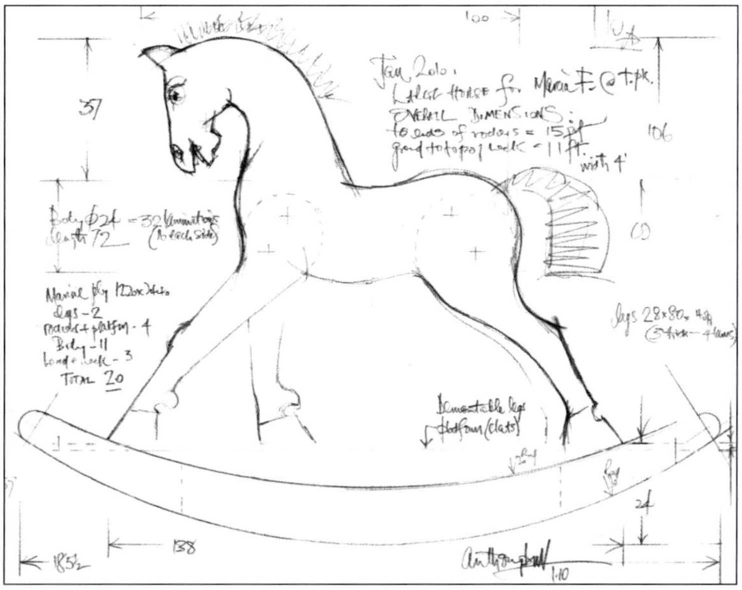

We gave them a quick-fire guided tour of the showroom, workshop and museum. On the way round Marcia told us her proposed artwork consisted of a monologue she intended to perform whilst sitting astride a big rocking-horse. It would be entitled The Horse is a Noble Animal, a phrase coined by her now elderly and much-loved mother. Marcia had been inspired, she said, by a rocking-horse she'd seen which was mounted on bows and white, which they thought would be a good colour.

'Or black,' Mole interjected.

'And big,' Marcia said.

'And masculine,' Mole added.

We showed them the hundred or so rocking-horses we had on the premises, of almost every type, size and style, but clearly none of them was what she was looking for.

'Can you give me some more clues, Marcia,' I said. 'I'm sure we can make the rocking-horse you have in mind, but I can't quite understand what that is. I mean, what about this one?'

We were standing beside one of my Extra Large Specials, the largest I'd made thus far.

'Oh I like it,' she said. 'But it's not, I mean, how shall I say, I was thinking, you know, bigger.'

'Bigger?' I said.

I looked out of the window across the yard to the stable where Bertie was standing with his head and neck hanging over the stable door, being snowed on. Bertie was a seventeen-hands high bay stallion owned by a woman in the village and he'd been with us on livery for some years. With all the wooden horses it was good to have a real one on the premises, and Bertie was an extremely handsome animal. He was my model: whenever I needed to remind myself what a horse was really like, I'd go and look at Bertie.

'Do you mean bigger like Bertie over there?'

'Yes, yes,' Marcia said, suddenly enthused. 'As big as him. Or bigger!'

At that moment the cab driver barged in to announce, 'I'm off back to York. You've gotta come now.'

We shook hands all round and watched the taxi disappear into the blizzard.

Jane said, 'So, she wants a masculine rocking-horse, coloured black or white, on bow rockers and bigger than Bertie. Hmm.'

My mind was whirring. I thought I'd done about all there was to do with rocking-horses but I'd never considered making a seriously huge one. I could already visualise it. I went into my office, made a sketch and emailed it to Marcia, telling her it would scale up to around 11 feet 6 inches high, 16 feet long. I was all fired up with enthusiasm and told her I could make the giant rocking-horse for her in short order, in time for her art exhibition, and inside her tight budget.

Straightaway she replied, 'Beautiful'!

I taped lining paper all over the biggest blank wall in Rocking House and enlarged my sketch to full size. Jane ordered thirty sheets of marine plywood and a couple of dozen tubes of glue. I made patterns, cut out the parts and did the initial assembly and carving in my studio, starting with the head and neck. Once carved it was so heavy I had to get help to lift it onto a sack barrow to wheel it across to The Rocking Horse Shop's main workshop where we'd been preparing the body and legs.

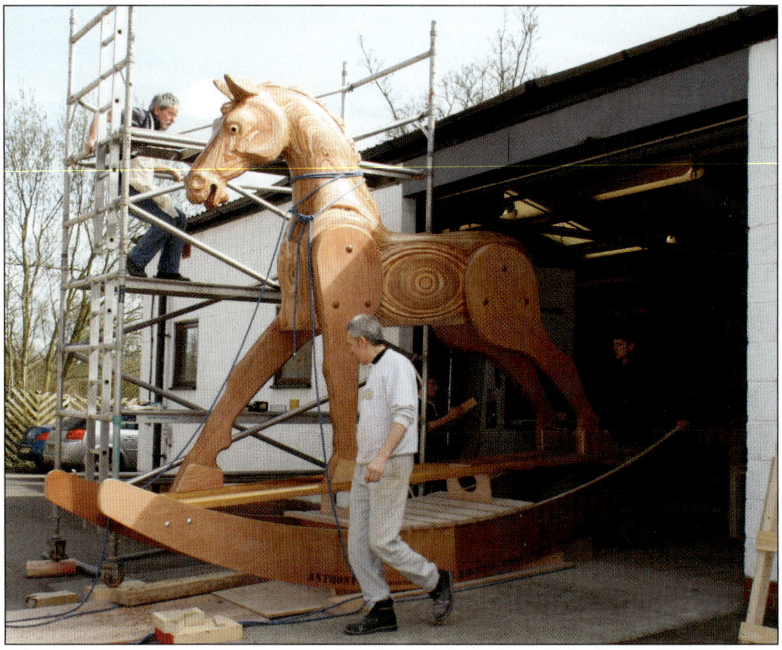

At this time Sam Glass had given up being a jobbing rocking-horse maker and come back to work full-time at The Rocking Horse Shop. We were also employing a highly competent time-served joiner named John, so I had skilled help on hand to assist with making Big Bertie, as we nick-named the giant rocking-horse. The body was basically a big plywood box, hollow for lightness, but when the head and neck was fixed on the three of us together couldn't lift it. We attached pulleys with ropes to the workshop roof-beams and when we were ready I asked everyone from the leather shop and office to come and help.

I said, 'When I give the word haul on these ropes and if he looks like he's tilting, hang on tight. We mustn't let him fall over.'

Slowly we hauled the huge head and body up towards the roof until it was high enough to bolt on the massive legs, each one taller than a man. I was in a sweat that the weight of Big Bertie would pull the roof down, or he'd fall over and squash someone, but up he went and on went the legs, lovely. The hooves were then bolted onto long rails running front to back. He wasn't even on his rockers yet but looked enormous. I was terrified he'd be too tall to go out through the door and I'd have to chop off the top of his head, or his legs. But when I measured the doorway it was 9 feet 6 inches high, giving a ¼ inch clearance above the top of his ears. I was so relieved I strutted round the workshop crowing, 'Well now, what great planning, eh?'

We varnished Big Bertie out in the yard and mounted him on his sixteen-foot long rockers. I bagged first go and shinned up a ladder to get onto his back. When the ladder was taken away and I was left sitting up there, suddenly I knew, for real, exactly how it is for a one-year-old child when they're plonked on the back of a big rocking-horse. You're very vulnerable, the horse feels dreadfully unsteady under you and won't stop moving, there's nothing much to hang onto and it's an awfully long way down if you fall. I leaned forward and Big Bertie tilted forward. I leaned back and back he went. I went faster. Big Bertie was so beautifully balanced I could make him rock as slowly or quickly as I wanted. Wheeeee! Exhilarating or what!

When I'd had my fill of rocking I climbed down and several of the others rushed to have a go. The press arrived and lots of photos were taken. Big Bertie brought us great publicity. When we delivered him to Marcia, his new owner, rolling along the motorway with a giant rocking-horse on a trailer and our shop's van with a yellow light flashing on the roof, rubberneckers leaned out of their car windows with their cameras, smiling and waving. Big Bertie appeared on TV news and in several national newspapers. Some of the pictures showed Marcia Farquhar sitting on his back wearing a green mackintosh, her arms up-stretched, declaiming 'The Horse is a Noble Animal'. Daughter Kate phoned to say she was on the Tube on her way to work in London one morning when she noticed that every person in her carriage was looking at a half-page colour photo of Big Bertie in the morning paper. She said she felt so proud she wanted to leap up and shout, 'Hey everybody, my Dad made that!'

For several months Big Bertie had been a big presence in our lives and everyone at The Rocking Horse Shop, including Jane, was sad to see him go.

'Let's make another one then,' I said. 'Better than Big Bertie and much, much bigger: A Bigger Bertie!'

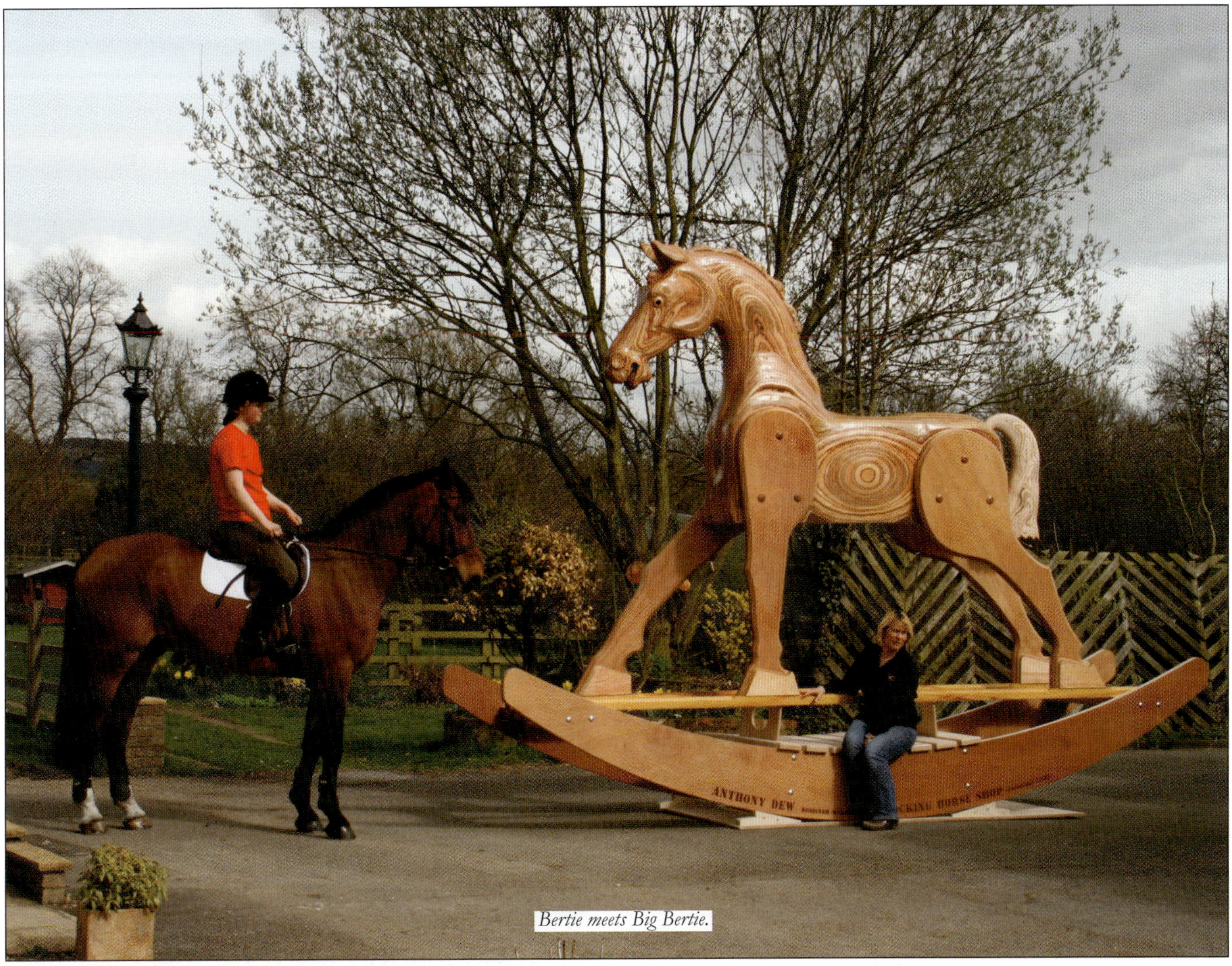

*Bertie meets Big Bertie.*

Size was everything with Bigger Bertie, which magnified the difficulty of every aspect of making him. For a start I didn't have a wall big enough to draw him full size. Every part was huge and heavy and we weren't geared up for it. John, the joiner who'd been so helpful when I'd made Big Bertie, had left. Sam Glass was still with us but he and the other staff were extremely busy with their everyday rocking-horse work and Jane said she could hardly spare them to help me. We'd been paid to make Big Bertie whereas Bigger Bertie would cost far more to build but with no promise of a return, a source of great anxiety for Jane. I maintained that the value of Bigger Bertie to The Rocking Horse Shop would be in all the great publicity he'd bring us. Jane didn't think so, didn't think he was worth it, and as the cost and arguments escalated she became increasingly unhappy with the project.

We couldn't build Bigger Bertie in the main workshop, we'd never have got him out. So most of the construction was done in the yard outside in a marquee The Rocking Horse Shop owned (bought to use at Fangfest). One afternoon I was away somewhere when a mighty gale blew up. I got back to Rocking Horse Yard to find the wind had ripped the marquee's guy-ropes out of the ground and Jane and the rest of the staff were in the pouring rain desperately hanging onto the huge white billowing canvas tent trying to stop it blowing away completely. We got it under control eventually but the marquee was badly ripped and Bigger Bertie got soaked.

Big Bertie had been a joy to design and build, exciting and fun for everyone involved. Bigger Bertie became a nightmare. He exhausted me, but if I left him for a day or two for a break he'd languish in the rain and deteriorate, or be altered. I kept going with him through sheer bloody-mindedness as he took forever to build and threatened to break The Rocking Horse Shop and us, both financially and emotionally.

Jane kept saying, 'Let's cut our losses and quit.'

I kept repeating, 'We have to finish him, we must. We can't quit now.'

Bigger Bertie didn't care.

Daughter Kate was working for the organisers of WorldSkills 2011 and through her we got a stand at the show. A huge exhibition, WorldSkills would be showcasing a wide array of trade and construction skills, with teams of students from dozens of countries coming to compete. It was to be held in London's ExCel Centre, tens of thousands of visitors were expected to attend and there would be extensive media coverage. A marvellous opportunity, I thought, to show off The Rocking Horse Shop to the world, and Bigger Bertie, even though he'd be unfinished.

Jane's brother Mark brought his big telescopic fork truck to lift the body, at this stage a rec-tangular hollow box, so we could bolt on the legs. He then lifted on the head and neck which I'd hand-carved in the studio, and then the whole lot onto the rockers, 28 feet (8.5m) long with massive turned end-pieces. The assembly and carving had to take place outside in the open air. I desperately wanted Bigger Bertie to be nearly, if not completely finished for WorldSkills, but despite rigging up

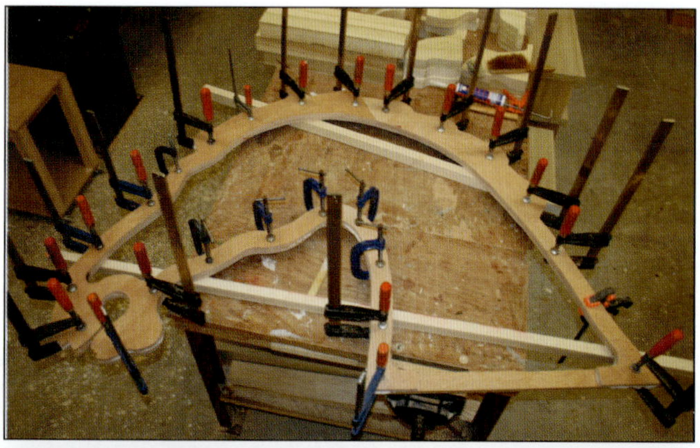

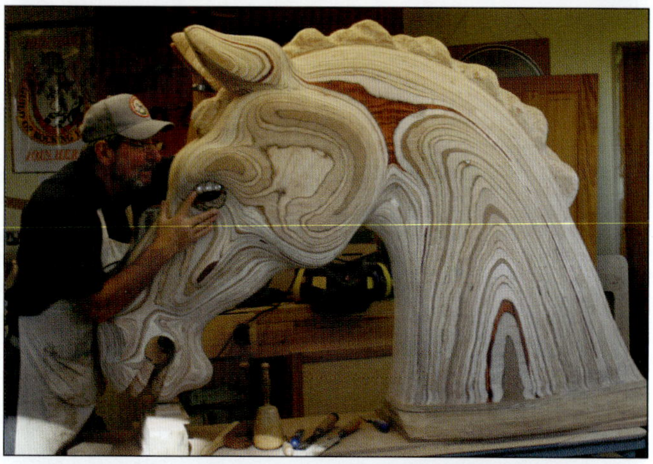

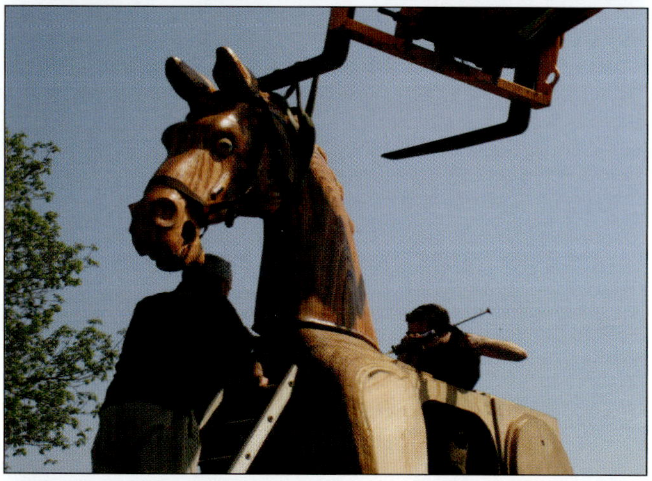

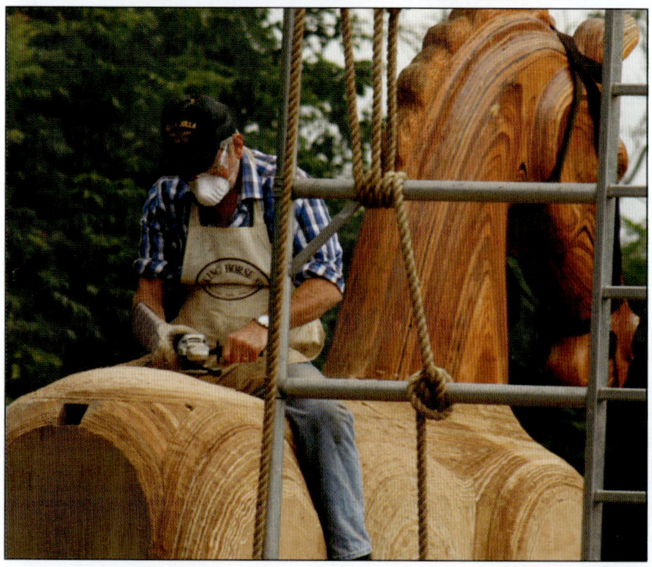

floodlights and working late every night, he wasn't anything like as far on as I'd hoped. I did give him a brain. There was room enough for me to climb inside his body and shuffle along to hang the tiny brain by a wire in his head. It was a shrivelled black walnut the size of a pullet egg. I reckoned even though Bigger Bertie was enormous his brain would be tiny. He never forgave me that insult.

I bought a low-load trailer to transport him, which doubled as his stage. Several of us climbed the ladder to have a go and in spite of his more than a ton and a half weight, Bigger Bertie rocked. I ordered some long banners to attach to the trailer and display on the stand at WorldSkills, with 'Bigger Bertie Rocks!' in great big letters. For transporting him and static display we bolted a pair of horizontal skids to the rockers, and with a few lengths of scaffold pole acting as rollers under these skids, he was surprisingly easy to move, at least on the flat. Rolling him up the ramp onto the trailer was more of a struggle, with Bigger Bertie complaining and creaking all the way before we got him positioned. Although his rockers were wide he was quite narrow and I worried about the stresses on his joints when we bumped along the road to London.

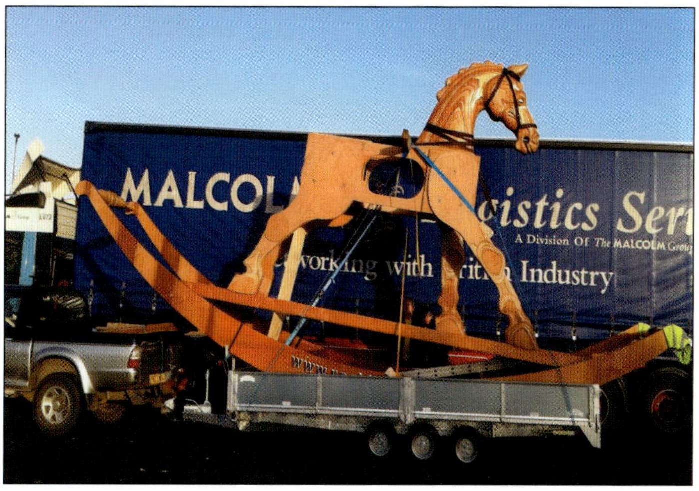


I intended spending the day before we set off for the exhibition doing last-minute carving and lashing Bigger Bertie securely to the trailer. But two TV crews came and, too good an opportunity to miss, we wound up posing for the cameras all day and it was evening before we got the lashings on. We had miles of rope and I'd borrowed webbing straps. Mark and I went for a test run and although Bigger Bertie swayed about alarmingly he was as secure as we could get him and I just hoped he'd survive the journey. We borrowed Mark's powerful black pick-up truck to tow Bigger Bertie to London on the trailer, escorted by The Rocking Horse Shop's maroon van with the yellow flashing light on the roof. I hardly slept. We met in the dark yard soon after five in the morning and were away by six. There were four of us: Jane, Helen (a work experience girl who'd help on the stand), Sam Glass and myself.

Overhanging branches brushed Bigger Bertie's face and we took it slowly and carefully along the potholed country roads to the motorway. On his trailer Bigger Bertie stood 4.85 metres high and motorway bridges are 5.1 metres. With barely a handspan to spare we drove slowly and with great trepidation under the first bridge. Then speeded up, had to. I was terrified we'd be late for our timed set-up slot at the ExCel Centre. I was also afraid that Bigger Bertie would shake himself to pieces en route (although it wasn't him cracking up as it turned out, it was me). Nevertheless we made good time until a police car flashed at us and hauled us over. A protracted argument ensued over the alleged legally permitted weight of our trailer.

The police also condemned a tyre on the borrowed tow vehicle and we had to drive off in search of a tyre company. It was hours before the tyre was replaced and the police let us go with an official caution. It still looked like we might make it but a hundred miles down the road the tow vehicle's engine started blowing smoke and died. Tempers flared, boiled over. We were at Watford Gap, seventy miles from our destination, and we'd definitely miss our slot. The four of us were stranded with a small van, a broken pick-up truck and a half-finished monster rocking-horse.

Jane phoned the RAC's breakdown service and a young man came to tow the pick-up back to Yorkshire. He stared up at Bigger Bertie and said, 'Bloody hell. What the eff is that!'

Miraculously, Jane found a local man named Ross Marshall with a tow-truck who cheerfully agreed to

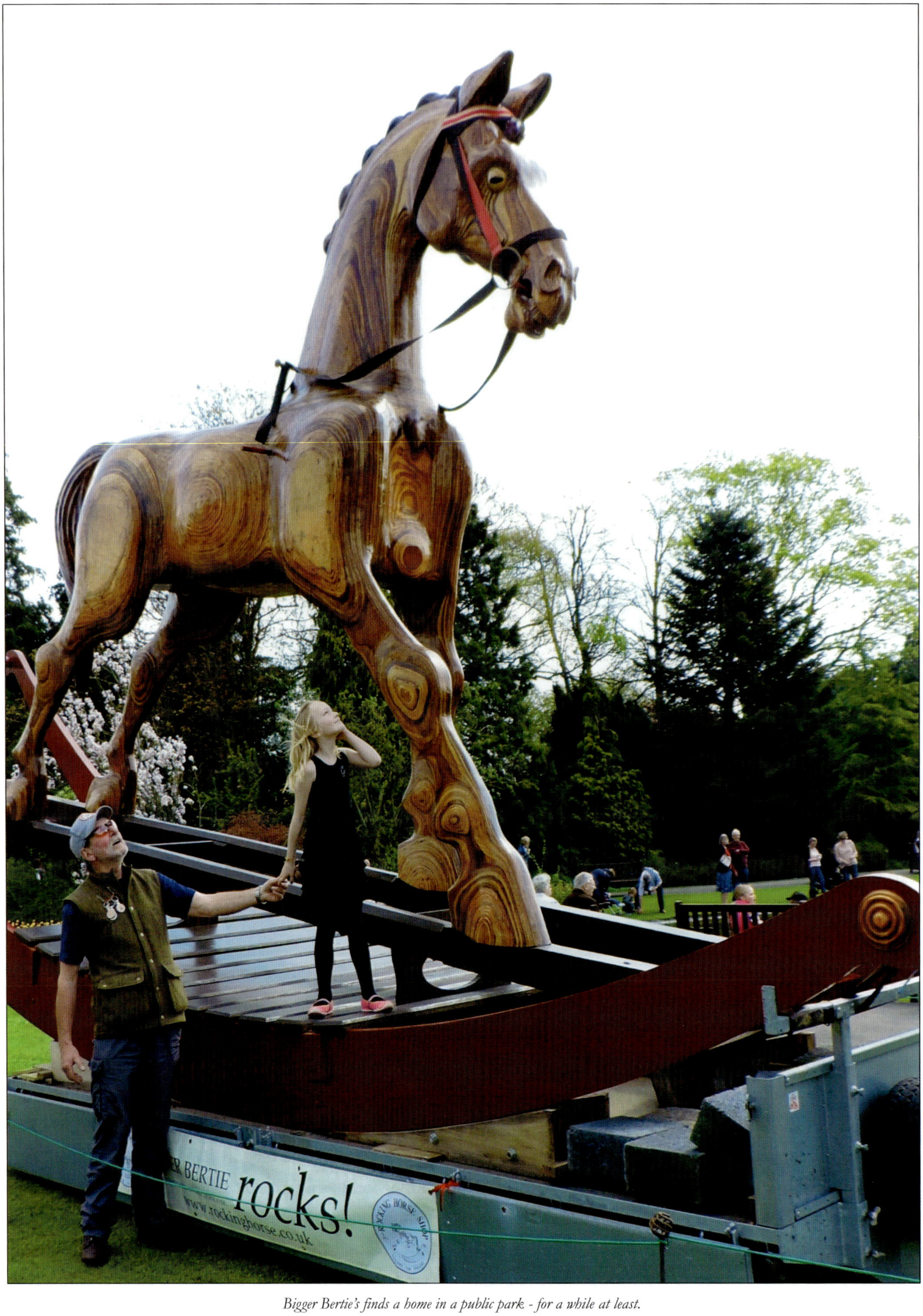


*Bigger Bertie's finds a home in a public park - for a while at least.*

tisement for The Rocking Horse Shop. It wasn't to be.

Any residual enthusiasm Jane may have had for Bigger Bertie had drained away completely during our nightmare journey to London. She said she regretted not over-ruling me and cancelling the whole project months ago. When Christies auction house in London, held a sale of 'Out of the Ordinary' items, she sent Bigger Bertie, hoping to recoup at least some of his cost. He'd be gone from the yard and she could forget about him. He failed to make his reserve.

For the second time Bigger Bertie returned from London and stood idle in the yard outside Rocking House, his great glass eye peering accusingly into Shirley's and my bedroom window. Shirley said it felt like he was watching her undress. The next I heard Jane sold him to a successful local business couple she'd befriended. Arrangements were being made for him to go on permanent display in the municipal park in Pocklington, home to the national collection of water lilies. It was a shame he'd have to be bolted permanently on his skids so he'd never rock, for Health and Safety reasons, but at least he'd be on public display. A grand opening party was organised with the town Mayor and other dignitaries present. On a lovely sunny day crowds gathered in the park to see Bigger Bertie wheeled in and presented to the town on permanent loan. It was an almost appropriate culmination to my forty year career as a rocking-horse person - but I wasn't quite done yet.

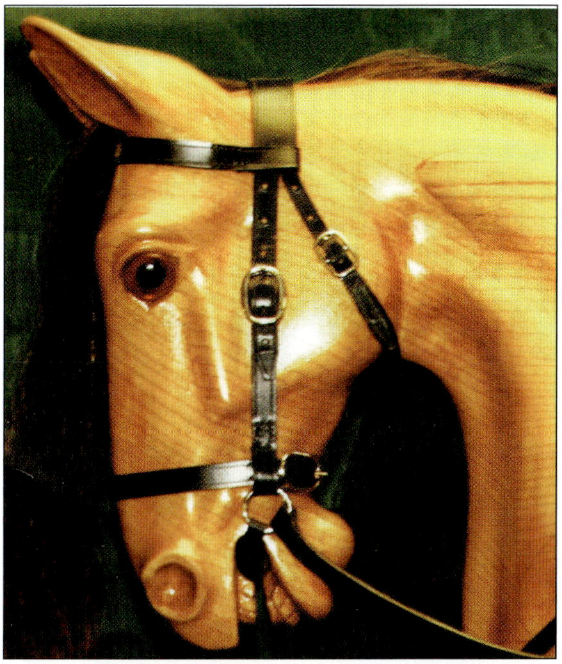

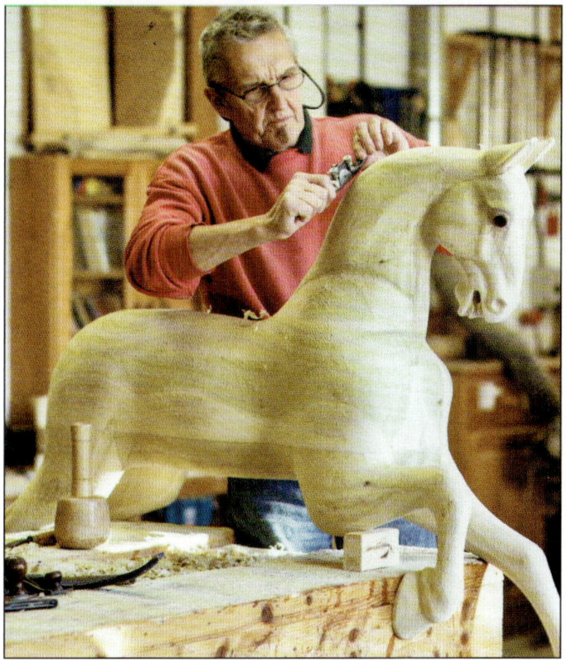

*AD's prototype (top) & Sam Glass at work on a 'Black Beauty'.*

After Bigger Bertie it seemed fitting to go small, so I designed a pair of half-size laminated rocking-horses for dolls or teddy bears. I also scaled up the Medium Rocky design - which now far out-sold The Rocking Horse Shop's traditional solid timber rocking-horse designs - and modified it to produce a Large Rocky plan. These were published in the Designs for Woodworkers series and accessories and timber packs for them went into our catalogue.

I drew a large traditional solid wood rocking-horse leaning forwards with one front leg lifted as if stepping out. I had in mind Lord Grantley's 1650 rocking-horse which I'd always admired, very refined and beautifully carved. This wouldn't be a plan for home-woodworkers but was intended to be one of the finest rocking-horses ever made. I hoped Jane would sell him finished, at a much higher price than all the others, because he'd clearly represent the highest standard of quality in our craft. This new top-of-the-range rocking-horse would also be a fresh and fascinating challenge for Sam Glass, and possibly his last chance to make a really superior horse, since he was approaching retirement too. I carved a prototype and took it to the workshop, Sam Glass took over and did a magnificent job of making them. The 'Black Beauty' would become the star of The Rocking Horse Shop's range of rocking-horses.

Despite these efforts the business was not progressing very well. Jane spoke of feeling like she was 'swimming in mud'. She discontinued several of the less profitable plans, cut costs wherever she could and declined to listen to advice, especially from me. Our relationship had become progressively worse through the months of the Bigger Bertie debacle and now, it seemed to me, almost every suggestion I made was greeted with an automatic no. I was retired, ostensibly, and resolved to try to forget all about rocking-horses, if I could.

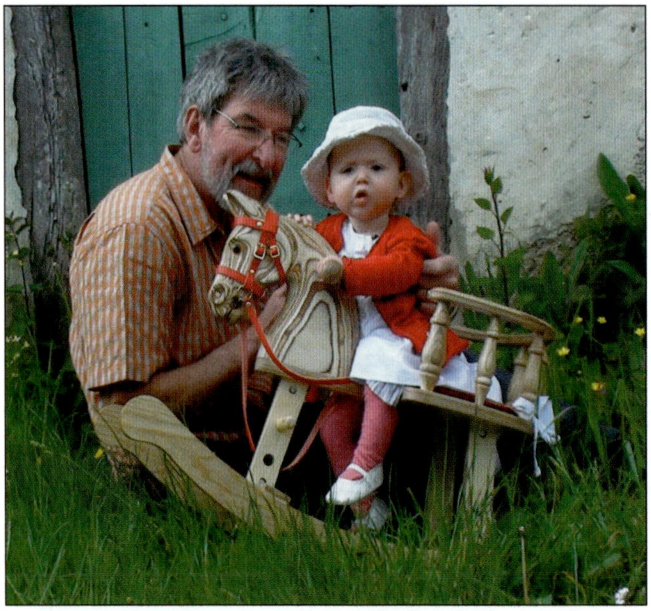

*Introducing granddaughter Eva to her first rocking-horse.*

Early one morning Jane phoned to tell me Bigger Bertie had had an accident. I drove straight to the park where he lived and found the giant horse lying on his side in a flower bed, his massive rockers smashed and broken plywood and crushed flowers everywhere. An elderly passerby told me he'd been walking his dog through the gardens, as he did every morning, when he'd heard Bigger Bertie make a high-pitched creaking sound. Seconds later he watched the horse keel over sideways and hit the ground with a terrible cracking, rending noise. Fortunately the man was some yards away or he'd have been squashed. As the park's manager politely put it, 'There appears to have been a structural failure…'

There were multiple reasons: poor quality marine plywood, inadequate hoof joints, too little adhesive and varnish, too many prolonged periods when Bigger Bertie stood out in the rain, and so on. But there was also the unfortunate fact that I'd forged ahead with the project without the whole-hearted support of The Rocking Horse Shop when I no longer had control. Bigger Bertie could have been great but…

I hated to give up on him and had long discussions with the industries manager of Her Majesty's Prison, Humber, with a view to getting prisoners to repair him under my direction. It wouldn't be viable to take Bigger Bertie into a prison for repair - shades of the Trojan Horse - but for a while it looked like some of the prison's more trusted inmates would be allowed to come out to work on him in Rocking Horse Yard. When that plan fizzled out I took my chain-saw and cut the remains of Bigger Bertie into pieces of liftable size. His head came back to Fangfoss and is in Sam's Wood, where it quietly rots. The rest went on a bonfire.

I've lost count of the number of rocking-horses I've been involved with over the years. Some of the ones I've made have been particularly special because, as well my skill and care, I poured all my love into them. After Eva, my beautiful first grandchild, was born to Lynn in France, I prepared the parts for a Little Rocky chair horse for her and took them over in a suitcase to assemble there. After that it occurred to me that Little Rocky could be fitted with removable heads. I made two horse heads, one carved and one that involved only easy shaping, and kangaroo, elephant and dinosaur heads. We now had an easy-to-make rocker with five interchangeable heads that simply bolted on. All the parts could be supplied ready-machined for home assembly and finishing.

All five new heads worked fine but I was particularly pleased with the rocking dinosaur. I'd had in mind a T-Rex, which all kids seem to love, but the problem had been T-Rex's huge teeth: I couldn't have a child's toy with sharp teeth. Then I read about a 66 million-year-old relative of T-Rex which had been discovered in China. This creature was covered in feathers, weighed around a ton and was reckoned to be eight or so metres long (on a par with Bigger Bertie!). It had rows of tiny teeth, which I could paint onto my version, so no Health and Safety problems, and I could make use (at last) of some of our stock of green cats eyes, which suited the dinosaur. It also had a very long snout, so I could hinge the mouth to make it fall open by gravity to reveal a bright red curved leather tongue. The rider pulled a handle attached to a cord to snap the mouth shut with a satisfying snicker-snack. Because of its very long nose the dinosaur was named Pinocchio Rex. Perfect!

I made prototypes, photographed the construction step-by-step, drew the plans, wrote the instructions and handed them over to Jane along with a marketing plan (which she ignored). The Little Rocky with five heads would be my last Design for Woodworkers.

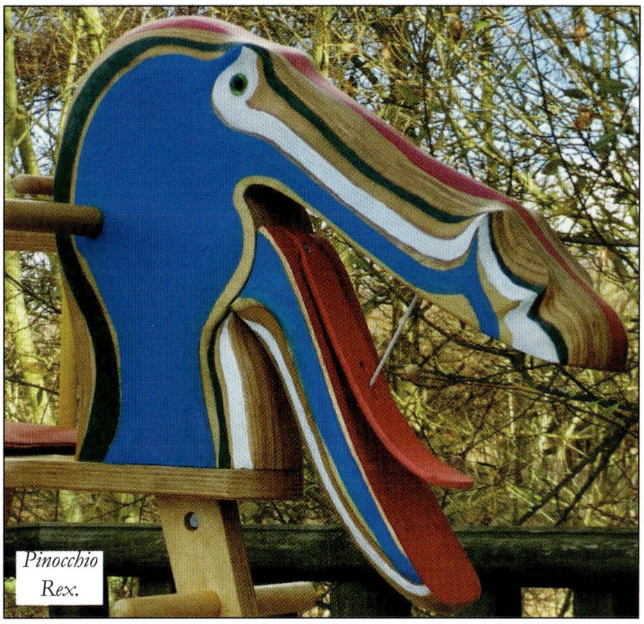

*Pinocchio Rex.*

In the early days Pat and I had gone to auctions of joinery workshops which were closing down following the owner's retirement. I welcomed the bargains we got but it always saddened me that what had obviously taken a lifetime to build would be disposed of in an hour or two. But there comes a time, perhaps when you've had enough or are simply too old and tired to carry on, when it is necessary to make a complete break. In 2016 Jane Cook and her husband bought the final tranche of shares in The Rocking Horse Shop Ltd. Now they owned the enterprise outright, including the workshops I'd built and all the tools, equipment and machinery in them. I'd had the run of the rocking-horse workshops for so long that, although it shouldn't have done, it came as a surprise when Jane took the keys and I realised I no longer had anywhere to make things.

My museum of old rocking-horses was doing nothing but gathering dust. Jane didn't want them so I sent the lot to auction and in a little over an hour my wonderful collection, around eighty rocking-horses, had all been sold. I hoped to individuals who'd care for them. Just four years later, in early 2020, I received an email from Jane's husband informing me that they'd sold The Rocking Horse Shop to a new owner. I'd seen him round the yard but didn't know him or hardly anything about him. I was well and truly out of it.

# 30

*Once upon a time there was a piece of wood*

The uncertainty I'd felt from the beginning, about what to do with my life, had been largely resolved by spending forty years designing and making rocking-horses. But now - 'retired' - I was at something of a loss. Banished from my workshop, I built a new smaller one in the yard - a 'man cave'. Here I can make anything that takes my fancy, including even the occasional rocking-horse for friends' children or grandchildren. And I've been making some animated rocking creations: they are toys, but not for children, necessarily. Sometimes my ideas work, sometimes they don't, but I don't worry about the time I'm wasting. And the great thing about woodwork is that nothing can go wrong that cannot be fixed. I don't employ anyone anymore, or make anything for money, and I don't have to bother about pleasing anyone.

Recently I made a Rocking Jesus Christ. Using wood off-cuts, wire and plastic plumbing pipe, Jesus has an egg-shaped tulipwood head and white wool hair and beard. He stands serenely in a rocking wooden boat in which the apostles huddle, eleven of them (Judas having been thrown out on a rope since, in this iteration, the Christians are less forgiving than they are often made out to be). Jesus's arms are outstretched in benediction but when you push a small lever hidden in his back he raises his arms to point heavenward.

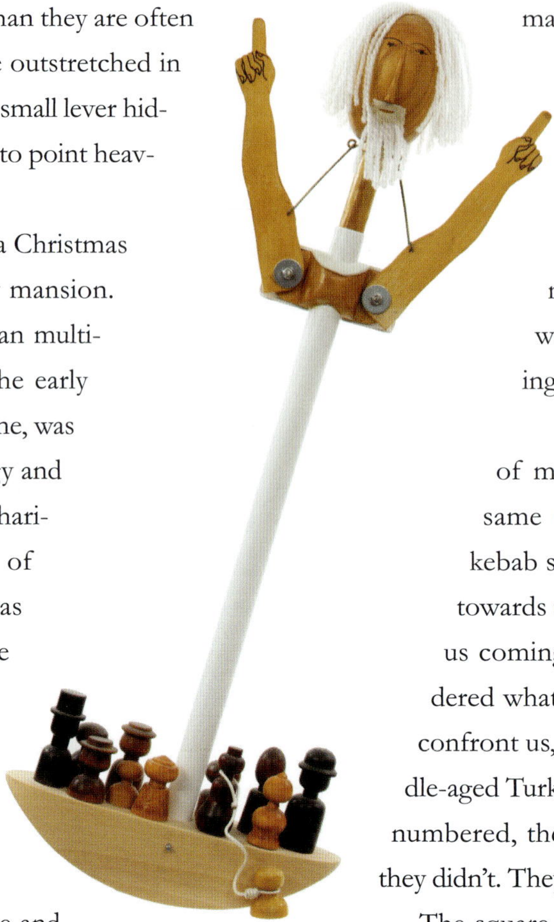

I took Rocking Jesus to a Christmas party in the annexe of a nearby mansion. The owner, Julian, was a Christian multi-millionaire who, having spent the early part of his life amassing his fortune, was now devoting his immense energy and a large chunk of his money to charitable works and the promotion of ethical capitalism. His hobby was drumming in his own three-piece band, with his lovely wife Rosie, who sang, and a guitarist. The band performed Christmas carols while Rocking Jesus stood on the piano, watching. Afterwards, Julian told me he and Rosie liked my piece and could they buy it?

'No, sorry,' I said. 'I'm not selling my work any more. I tell you what though, I have in mind another Rocking Jesus, a second coming as it were, bigger and better than this one. I don't know when I'll make it but when I do, if you like it, I'll give it to you.'

Next time I saw Julian he said, 'Rosie and I would love you to make something for us. But we must pay you, I insist.'

'In that case forget it,' I said. 'I no longer make for money and I can't be doing with descriptions and commissions and deadlines and all that. Sorry.'

I amazed myself. For forty years I'd worked my socks off to make a living out of my craft and here was a multi-millionaire offering to pay me to make a piece of artwork, a piece I intended making anyway, and I'm telling him to keep his money.

If I'm lucky (and I am, mostly) when I drive into York I can find a parking place in a square near the city centre. One evening as I parked I saw a young man, maybe sixteen years old, riding a bicycle across the far side of the square. Suddenly half a dozen youths came screaming out of a side street, hollering and waving their arms. They charged at the young man, knocked him off his bike and with shocking violence started punching and kicking him.

Without thinking I jumped out of my car and ran towards them. At the same time the Turkish man who ran a kebab stall nearby came out and he too ran towards the fight. The youths looked up, saw us coming, and stopped. I might have wondered what would happen if they'd decided to confront us, a skinny old Brit and a plump, middle-aged Turk. They were young and we were outnumbered, they could easily have beaten us. But they didn't. They ran away, back down the side street.

The square was quiet and peaceful again as we helped the young man to his feet. He was badly shaken but not injured.

'What was all that about?'

'I don't know,' he said. 'I don't know them. I'm alright. I'm alright, I'm alright.'

He picked up his bike and rode off. As we walked back across the square the kebab seller shook his head sadly and said, 'Those bloody people, all they do is fight. But they could do anything they want here. Don't they know this country is paradise?'

I know England is no paradise. But, since everything is relative and there are a great many places far, far worse, perhaps this country is paradise, for some. I've been lucky, mostly, and it's true that here I've been free to do more or less whatever I chose. And I have. It would have been foolish not to.

After our divorce Pat studied theology and took up wild swimming. These days my wife Shirley and I are on good, friendly terms with her. Given the long history Pat and I share, as well as our children and grandchildren, that is as it should be. Shirley refers to Pat as my first wife and herself as my last wife because we're going to be together for the duration. That's a promise, Shirley says (not a threat). We're very different but we rub along together pretty well most of the time. Shirley is a Christian and believes she'll live for ever in paradise, but the thought of endless life after this one appals me. And what a bizarre scene, if she goes first and is happily reunited in heaven with her first husband John, the love of her life, and I show up. I love Shirley but I'm as sure as I can be that after I die I won't see her again.

No, I don't believe in paradise, except it's here. One of these days (not yet, but before I go completely gaga) I intend to take off on my paraglider (which in my dreams is a giant rocking-horse who has kicked off his rockers and acquired wings) and fly up to the clouds. And then keep going.

James and Becca, the new owners of The Rocking Horse Shop, took control in January 2020 just as the Covid virus pandemic was starting to take hold. Not great timing. But he got on with the job as best he could and I didn't see much of him. Odd times when we met in the yard we chatted amiably enough and he admitted he had an awful lot to learn about rocking-horses and the business. I said I was sitting on forty years worth of experience and would be happy to help in any way I could. Since my fondest wish was for the enterprise to survive and thrive into the future, he only had to ask. Now and then he has asked, and we've got to know each other better.

James Honey is an excellent carver and manager and, surprisingly, the Covid virus lock-downs turned out to be good for The Rocking Horse Shop. The showroom had to close to visitors but the workshop was big enough for most of the staff to socially distance and keep working. Some customers decided that if they were going to be stuck at home for extended periods they'd make a rocking-horse, so the mail order sales of plans, timber packs and accessories boomed. At the same time other customers were thinking that if they couldn't go on holiday they'd spend their money on a special toy for their children or grandchildren instead, so the finished rocking-horse side of the business flourished. After ten years limping along at a relatively low level, The Rocking Horse Shop's fortunes were looking up again.

We are in a good place too, Shirley and I. She paints in her garden studio on one side of Rocking House, I make things in my man-cave on the other side, and we meet in the middle. I fly whenever the weather allows and intend to keep doing so for as long as I'm able. We've 'future-proofed' Rocking House so we'll be able to stay here until carried out feet first. We look after Sam's Wood and tend our garden. And, most gratifying, the swallows are back. Not as many as before, but still...

One afternoon James stopped me in the yard and said, 'I've only a few copies left of *The Complete Rocking Horse Maker*. Would you be interested in writing a new edition?'

'I'd love to,' I said.

The basic techniques of rocking-horse making haven't changed much but I knew there were lots of ways I could update the book to include several new designs as well as variants and wrinkles the earlier edition missed, and add new photographs and write more about the history of rocking-horses and restoration. We'd call the new book *The Complete Rocking Horse Maker 2* and hope it would introduce a whole new generation to our beautiful craft. James liked that idea.

He also liked the idea of a companion volume to tell the back-story: something of the history and practice of our craft, but focussing on the founding and development of our enterprise and the people involved. And because the skills and experience we've acquired are transferable, I hoped it would convey something useful about the reality of living a hands-on creative life in the twenty-first century. It's not easy, but it's worthwhile and sustainable and (in a world heading for oblivion) I hope it catches on. I doubt these books will be the last words on the subject, but they'll almost certainly be mine, and I'd like to end on a positive note. Keep on rocking...

*Anthony Dew,*
*Rocking House, Fangfoss, October 2021.*

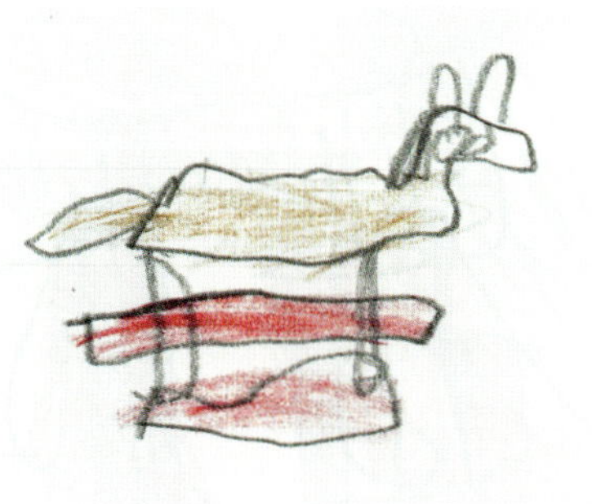

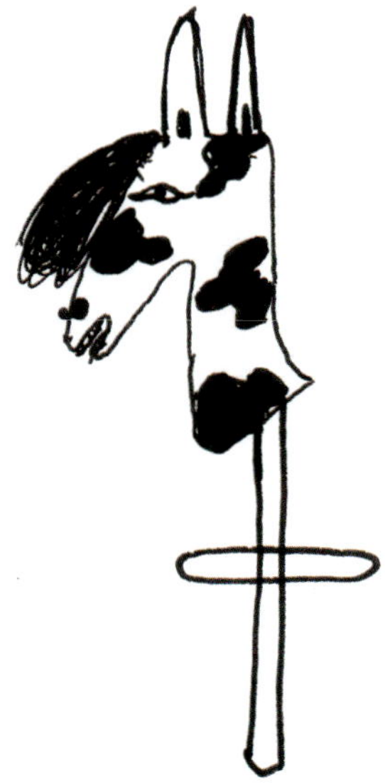

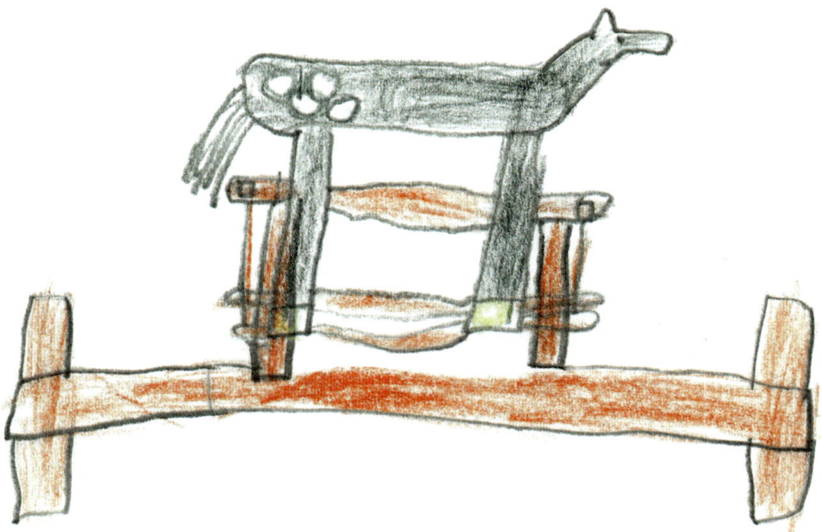

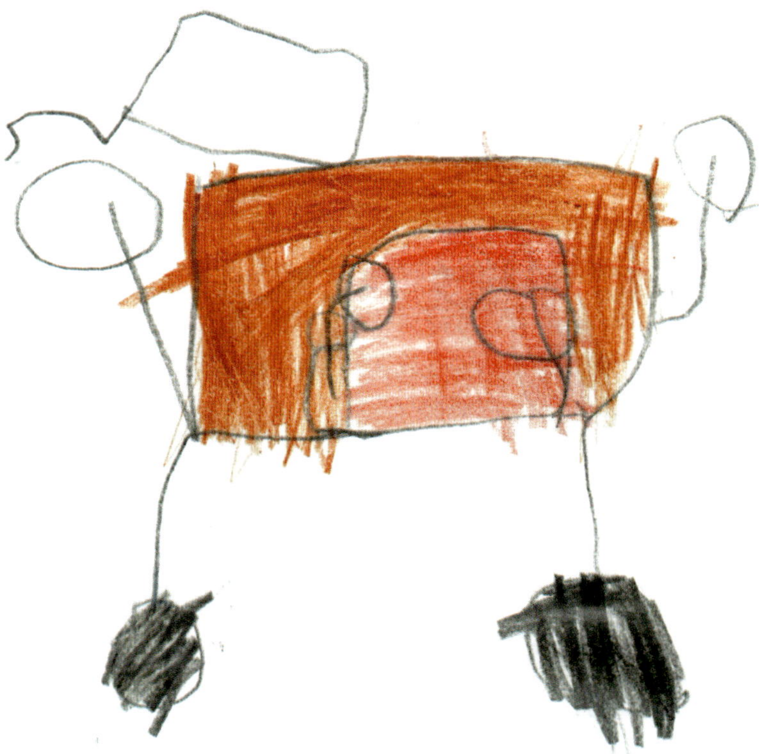

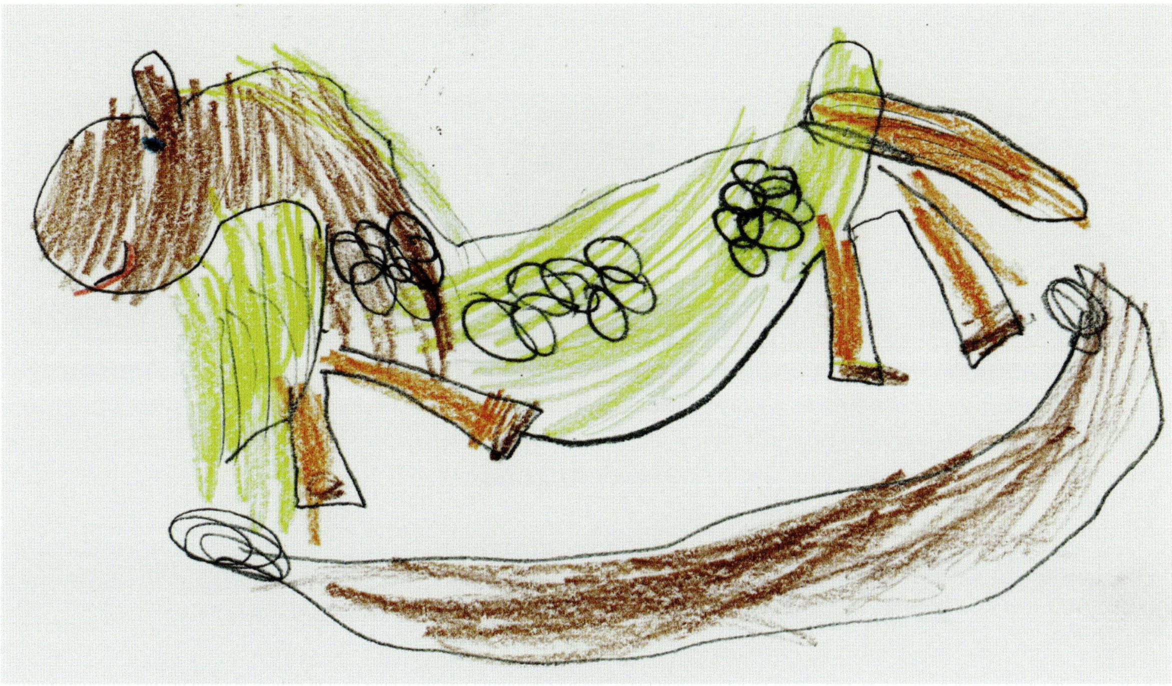

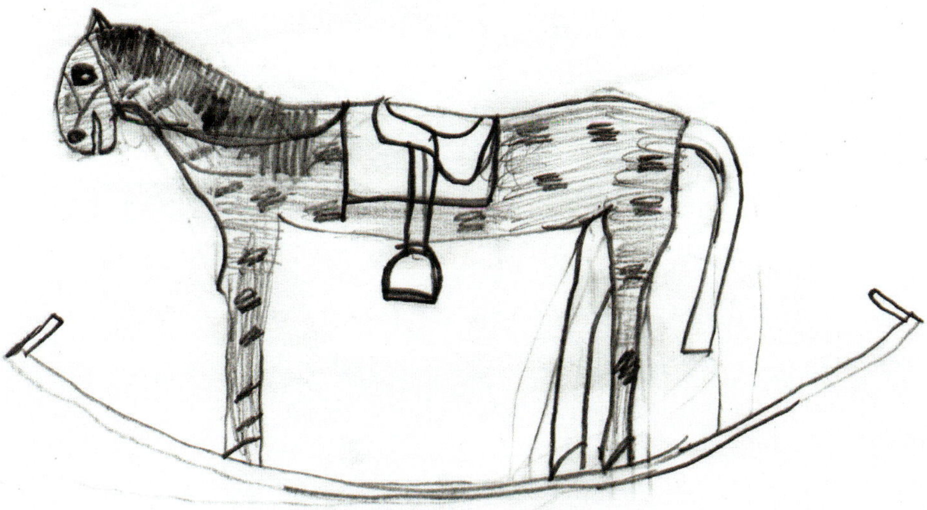

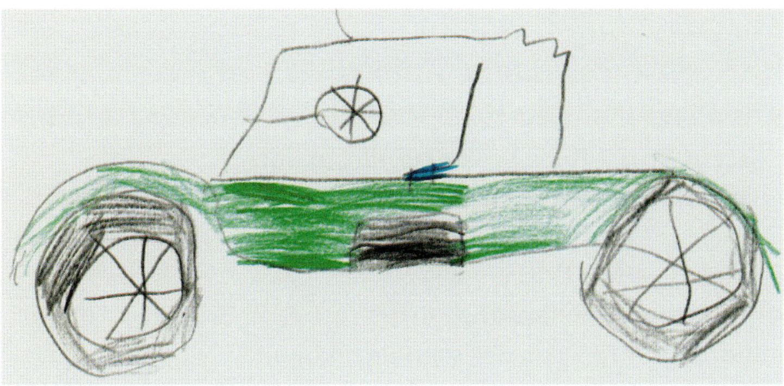

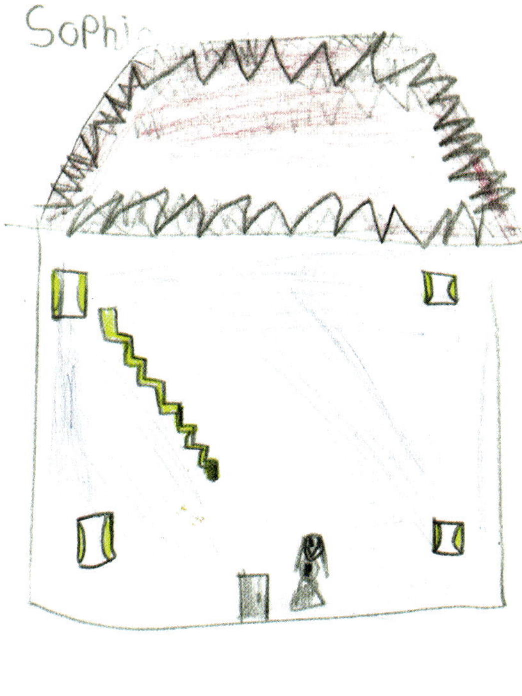
Sophi

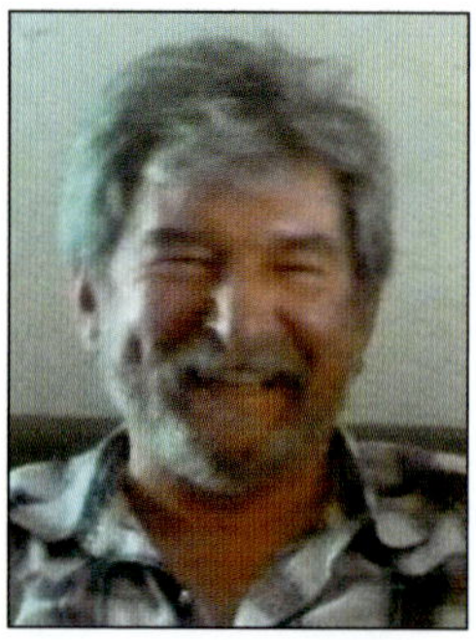

Acknowledgements

I am forever thankful to
my first wife Pat
who made our rocking good life together for so many years,

our children - Sam, Kate and Lynn,

and my ever-supportive (and last) wife, Shirley.

In my writing I have been greatly encouraged by
Harry Bayman, Chris Bridge, Carole Bromley, James Harrison and Dave Nicholson.

For help and advice with this book I thank
James and Becca,
Julia Cockman, Mary Ann Dearlove, Jocelyn Hudson, Bethany Wright,
and the artists Peter Schoenecker and Jim Stafford
.
I owe particular thanks to Janet Cochrane and Jane Allen
and especially to the brilliant Lara Stafford.

The story is as true as my memory of events allows,
informed by my journals written at the time and confirmed
by third party information where possible or appropriate.

The order of some events has been modified and some names have been changed.
Any errors that remain are entirely mine.

Cover design, title page and 'Embryology & Ascent of the Rocking-Horse' illustrations
by ace paraglider & artist Steve Ham.

Photograph on page 6 by Paul & Angie Boyer.
Photographs on Page 115 by Martyn f. Chillmaid.
Drawings on pages 144 to 147 by Fangfoss and Bugthorpe primary school children.

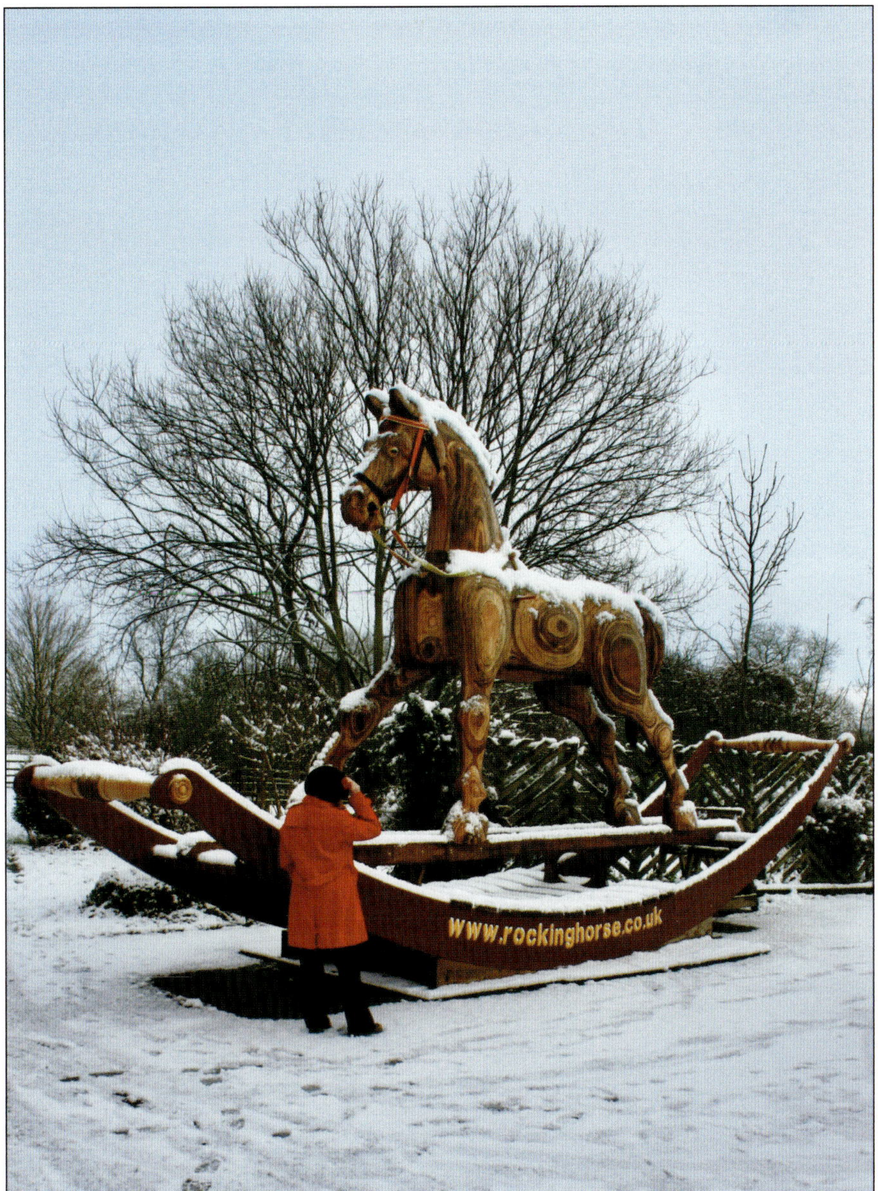
www.rockinghorse.co.uk

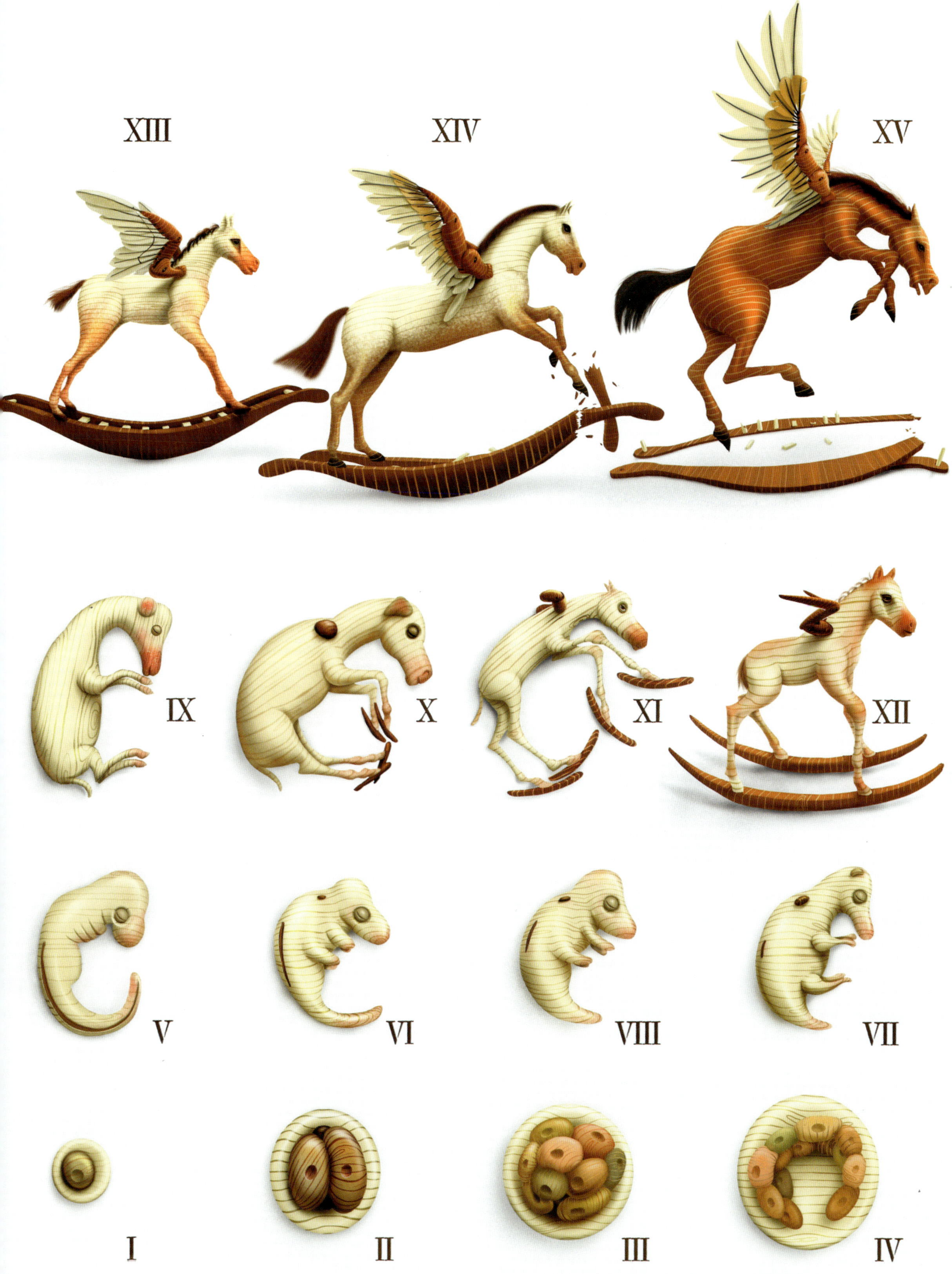
XIII
XIV
XV
IX
X
XI
XII
V
VI
VIII
VII
I
II
III
IV